# ST ANTONY'S/MACMILLAN SERIES

*General editors: Archie Brown (1978–85) and Rosemary Thorp (1985–   ), both Fellows of St Antony's College, Oxford*

Roy Allison FINLAND'S RELATIONS WITH THE SOVIET UNION, 1944–84
Said Amir Arjomand (*editor*) FROM NATIONALISM TO REVOLUTIONARY ISLAM
Anders Åslund PRIVATE ENTERPRISE IN EASTERN EUROPE
Omer Bartov THE EASTERN FRONT, 1941–45, GERMAN TROOPS AND THE BARBARISATION OF WARFARE
Gail Lee Bernstein and Haruhiro Fukui (*editors*) JAPAN AND THE WORLD
Archie Brown (*editor*) POLITICAL CULTURE AND COMMUNIST STUDIES
Archie Brown (*editor*) POLITICAL LEADERSHIP AND THE SOVIET UNION
Archie Brown and Michael Kaser (*editors*) SOVIET POLICY FOR THE 1980s
S. B. Burman CHIEFDOM POLITICS AND ALIEN LAW
Helen Callaway GENDER, CULTURE AND EMPIRE
Renfrew Christie ELECTRICITY, INDUSTRY AND CLASS IN SOUTH AFRICA
Robert O. Collins and Francis M. Deng (*editors*) THE BRITISH IN THE SUDAN, 1898–1956
Roger Cooter (*editor*) STUDIES IN THE HISTORY OF ALTERNATIVE MEDICINE
Wilhelm Deist THE *WEHRMACHT* AND GERMAN REARMAMENT
Robert Desjardins THE SOVIET UNION THROUGH FRENCH EYES, 1945–85
Guido di Tella ARGENTINA UNDER PERÓN, 1973–76
Guido di Tella and Rudiger Dornbusch (*editors*) THE POLITICAL ECONOMY OF ARGENTINA, 1946–83
Guido di Tella and D. C. M. Platt (*editors*) THE POLITICAL ECONOMY OF ARGENTINA, 1880–1946
Simon Duke US DEFENCE BASES IN THE UNITED KINGDOM
Julius A. Elias PLATO'S DEFENCE OF POETRY
Ricardo Ffrench-Davis and Ernesto Tironi (*editors*) LATIN AMERICA AND THE NEW INTERNATIONAL ECONOMIC ORDER
David Footman ANTONIN BESSE OF ADEN
Bohdan Harasymiw POLITICAL ELITE RECRUITMENT IN THE SOVIET UNION
Neil Harding (*editor*) THE STATE IN SOCIALIST SOCIETY
Richard Holt SPORT AND SOCIETY IN MODERN FRANCE
Albert Hourani EUROPE AND THE MIDDLE EAST
Albert Hourani THE EMERGENCE OF THE MODERN MIDDLE EAST
J. R. Jennings GEORGES SOREL
A. Kemp-Welch (*translator*) THE BIRTH OF SOLIDARITY
Paul Kennedy and Anthony Nicholls (*editors*) NATIONALIST AND RACIALIST MOVEMENTS IN BRITAIN AND GERMANY BEFORE 1914
Richard Kindersley (*editor*) IN SEARCH OF EUROCOMMUNISM
Maria D'Alva G. Kinzo LEGAL OPPOSITION POLITICS UNDER AUTHORITARIAN RULE IN BRAZIL
Bohdan Krawchenko SOCIAL CHANGE AND NATIONAL CONSCIOUSNESS IN TWENTIETH-CENTURY UKRAINE
Gisela C. Lebzelter POLITICAL ANTI-SEMITISM IN ENGLAND, 1918–1939
Nancy Lubin LABOUR AND NATIONALITY IN SOVIET CENTRAL ASIA
C. A. MacDonald THE UNITED STATES, BRITAIN AND APPEASEMENT, 1936–39
Robert H. McNeal TSAR AND COSSACK, 1855–1914
David Nicholls HAITI IN CARIBBEAN CONTEXT
Patrick O'Brien (*editor*) RAILWAYS AND THE ECONOMIC DEVELOPMENT OF WESTERN EUROPE, 1830–1914
Amii Omara-Otunnu POLITICS AND THE MILITARY IN UGANDA, 1890–1985

Roger Owen (*editor*) STUDIES IN THE ECONOMIC AND SOCIAL HISTORY OF PALESTINE IN THE NINETEENTH AND TWENTIETH CENTURIES

Ilan Pappé BRITAIN AND THE ARAB–ISRAELI CONFLICT, 1948–51

D. C. M. Platt and Guido di Tella (*editors*) ARGENTINA, AUSTRALIA AND CANADA: STUDIES IN COMPARATIVE DEVELOPMENT, 1870–1965

Irena Powell WRITERS AND SOCIETY IN MODERN JAPAN

Alex Pravda (*editor*) HOW RULING COMMUNIST PARTIES ARE GOVERNED

T. H. Rigby and Ferenc Fehér (*editors*) POLITICAL LEGITIMATION IN COMMUNIST STATES

Hans Rogger JEWISH POLICIES AND RIGHT-WING POLITICS IN IMPERIAL RUSSIA

Marilyn Rueschemeyer PROFESSIONAL WORK AND MARRIAGE

A. J. R. Russell-Wood THE BLACK MAN IN SLAVERY AND FREEDOM IN COLONIAL BRAZIL

Nurit Schleifman UNDERCOVER AGENTS IN THE RUSSIAN REVOLUTION-ARY MOVEMENT

Amnon Sella and Yael Yishai ISRAEL THE PEACEFUL BELLIGERENT, 1967–79

Aron Shai BRITAIN AND CHINA, 1941–47

Lewis H. Siegelbaum THE POLITICS OF INDUSTRIAL MOBILIZATION IN RUSSIA, 1914–17

H. Gordon Skilling *SAMIZDAT* AND AN INDEPENDENT SOCIETY IN CENTRAL AND EASTERN EUROPE

David Stafford BRITAIN AND EUROPEAN RESISTANCE, 1940–45

Nancy Stepan THE IDEA OF RACE IN SCIENCE

Verena Stolcke COFFEE PLANTERS, WORKERS AND WIVES

Jane E. Stromseth THE ORIGINS OF FLEXIBLE RESPONSE

Marvin Swartz THE POLITICS OF BRITISH FOREIGN POLICY IN THE ERA OF DISRAELI AND GLADSTONE

Rosemary Thorp (*editor*) LATIN AMERICA IN THE 1930s

Rosemary Thorp and Laurence Whitehead (*editors*) INFLATION AND STABILISA-TION IN LATIN AMERICA

Rosemary Thorp and Laurence Whitehead (*editors*) LATIN AMERICAN DEBT AND THE ADJUSTMENT CRISIS

Rudolf L. Tökés (*editor*) OPPOSITION IN EASTERN EUROPE

Robert Wihtol THE ASIAN DEVELOPMENT BANK AND RURAL DEVELOP-MENT

Toshio Yokoyama JAPAN IN THE VICTORIAN MIND

---

### Series Standing Order

If you would like to receive future titles in this series as they are published, you can make use of our standing order facility. To place a standing order please contact your bookseller or, in case of difficulty, write to us at the address below with your name and address and the name of the series. Please state with which title you wish to begin your standing order. (If you live outside the UK we may not have the rights for your area, in which case we will forward your order to the publisher concerned.)

Standing Order Service, Macmillan Distribution Ltd, Houndmills, Basingstoke, Hampshire, RG21 2XS, England.

# The Asian Development Bank and Rural Development

## Policy and Practice

Robert Wihtol

**M**

MACMILLAN
PRESS

in association with
ST ANTONY'S COLLEGE
OXFORD

First published 1988

Published by
THE MACMILLAN PRESS LTD
Houndmills, Basingstoke, Hampshire RG21 2XS
and London
Companies and representatives
throughout the world

Printed in Hong Kong

British Library Cataloguing in Publication Data
Wihtol, Robert
The Asian Development Bank and rural
development: policy and practice.—
(St Antony's/Macmillan series).
1. Asian Development Bank  2. Rural
development—Asia  3. Asia—
Economic conditions—1945–
I. Title  II. Series
330.95′0428      HC412
ISBN 0-333-46436-2

The views and interpretations in this
book are the responsibility of the
author and should not be attributed
to the International Labour
Organisation/Office.

# Contents

# List of Tables and Figures

**TABLES**

**FIGURES**

# List of Abbreviations

| | |
|---|---|
| ADB | Asian Development Bank |
| ADBN | Agricultural Development Bank of Nepal |
| ADF | Asian Development Fund (of the ADB) |
| AFDB | African Development Bank |
| ASEAN | Association of Southeast Asian Nations |
| ASF | Agricultural Special Fund (of the ADB) |
| CIF | Cost, Insurance, Freight |
| DAC | Development Assistance Committee (of the OECD) |
| DMC | Developing Member Country (of the ADB) |
| EC | European Community |
| ECAFE | Economic Commission for Asia and the Far East (UN) |
| EDF | European Development Fund |
| EIRR | Economic Internal Rate of Return |
| ESCAP | Economic and Social Commission for Asia and the Pacific (UN) |
| FAO | Food and Agriculture Organisation |
| GNP | Gross National Product |
| HYV | High-Yielding Variety |
| IBRD | International Bank for Reconstruction and Development |
| ICB | International Competitive Bidding |
| IDA | International Development Association |
| IDB | Inter-American Development Bank |
| IDS | Institute of Development Studies (University of Sussex) |
| IFAD | International Fund for Agricultural Development |
| IFC | International Finance Corporation |
| ILO | International Labour Organisation/Office |
| IMF | International Monetary Fund |
| IRRI | International Rice Research Institute |
| MOF | Ministry of Finance (Japan) |
| MPSF | Multi-Purpose Special Fund (of the ADB) |
| OCR | Ordinary Capital Resources (of the ADB) |
| ODA | Official Development Assistance |
| OECD | Organization for Economic Cooperation and Development |

| | |
|---|---|
| OECF | Overseas Economic Cooperation Fund (Japan) |
| PBME | Project Benefit Monitoring and Evaluation |
| PCR | Project Completion Report (of the ADB) |
| PNG | Papua New Guinea |
| PPAR | Project Performance Audit Report (of the ADB) |
| SFR | Special Fund Resources (of the ADB) |
| SIDA | Swedish International Development Authority |
| TASF | Technical Assistance Special Fund (of the ADB) |
| UK | United Kingdom |
| UN | United Nations |
| UNCTAD | United Nations Conference on Trade and Development |
| UNDP | United Nations Development Programme |
| US | United States of America |
| USAID | United States Agency for International Development |
| USSR | Union of Soviet Socialist Republics |

# Preface

The Asian Development Bank has come under growing criticism in the 1980s for emphasising the quantitative aspects of its operations, particularly the annual expansion of loan approvals, while at the same time disregarding developmental, technical and economic aspects of its projects. This tendency was evident in the 1970s but has become more pronounced in the 1980s following the strong push by Fujioka Masao, who took over the presidency of the Bank in 1981, to increase lending at a time of stagnation or decline in the demand for ADB loans among the Bank's borrowers. The conflict between management's annual lending targets and the Bank's developmental concerns in 1986–7 led donor representatives on the Bank's board of directors to question the approval of a number of projects on grounds of poor quality, and resulted in a harshly critical twentieth anniversary assessment of the Bank in the *Far Eastern Economic Review* in November 1986. At the Bank's annual meeting in April 1987 several donors drew further attention to the problematic relationship between lending quantity and project quality.

This study examines the ADB's policies and lending of relevance to rural development, focusing on the question of why effectively tackling rural development has proved so difficult for the Bank. The main themes – the gap between stated policies and lending practice, political and organisational constraints on lending, and the relationship between management objectives and broader development objectives – have a direct bearing on many of the issues at present being discussed by the Bank and its members. While it is important for a study of this nature to be up-to-date, it is virtually impossible for a topical book not to be overtaken by events in one area or another. ADB policies are examined mainly from 1967, when the Bank started operating, to 1985, but the implications of more recent policy developments are considered wherever possible. Tables on aggregate lending include data from the Bank's 1986 *Annual Report*, but owing to difficulties in obtaining source material, individual projects are examined mainly in 1967–83.

For the sake of uniformity, a number of conventions have been adopted. In the text and end-notes Japanese, Chinese and Korean names are given in their original order, with the surname first, regardless of the varying practices in different sources. Throughout the text $ refers to US dollars, one billion equals one thousand million and tons are metric. Abbreviations are listed on pages ix–x.

The author wishes to thank the many individuals who have contributed to this study with their guidance, suggestions and comments. Initial thanks are due to Mauri K. Elovainio for encouraging the author to take up research, and to Vilho Harle for pointing out the lack of research on the ADB. Particular thanks are owed to the many staff members of the Bank who contributed generously of their time and experience, but who must remain anonymous. The careful guidance of Professor J. A. A. Stockwin throughout the drafting of the study is acknowledged with gratitude. Thanks are also due to Professor Robert Cassen and John White for helpful criticism and to Geoffrey Hurley and Bertil Nilsson for their comments on different parts of the draft. Much of the writing was done while the author was at St Antony's College, Oxford, in 1985. The author is also grateful for being granted the use of the facilities of the Department of Political Science at the University of Helsinki at different stages of the work. Finally, the author acknowledges warmly the work of Elizabeth Bullock and Wendy Rimmer, who typed and retyped the various drafts with great efficiency.

Financial support for the study was received from the Academy of Finland, the Overseas Research Student Award Scheme of the United Kingdom, the Tampere Peace Research Institute (Finland) and the Scandinavian Institute of Asian Studies, and is gratefully acknowledged.

*Oxford, July 1987*                                    Robert Wihtol

# 1 Introduction

Is it possible for a multilateral development bank,[1] funded primarily by the developed market economies, to implement effectively a lending programme in the developing countries aimed not only at promoting economic growth but at alleviating poverty and raising living standards in rural areas? This was one of the principal challenges put to the multilateral banks in the early 1970s, as the development priorities of the international donor community shifted from the straightforward promotion of growth to policies and programmes aimed more directly at reducing poverty, narrowing income disparities and creating employment in developing countries. It is also a challenge to which the extensive literature assessing the role and performance of aid agencies suggests that these banks have been less than successful in responding.

A number of studies indicate that the multilateral banks have to a limited extent been able to direct their programmes to the poor, while numerous others suggest that they have not been able to channel their loans to the lowest income groups. Yet others claim that multilateral aid programmes in fact significantly contribute to perpetuating the economic relationships which are at the root of rural poverty. Virtually all research, however, indicates that the reorientation of the programmes of multilateral aid agencies toward poverty alleviation has encountered severe political and organisational constraints, and raises the question of how these constraints can be overcome. This study examines the question in the light of the lending policy and practice of the Asian Development Bank (in this study referred to as the ADB or the Bank) between 1967 and the mid-1980s.

In the 1960s, development aid concentrated on promoting economic growth and directed investment mainly towards the 'traditional' sectors of infrastructure and industry. In the rural sector, growth-oriented strategies led to investment in increasing agricultural production through the introduction of the high-yielding foodgrain varieties of the 'green revolution'. Following the worldwide foodgrain shortages of the early 1970s and the growing international awareness that poverty and unemployment, particularly in rural areas, had increased in spite of growth-oriented development efforts, in the early 1970s the international donor community and the agencies providing finance and technical assistance for the rural sector undertook a major review of their policies to develop more direct solutions to the problems of hunger, poverty and unemployment.

In his address to the World Bank board of governors in September 1973, in what has since become his most widely quoted policy statement, the President, Robert McNamara, noted that the benefits of international aid had not reached the majority of the poor and announced a major shift in the World Bank's lending policies towards a 'rural development strategy' focusing on the problem of rural poverty.[2] This was followed in 1974 by the convening of a World Food Conference by the Food and Agriculture Organisation (FAO) and a World Employment Conference in 1976 by the International Labour Organisation (ILO). In 1974–5, the main sources of development finance, the World Bank, the Inter-American Development Bank (IDB), the ADB, the European Development Fund (EDF) and a number of bilateral agencies including the United States Agency for International Development (USAID) significantly increased their funding for the rural sector in both real and relative terms. This was accompanied by a reorientation of development policies in what can be described as a shift from agricultural development, centred around economic growth, to rural development combining the three objectives of growth, employment and income distribution.

In the ADB this shift took the form of both a substantial increase in the allocation of funds for the rural sector and a revision of the Bank's development policy. The annual distribution of ADB lending commitments by sector is set out in Tables 1.1 and 1.2, and shows that the rural sector's allocation has increased steadily from an average of 16.8 per cent in 1968–72 to 28.6 per cent in 1974–8, and further to 34.2 per cent in 1979–86. The sharpest rise took place in 1973–5: in 1973 rural lending more than doubled, and in both 1974 and 1975 it increased in real terms by over 80 per cent. In the latter half of the 1970s, rural lending increased at a slower pace, and since 1979 the ADB has continuously allocated one third of its resources to agriculture and rural development, making it the single most important sector of Bank lending. The tables indicate a number of general trends in the Bank's lending priorities. Lending for agriculture, agro-industry and energy has increased very significantly in real and relative terms, followed by social infrastructure (urban development, education, health and population), and lending for water supply and sanitation has increased in real terms but maintained a constant relative share, while lending for industry and development

Table 1.1 Distribution of ADB annual loan commitments by sector, 1968–86 ($ million)

| | Agriculture & agro-industry | Energy | Industry & non-fuel minerals | Development banks | Transport & communications | Water supply & sanitation | Urban development, education, health & population | Multi-sector | Total lending |
|---|---|---|---|---|---|---|---|---|---|
| 1968 | 2.0 | – | 10.2 | 15.0 | 7.2 | 7.2 | – | – | 41.6 |
| 1969 | 27.3 | 3.1 | 3.8 | 35.0 | 28.9 | – | – | – | 98.1 |
| 1970 | 45.8 | 43.1 | 37.0 | 40.0 | 63.5 | 13.3 | 3.0 | – | 245.6 |
| 1971 | 49.3 | 105.5 | 4.2 | 42.0 | 44.2 | 8.8 | – | – | 254.0 |
| 1972 | 32.8 | 121.1 | – | 32.0 | 67.6 | 58.9 | 3.7 | – | 316.1 |
| 1973 | 74.3 | 92.5 | – | 79.6 | 125.0 | 43.7 | 6.4 | – | 421.5 |
| 1974 | 134.0 | 76.6 | 104.9 | 82.0 | 81.5 | 68.8 | – | – | 547.7 |
| 1975 | 245.9 | 152.1 | 17.5 | 111.0 | 81.6 | 37.8 | 14.5 | – | 660.3 |
| 1976 | 200.9 | 128.7 | 51.5 | 153.0 | 166.6 | 75.3 | – | – | 775.9 |
| 1977 | 262.0 | 217.6 | 40.4 | 95.0 | 146.0 | 84.8 | 40.7 | – | 886.5 |
| 1978 | 310.7 | 249.2 | 124.6 | 157.5 | 138.1 | 94.1 | 84.5 | – | 1158.7 |
| 1979 | 411.6 | 325.3 | 20.2 | 137.0 | 114.8 | 108.2 | 133.3 | 1.2 | 1251.6 |
| 1980 | 467.9 | 382.4 | 6.2 | 127.0 | 223.4 | 107.2 | 120.6 | 1.0 | 1435.7 |
| 1981 | 541.6 | 480.1 | 13.0 | 204.0 | 72.4 | 123.7 | 241.1 | 1.7 | 1677.6 |
| 1982 | 621.3 | 513.7 | 16.2 | 148.5 | 257.4 | 57.9 | 115.6 | – | 1730.6 |
| 1983 | 648.4 | 450.8 | 95.0 | 205.0 | 65.5 | 186.6 | 234.8 | 7.2 | 1893.2 |
| 1984 | 758.0 | 766.7 | – | 54.0 | 381.2 | 103.6 | 136.0 | 34.8 | 2234.3 |
| 1985 | 559.5 | 244.7 | 15.8 | 227.0 | 310.0 | 206.1 | 337.6 | 7.4 | 1980.1 |
| 1986 | 822.2 | 514.9 | 10.0 | 100.0 | 178.8 | 54.0 | 218.5 | 103.0 | 2001.3 |
| Total | 6173.9 | 4887.2 | 512.0 | 2044.0 | 2546.6 | 1437.6 | 1691.5 | 197.7 | 19491.4 |

Note: All figures do not tally due to rounding, minor changes over time in the Bank's sector classification of projects and the fact that the 1982 total was originally given as $1730.6 million but has subsequently been revised to $1683.6 million.

Sources: Annual figures are from ADB, Annual Report (1968–86). The totals on the bottom line are from ADB, Annual Report (1986).

Table 1.2 Distribution of ADB annual loan commitments by sector, from 1968–70 to 1984–6 (per cent, based on three-year moving averages)

| | Agriculture & agro-industry | Energy | Industry & non-fuel minerals | Development banks | Transport & communications | Water supply & sanitation | Urban development, education, health & population | Multi-sector | Total lending |
|---|---|---|---|---|---|---|---|---|---|
| 1968–70 | 19.5 | 12.0 | 15.0 | 23.4 | 24.1 | 5.3 | 0.7 | – | 100.0 |
| 1969–71 | 20.5 | 25.4 | 8.7 | 19.5 | 21.7 | 3.7 | 0.5 | – | 100.0 |
| 1970–72 | 15.7 | 33.1 | 5.0 | 14.0 | 21.5 | 9.9 | 0.8 | – | 100.0 |
| 1971–73 | 15.8 | 32.2 | 0.4 | 15.5 | 23.9 | 11.2 | 1.0 | – | 100.0 |
| 1972–74 | 18.8 | 26.7 | 4.0 | 15.1 | 21.3 | 13.3 | 0.8 | – | 100.0 |
| 1973–75 | 27.9 | 23.0 | 4.2 | 16.7 | 17.7 | 9.2 | 1.3 | – | 100.0 |
| 1974–76 | 29.3 | 21.3 | 5.5 | 17.4 | 16.6 | 9.1 | 0.8 | – | 100.0 |
| 1975–77 | 30.5 | 22.0 | 4.2 | 15.5 | 17.0 | 8.4 | 2.4 | – | 100.0 |
| 1976–78 | 27.4 | 21.5 | 7.2 | 14.4 | 16.0 | 9.0 | 4.5 | – | 100.0 |
| 1977–79 | 29.8 | 24.0 | 5.7 | 11.8 | 12.1 | 8.7 | 7.9 | – | 100.0 |
| 1978–80 | 30.9 | 24.9 | 3.9 | 11.0 | 12.4 | 8.0 | 8.8 | 0.1 | 100.0 |
| 1979–81 | 32.6 | 27.2 | 0.9 | 10.7 | 9.4 | 7.8 | 11.3 | 0.1 | 100.0 |
| 1980–82 | 34.0 | 27.7 | 0.7 | 10.0 | 11.5 | 6.0 | 10.0 | 0.1 | 100.0 |
| 1981–83 | 33.7 | 26.6 | 2.4 | 10.6 | 7.5 | 7.0 | 11.2 | 1.0 | 100.0 |
| 1982–84 | 34.2 | 29.0 | 1.9 | 7.0 | 12.1 | 6.0 | 8.4 | 1.4 | 100.0 |
| 1983–85 | 31.9 | 24.2 | 1.8 | 8.0 | 12.5 | 8.2 | 11.7 | 1.5 | 100.0 |
| 1984–86 | 34.8 | 24.8 | 0.4 | 6.2 | 14.2 | 5.9 | 11.3 | 2.4 | 100.0 |
| Total (1968–86) | 31.7 | 25.1 | 2.6 | 10.5 | 13.1 | 7.4 | 8.7 | 1.0 | 100.0 |

Note: Figures may not tally due to rounding.
Source: ADB, Annual Report (1984–6).

banks and infrastructure (transport and communications) has increased somewhat in real terms but declined markedly in relative terms. The increase in rural lending was accompanied by a fundamental revision of the ADB's development policy for the rural sector. The Bank's rural policy has been guided by two major surveys and can accordingly broadly be split into two periods. The first *Asian Agricultural Survey* was published by the Bank soon after its establishment, in 1968, and recommended a strategy of agricultural modernisation based on raising foodgrain production through the widespread introduction of new foodgrain varieties and extensive investment in irrigation and agricultural inputs.[3] The survey laid the foundations for the Bank's rural policy and served as a blueprint for the Bank's rural lending into the early 1970s. In connection with the new development strategies espoused by the donor community in the early 1970s and following the lead of the World Bank, in 1974–5 the ADB initiated a number of changes in its rural lending and undertook a major policy review of the Asian rural sector. The second survey, *Rural Asia: Challenge and Opportunity*, was published in 1977 and took a critical view of the first survey's growth-oriented approach.[4] In line with the policy changes of other international agencies, the second survey drew attention to the question of rural poverty and recommended that lending be reoriented to tackle the problems of income distribution and rural employment creation alongside that of food production. It also outlined the required modifications in the Bank's operational policies and practices. Although the international political setting for development assistance underwent major changes in the early 1980s, the Bank has continued to recognise the validity of the policy objectives set out in the second survey for rural development in the 1980s.[5]

While the ADB has increased its rural lending and adopted a rural development policy emphasising both growth and poverty alleviation, it does not automatically follow that Bank projects are more effectively narrowing income gaps, increasing employment, and providing essential social services to the poorest segments of the rural population. For policies to have the intended impact, effective steps must be taken to translate them into practice, which means that management objectives, operational policies, project identification criteria, planning procedures, loan modalities and lending practices also need to be appropriately revised. A major conclusion of Chapters 7 and 8 of this study is that the change in the Bank's development policy has led to only very limited changes in project content, and that as a result the Bank's lending even in the late 1970s and early 1980s has continued to focus on agricultural production, with little tangible impact in rural poverty. This study is concerned with the reasons for this gap between policy and practice, and their implications for Bank policy and operations.

## Research on Development Banks

Multilateral development banks are a recent phenomenon in international relations, as is the literature on the banks. The International Bank for Reconstruction and Development (IBRD) was established in 1944, to fund post-war reconstruction, and the thrust of its lending shifted to the developing countries only in the late 1950s. Its concessional affiliate, the International Development Association (IDA), was set up in 1960, and by the late 1960s the World Bank had become the largest single source of international development finance. At the same time, the growing demand for development finance at the regional level together with various political factors led to the establishment of the IDB in 1959, the African Development Bank (AFDB) in 1963, and the ADB in 1966. While the IDB was operational throughout the 1960s, the other two regional banks only started lending in the late 1960s and consolidated their lending programmes in the 1970s.

A few studies on the World Bank were written in the 1950s and 1960s, but the bulk of the research on the multilateral banks has been published since 1970. Research has tended to focus on the World Bank, owing partly to its leading role and partly to the comparatively recent emergence of the regional banks. Generally, this literature can be classified in three groups: historical accounts, structural and comparative studies of the banks as institutions, and analyses of the banks' development policies and the impact of their operations.

Much of the early research concentrates on the banks' historical development and the description, comparison and analysis of their structure. Mason's and Asher's comprehensive study of the World Bank has become widely accepted as a semi-official history, and at the same time contains substantial critical discussion of central policy issues.[6] While the study covers the entire period from the World Bank's establishment until 1971, it does not extend to McNamara's rural development strategy of the 1970s. Dell's study of the IDB examines the organisation and administration of the bank, and its operational policies, and briefly looks at sectoral lending policies, but does not discuss the IDB's development policy nor assess the impact of its projects.[7] Within a more formal framework, Amegavie describes the structure and modes of operation of the AFDB, while Fordwor provides a personal account of the AFDB's institutional and political problems prior to and during his term as its president.[8]

The first comparative study was White's *Regional Development Banks*, which systematically compares the three regional banks' history, structure and operations. White's discussion of the IDB's lending has the perspective of a full decade, but his treatment of the operations of the ADB and the AFDB, which had both at the time of writing been lending for only one or two years, is by necessity more superficial.[9] An article by Krasner published in 1981 serves to update White's study and draws significant conclusions about the differences in the regional banks' political power structures and operational development.[10] Syz, again, adopts a legalistic approach in his analysis of the multilateral banks' structure and modes of operation, but also points out differences between the banks.[11]

Of more relevance to the present study is the research on the banks' policies and operations, which can broadly be subdivided into reformist policy analyses and more fundamentally critical studies. This literature has to a large extent centred on the evolution of the World Bank's policies during the 1970s. Reformist research, mainly from within the framework of international institutions concerned with development, has concentrated on the problems in effectively implementing rural development programmes and projects, often with a view to recommending changes in the policies and institutions concerned. One of the earliest comprehensive assessments of the World Bank was undertaken by Reid who, after leaving the bank's staff in 1965, published an essay discussing various operational issues and recommending changes in the bank's policies and projects with a view to enhancing its developmental role.[12] In a book published in 1973, which expands on the themes of the essay, Reid examines a wide range of operational issues and puts forward detailed proposals for making the bank more effective, with particular emphasis on the institutional means of increasing the impact of projects on employment creation and strengthening local institutions in the borrowing countries.[13]

Tendler's study of foreign aid, which was published in 1975 and examines both World Bank and USAID projects, is similarly concerned primarily with the role of organisational factors in determining the content of aid programmes.[14] Van de Laar, whose book on the World Bank was published in 1979, six years after McNamara announced the shift in emphasis in the bank's lending, questions whether the bank has been able to reorient its lending to benefit the poor. In seeking to explain the lack of impact of World Bank lending on poverty, van de Laar concentrates on institutional issues and the need for changes in the organisation of the bank.[15] The most recent reformist study of the World Bank, by Ayres, describes the political and administrative constraints within which policy change has taken place, but in contrast to van de Laar's study takes a cautiously positive view of the bank's poverty-oriented lending.[16]

At the same time a much more critical body of literature has emerged which views the multilateral banks primarily as a means of promoting the economic and political interests of the leading donor countries and the often authoritarian governments and predominantly urban élites of the major borrowers, to the detriment of the interests of the urban and rural poor. The World Bank's rural development strategy and the increased flows of development finance to the rural sector are considered a response to the rapidly expanding involvement of the capitalist countries' private sector in Third World agriculture, rather than a genuine response to the problems of rural poverty. Within this context, rural development programmes are seen as a way of integrating small farmers into an exploitative capitalist economy, but are not considered of any significant benefit to the lowest income groups.

*Aid as Imperialism* (Hayter, 1974) was one of the earliest critical studies, but because it attempts to cover the aid programmes of a number of organisations, its analysis is superficial and pays little attention to either the political pressures on aid agencies or the political differences between them.[17] In the late 1970s, a number of studies on the World Bank's rural lending, particularly by Feder, Payer and the Institute for Food and Development Policy, gradually gave more depth to the critical research on development banks.[18] These were followed in 1982 by the study of Bello, Kinley and Elinson concerning World Bank lending in the Philippines, which concludes that its principal impact has been to support an authoritarian regime, while contributing to a deterioration in the economic position of the rural and urban poor.[19] The most comprehensive critical study is *The World Bank, A Critical Analysis* (Payer, 1982), which discusses the political forces behind the bank and examines in considerable detail the bank's policies and the impact of its lending in each major sector. Based on numerous case examples, Payer concludes that the World Bank's programmes are in close congruence with the economic interests of the US and are supporting the expansion of multinational corporations into the Third World, and that even its poverty-oriented projects are not benefiting the poor.[20]

Owing to the ADB's relatively short existence, the literature on the Bank focuses on its history and a predominantly structural analysis of how the Bank functions, but is markedly lacking in analysis of the Bank's policies and operations. Two historical studies examine the founding of the Bank. Krishnamurti provides a detailed insider's account of the negotiations on the drafting of the Bank's charter between 1963 and 1966, but in reading this study one should bear in mind that it was written at the Bank's request and published by the Bank.[21] Huang's book is also mainly a history of the events leading to the establishment of the Bank, although it briefly examines the Bank's operations between 1968 and 1974.[22] These are supplemented by the memoirs of the Bank's first President, Watanabe Takeshi, which constitute a more personal account of the Bank's founding and its operations from 1968 to 1971.[23]

Several studies touch on aspects of the ADB's policies and operations, but to date no comprehensive policy analysis or assessment has been undertaken. White provides a detailed discussion of the Bank's operational structure, but his coverage of actual operations is brief and dated.[24] Tsao's dissertation is mainly concerned with the Bank's internal workings, and is similarly constrained by the fact that it was written relatively soon after the Bank was established.[25] Krasner's article is much more recent, and provides considerable insight into the political nature of the ADB, but is too brief to go into policies in any detail.[26] Yasutomo, again, provides a useful historical account of Japan's role in the Bank, but discusses Bank policies only briefly and mainly in relation to Japanese policies and interests.[27]

**Political and Organisational Explanations**

The literature assessing multilateral aid agencies and programmes suggests two broad explanations for the limited focus and impact of the banks' lending programmes on poverty – one related to the political power structures and national interests underlying the banks, and the other to the role of organisational factors in shaping and constraining project formulation and implementation. The banks' radical critics emphasise that the World Bank, the IDB and the ADB are political institutions working within a framework determined by the US and a few other industrial countries, promoting capitalism and the role of the private sector in Third World countries, with the inherent economic function of securing sources of supply for the industrial economies and promoting exports of their capital goods and technology to developing countries. These political and economic interests are seen as the main obstacle to the effective redirection of the banks' lending programmes towards poverty alleviation. However, the high degree of political control exerted over the banks' policies and operations is also stressed by researchers more closely affiliated with the realist school of political thought.[28]

On the other hand, particularly since the growth in emphasis placed by donors and aid agencies on poverty-oriented development strategies, a substantial body of research has emerged identifying organisational and administrative factors as the principal constraint on the redirection of aid programmes. Tendler highlights the role of the organisational rather than political environment in determining the content of projects, and notes that, seen from the point of view of an administrator or project planner working inside an organisation, aid agencies have abundant capital resources which they are under constant pressure to commit. According to Tendler, this basic organisational objective of 'moving money', combined with the fact that funds are largely earmarked to cover foreign exchange costs, leads to a strong emphasis on large-scale, standardised capital investment projects and works against projects which do not meet these requirements.[29] More recently the Development Assistance Committee (DAC) has termed this the 'fund-channelling function' of aid agencies.[30]

Rondinelli is more concerned with the complex international procedures for project formulation and implementation which the policy changes of the early 1970s gave rise to, and the disjunction between these procedures, on the one hand, and the borrowing countries' political, administrative and cultural constraints and developmental interests, on the other.[31] He suggests that more appropriate and effective projects can only be achieved by increasing the adaptability of planning and introducing administrative procedures that facilitate innovation. Ascher, again, draws attention to the central role played by agency staff in resisting the adoption of priorities and practices required to pursue new development strategies.[32] In contrast, Ayres discusses the impact of organisational factors alongside that of political constraints.[33]

This study argues that the ADB's approach to rural development is determined by both political and organisational factors, and that a clear distinction can be made between the respective roles of these factors in shaping and constraining Bank policies and operations. Due to the close relationship between financial contributions and real influence in the ADB, its broad policies are largely determined by the policies and interests of its two major donors, Japan and the US. Project formulation, again, is more directly constrained by organisational factors, in particular the operational priorities and objectives set by the Bank's management. Following the Bank's founding its management was concerned with establishing the Bank's reputation and credit rating on the international financial markets and laid strong emphasis on loans conforming to 'sound' banking principles. Once the Bank's financial base was established, management's emphasis shifted towards ensuring a steady expansion of loan commitments and disbursements corresponding to the growth of the Bank's resources. It is the contention of this study that this organisational concern with fund-channelling constrains the ADB to a conventional banking role, and impedes the achievement of broader development objectives. While donor policies and interests determine the parameters of the Bank's development policy and lending, organisational factors determine how policies are implemented, are central to explaining the Bank's very limited involvement in poverty alleviation, and provide the key to any significant change in Bank operations.

**The Framework of this Study**

Policy formulation and implementation in the ADB is examined at four levels. The Bank's *development policy* is defined as the broad socio-economic objectives with which the Bank is concerned, and the overall strategy for achieving these objectives (for example, increased agricultural production, increased rural employment and the more equitable distribution of rural incomes, combined as a 'rural development' strategy). The Bank's *operational policies and lending practices* are the specific decisions and activities undertaken towards achieving policy objectives (for example, the allocation of resources by sector, subsector and country, and specific policies related to project formulation and implementation). The ADB's principal policy outputs are *projects*, but these should be distinguished from *project impact* which may or may not meet policy objectives (for example, farm output increased, rural jobs created, and income disparities reduced).[34]

The main difficulty in analysing policy formulation and implementation in the Bank is the large number of factors which shape the different stages of the process. Corresponding to the levels of the policy process, four major groups of factors can be distinguished. The Bank's development policy follows broad trends in international development policy, but is also shaped by the specific policies and interests of the Bank's major donors. Operational policies, again, are shaped within a political and an organisational context, and their practical implementation takes place within the framework of goals and objectives set by management. The borrowing countries obviously also influence the above two stages, but the role of their policies and vested political interests is more prevalent at the stage of project formulation. Projects are prepared within the context of government programmes, although the Bank may play a role in formulating these programmes. Finally, whether projects have the intended impact or not is also determined by the socio-economic conditions in the borrowing country. The different levels of policy formulation and implementation and the main factors influencing the process are set out in Figure 1.1, which also serves as a basis for the structure of this study.

Following a review in Chapter 2 of the Bank's operational structure and the distribution of influence among its member countries, Chapter 3 discusses the role of the donor governments in shaping ADB policy. In examining the Bank's policies it is particularly significant that the donor countries wield about 55 per cent of formal voting power and contribute about 90 per cent of the Bank's resources. The ADB's donors can be divided into three groups. Japan and the United States account for 41.8 per cent and 16.1 per cent of ADB resources respectively, and both have a strong independent influence on ADB policies, while the influence of the other donors, who have contributed 32.1 per cent of Bank resources, is more fragmented. The primary source for the donors' policies toward the Bank are their governors' statements at the Bank's annual meetings.

Chapter 4 examines the development of the ADB's policy for the rural sector, the Bank's initial policy of agricultural modernisation, its shift towards a policy of rural development in the mid-1970s, and

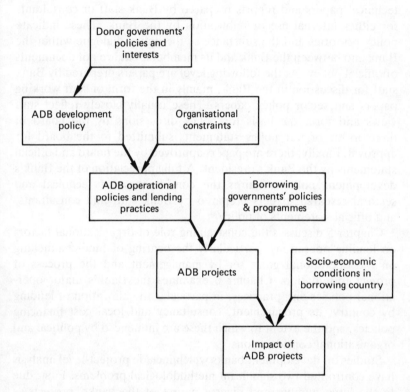

*Figure* 1.1 Factors influencing the formulation and implementation of ADB policy and projects

policy changes in the early 1980s. In contrast to the relatively clear-cut source material on donor policies, material on Bank development policy is difficult to define and can broadly be classified into three groups, according to the degree of formal approval it has within the Bank. At the bottom of this hierarchy are major sectoral surveys, technical papers and reports prepared by Bank staff or consultants for either internal use or publication by the Bank. These indicate policy priorities and the substance of the policy dialogue within the Bank and between the Bank and its members, but are not documents of official policy. At the following level are papers prepared by Bank staff for discussion in the Bank, mainly in the form of staff working papers and sector policy papers. These usually closely reflect staff views and form the basis for policy discussions by the board of directors or briefer policy statements submitted to the board for approval. Finally, there are papers approved by the board and official statements by the Bank's president. A full appreciation of the Bank's development policy requires the consideration of technical and sectoral research, papers prepared by Bank staff and consultants, and official statements of policy.

Chapter 5 discusses the constraining role of organisational factors on lending operations, particularly the bearing of fund-channelling on the operational goals set by management and the process of project formulation. Chapter 6 examines the Bank's major operational policies and practices, in particular the allocation of lending by country, its procurement, consultancy and local cost financing policies, and the extent to which these are influenced by political and organisational considerations.

Studies on development banks which include project-level analysis have confronted two significant methodological problems. First, due to the large number and diverse nature of the banks' projects, a suitable balance must be struck between the detailed examination of specific projects and the need to draw general conclusions. One of the earliest project studies is Hirschman's analysis of eleven World Bank projects.[35] However, as van de Laar points out, the small number of projects selected casts some doubt on the general applicability of the conclusions.[36] In their recent analyses of the World Bank, both Payer and Ayres adopt a more satisfactory approach, supplementing a discussion of sectoral policies with numerous case examples.[37] The nature of the problem in the ADB is demonstrated by the fact that between 1968 and 1986 the Bank approved 746 loans with a total value of $19.5 billion.

The second problem relates to the selection and availability of information on projects. The ADB's project cycle is based on that of the World Bank and can be divided into six stages: identification, preparation, appraisal, loan negotiations and approval, implementation, and post-evaluation.[38] From the point of view of providing information on projects and their impact, the appraisal and post-evaluation stages are the most important. The appraisal report, which is prepared by Bank staff, covers the technical, institutional, economic and financial aspects of a project, serves as a basis for loan negotiations, and forms an integral part of the loan agreement. It is a reliable source of information on the objectives and intended impact of a project, but not of its *actual* implementation or impact. When a project is completed, a project completion report (PCR) is prepared by the responsible technical division, and some months later a project performance audit report (PPAR) is prepared by the Bank's Post-Evaluation Office, an independent unit which reports directly to the president.[39] The PPAR is a relatively critical in-house assessment intended 'to identify lessons from experience that can be applied to improve future development assistance from the bank',[40] but while it is of considerable use in assessing a project's impact, as the life-cycle of a typical project lasts from six to ten years, PPARs are not available for recent projects. At the same time, as Payer points out with regard to the World Bank, official project reports need to be supplemented with independent accounts.[41]

Chapters 7 and 8 look at the Bank's rural sector projects, in particular the extent to which policy changes have or have not led to innovations and changes in projects, and the impact of rural projects in the borrowing countries. To narrow down the focus of the discussion, the three most important subsectors of rural lending have been selected – irrigation and rural development, rural credit and road construction.[42] In each area the chapters examine whether projects have changed, and the projects' impact on three key policy objectives: agricultural production, employment and income distribution. The discussion is centred on five clusters of projects: irrigation and rural development in Indonesia and the Philippines, agricultural credit in Nepal, fisheries credit in Sri Lanka, and road construction in the Philippines. The chapter is based on appraisal reports, PCRs and PPARs, supplemented with relevant reports by other agencies and available independent accounts.

# 2 The Asian Development Bank

An important distinction between most specialised agencies of the UN system[1] and the multilateral banks is that in the former each member government has one vote, while in the latter voting power and influence is much more closely related to financial contributions and emphasises the relative role of the banks' donors. Both the ADB's decision-making structure and the positions taken by its members on key institutional and policy issues highlight the fact that a fundamental conflict in the Bank is that between the interests of the donors and the developing member countries (DMCs) in exerting control over the Bank's operations. Following a brief outline of how the Bank operates, this chapter discusses the question of political influence in the Bank, and compares voting power and formal influence with the more realistic financial influence.

## How the Bank Operates

The ADB was established in December 1966 as the result of a series of preparatory meetings held between 1963 and 1966 under the auspices of the UN Economic Commission for Asia and the Far East (ECAFE).[2] On the one hand, the Bank was set up in response to the perceived need among the Asian countries for a source of development finance catering to the specific needs of the region. In the early 1960s there was considerable dissatisfaction among the Asian countries with World Bank lending, which in Asia was concentrated mainly in India and Pakistan and on infrastructure as opposed to agriculture or industry. On the other hand, the main incentive for the financial participation of the industrialised countries lay in the opportunity the Bank offered as a means for promoting their development policies and economic and political interests. Japan played a particularly central role in establishing the Bank, due to the vital importance of the Asian developing countries both as a source of raw materials and food and as an outlet for expanding exports and foreign investment for the Japanese economy.

The Bank had 31 founding members, and by 1987 its membership had increased to 47, consisting of 29 Asian and Pacific developing countries and 18 industrial countries, three from the region (Japan, Australia and New Zealand), two from North America (the US and Canada) and 13 from Western Europe (Austria, Belgium, Denmark, Finland, France, Italy, the Netherlands, Norway, Spain, Sweden, Switzerland, the UK and West Germany). The industrial members constitute the main source of funds for Bank operations, while the DMCs, with three exceptions, are the Bank's borrowers. When the Bank was established, it was agreed that India would not be included among the borrowers; this policy was recently revised, and in 1986 the Bank initiated a lending programme in India. Taiwan, Hong Kong and Singapore, again, have been 'graduated' by the Bank from the status of borrowing countries.

The ADB's principal mode of operation is the provision of capital assistance for development projects, in the form of loans on either ordinary or concessional terms. Loans from the Bank's ordinary capital resources (OCR) have a 2- to 7-year grace period and a maturity period of 10 to 30 years, and have carried interest rates varying from 6.875 per cent in the late 1960s to 10.5 per cent in 1983; in 1986 the Bank introduced a standard variable interest rate which was initially set at 7.65 per cent and revised in 1987 to 7.03 per cent. Concessional loans from the Bank's special fund resources (SFR), again, have a 10-year grace period, a maturity period of 40 years, and carry interest only in the form of a 1 per cent service charge. Ordinary loans are made for all sectors of Bank activity, and have concentrated on the member countries with a relatively high gross national product (GNP) per capita, particularly the Association of Southeast Asian Nations (ASEAN) countries and the East Asian developing countries. Concessional loans, again, have been granted mainly to the least developed members, particularly in South Asia, and are often more directly poverty-oriented, focusing predominantly on agriculture and rural development. By the end of 1986, the Bank had committed ordinary loans totalling $13 316.7 million and concessional loans worth $6174.7 million.

In addition to its lending activities, the Bank provides technical assistance grants and has carried out various regional activities. Technical assistance is intended mainly to help the borrowing countries in project preparation and implementation, and has concentrated on the least developed member countries. The Bank's regional activities, again, include the undertaking or commissioning of various regional surveys and studies, and the organising of meetings, seminars and workshops. Technical assistance and regional activities provide the ADB with a means of influencing the formulation of development policies in its borrowing countries, and there has been a clear shift from the provision of policy guidance at the regional level, including the two agricultural surveys, to the enhancement of the Bank's role in country-level policy formulation in the 1980s. Compared with the World Bank, which often makes loans conditional on policy changes, the initial thrust of ADB operations was at the project rather than the policy level. Although recently the Bank has increasingly attached policy conditions to its loans, it is confined by its charter to lending for projects. By 1986, the Bank had provided $241.6 million in technical assistance grants, of which $204.2 million was for technical assistance to individual countries and $37.4 million for regional activities.

ADB operations are funded through three channels, which correspond to the Bank's modes of operation. The Bank's ordinary capital resources form the basis for ordinary lending operations, while the Asian Development Fund (ADF) provides concessional loans. Technical assistance grants are funded mainly through the Bank's Technical Assistance Special Fund (TASF), but these are supplemented with grants from other sources, mainly the donors' bilateral programmes and the United Nations Development Programme (UNDP).

The Bank's OCR consist of three main categories: subscribed capital stock, funds raised by the Bank through borrowing, and funds received by the Bank as repayment of and income from OCR loans. Based on its subscribed capital stock, the Bank borrows on the international capital markets, and lends to its developing members on terms which broadly reflect the Bank's own borrowing costs and administrative expenses. Member countries' subscriptions to Bank capital are divided into paid-in and callable shares, of which the paid-in portion has ranged from 50 per cent of subscriptions to the original capital stock to 5 per cent of subscriptions to the third general increase in 1983. The paid-in shares are paid partly in convertible currency and partly in the national currency of the member, while the callable shares in effect constitute a government guarantee from each member country. By 1986, Bank members had subscribed a total of $19 475.9 million of their entitlements, of which $2354.4 million (12.1 per cent) was paid in and $17 121.6 million (87.9 per cent) was callable.

At the time of establishment of the ADB, there was considerable disagreement among the member countries regarding the importance of special funds and the form such funds should take. Consequently, no general fund comparable to the World Bank's concessional 'window', the IDA, was established, and the ADB charter merely set out the general terms for eventual special funds. Once the Bank was operational in 1968 three special funds were set up, the Multi-Purpose Special Fund (MPSF), the Agricultural Special Fund (ASF) and the Technical Assistance Special Fund (TASF). The MPSF provided loans on concessional terms for all sectors, while the ASF, which was funded mainly by Japan, provided concessional loans for agricultural projects. Initially donors contributed to the MPSF and ASF at their own initiative on a bilateral basis, and under terms which varied considerably. As the Bank's concessional lending expanded, the need to regularise the mobilisation of additional resources for the special funds and achieve uniformity in the terms and administration of concessional lending led to the establishment in 1974 of the ADF, which gradually became the Bank's only source of concessional loans.

ADF resources consist of contributions from donor countries, funds recieved as payment and income from ADF loans, and a small portion of so-called set-aside resources from the Bank's OCR. Because of the concessional terms of its loans, the ADF cannot sustain itself on repayments and income and is almost completely reliant on replenishments to maintain and expand its lending. Consequently, while ADF loans have accounted for only 31.7 per cent of Bank lending, as contributions to the fund are paid in full, by 1986 contributions to the ADF constituted 75.9 per cent of funds actually paid in to the Bank by donors. The replenishment negotiations for the ADF, at which both the size of each replenishment and the formula for cost-sharing among donors are worked out, are held at 4-year intervals. The negotiations have proved sensitive to changes in donor policies and have become increasingly politicised, with some contributions being used directly as a means of achieving leverage over Bank policies, particularly by the US. Due to the ADF's direct dependence on contributions, delays in payment and in replenishment negotiations have on several occasions restricted and threatened to halt ADF lending.

Although small in volume compared with the Bank's capital assistance, technical assistance is used mainly for project preparation and therefore plays an important role in determining project content. Compared with the ADF, which unified the terms of the Bank's concessional lending, contributions to the TASF, as well as other technical assistance contributions, are made by donors on a bilateral basis, giving them considerable influence on the use to which their contributions are put. Procurement and consultancy contracts under Bank and ADF loans are governed by international competitive bidding (ICB) and Bank procedures for the selection of consultants, but while an effort has been made by the Bank to untie consultancy services provided under technical assistance grants, these continue to be tied in varying degree to the donor country.[3]

## Voting Power and Financial Influence

In examining the power structure of the ADB, a distinction should be made between formal voting power and actual influence on Bank operations. Formal voting power is predominantly proportional to economic contributions, and is based 80 per cent on capital subscriptions and 20 per cent on an equal distribution of votes. However, the formula does not reflect the real influence of the Bank's dominant donors as it takes account of neither special fund contributions, which in fact constitute a much larger financial contribution from donors than capital subscriptions, nor the weight carried by the potential threat that contributions will not be renewed unless the donors' policy requirements are met.

In the negotiations on the drafting of the ADB charter, a number of decisions of key importance to the power structure and decision-making process of the Bank were worked out. The two most important were the distribution of voting power and the size of and distribution of seats on the board of directors. Underlying the question of voting power were two issues, the need to balance the regional and non-regional countries' power, to ensure the regional nature of the Bank, and the need to strike a balance between proportionality, in relation to financial contributions, and equality. The latter principle was important to guarantee a degree of voting power to the Bank's DMCs, but relating voting to economic contributions was important as an incentive for the financial participation of the donors.

To ensure that control of the Bank remained with the regional countries, it was decided that a minimum of 60 per cent of total voting strength should be reserved for the regional countries. With regard to financial proportionality and equality, it was agreed, following the example of the other multilateral banks, to adopt a system consisting of basic votes distributed on an equal basis and additional votes based on the number of shares subscribed.[4] The percentage of basic votes, which was crucial in determining how financially weighted the voting system would be, however, was the subject of extensive and controversial discussion.

Both the developing countries and the socialist countries participating in the negotiations favoured a large share of basic votes, while Japan, the US and the other donors wanted higher financial proportionality, to ensure their control over Bank operations. Afghanistan initially favoured a fully equal distribution of votes, and later adopted the position that at least 50 per cent should be distributed equally. South Korea also favoured allocating 50 per cent of votes equally, while the other developing countries wanted at least 20 per cent of votes to be distributed on an equal basis.[5] Both the USSR and Czechoslovakia, who participated in the initial ECAFE negotiations on the ADB, supported the fully equal distribution of votes, and cited the unequal distribution of votes as one of their main reasons for not joining the Bank.[6]

The Japanese Ministry of Finance instructed its representatives to press for a single digit percentage and established 10 per cent as its upper limit, in line with the model of the World Bank.[7] The US also favoured a solution along the lines of the World Bank, putting its preference at between 5 and 10 per cent and setting 20 per cent as an absolute ceiling. The other donors supported percentages ranging from 10 to 20. Eventually, a consensus in support of 20 per cent was reached, although Japan, already having amended its upper limit by going up to 15 per cent, only agreed on the condition that the board of directors have ten seats rather than the twelve demanded by the developing countries.[8]

Table 2.1 sets out the distribution of voting power and total paid-in financial contributions (OCR and SFR) to the Bank by member country. The distribution of voting power can be examined in terms of regional and non-regional countries, as stressed by the Bank, or in terms of donors and DMCs, which is more relevant for most policy issues.[9] The voting power of the regional members, including Japan, Australia and New Zealand, has been well over 60 per cent, but it is considerably more significant that the donors have had continuous control over the Bank, with mean voting power of approximately 59 per cent compared with the DMCs' 41 per cent. Over time the DMCs' voting power has increased somewhat, most recently following the Bank's acceptance of China as a member in 1986. At the same time

*Table* 2.1 Voting power in and total financial contributions to the ADB by member country (per cent)

| | Voting power in 1968 | Voting power in 1976 | Voting power in 1986 | Share of total paid-in financial contributions by 1986 (OCR and SFR) |
|---|---|---|---|---|
| Afghanistan | 1.0 | 0.8 | 0.5 | * |
| Bangladesh | – | 1.5 | 1.3 | 0.3 |
| Bhutan | – | – | 0.4 | * |
| Burma | – | 1.0 | 0.9 | 0.1 |
| Cambodia | 0.9 | 0.7 | 0.5 | * |
| China | – | – | 6.2 | 1.7 |
| Cook Islands | – | 0.5 | 0.4 | * |
| Fiji | – | 0.5 | 0.5 | * |
| Hong Kong | – | 1.0 | 0.9 | 0.2 |
| India | 8.3 | 6.6 | 6.1 | 1.7 |
| Indonesia | 2.7 | 5.7 | 5.3 | 1.5 |
| Kiribati | – | 0.5 | 0.4 | * |
| Laos | 0.7 | 0.5 | 0.4 | * |
| Malaysia | 2.3 | 3.1 | 2.8 | 0.7 |
| Maldives | – | – | 0.4 | * |
| Nepal | 0.8 | 0.6 | 0.6 | * |
| Pakistan | 3.3 | 2.6 | 2.4 | 0.6 |
| Papua New Guinea | – | 0.6 | 0.5 | * |
| Philippines | 3.5 | 2.8 | 2.5 | 0.6 |
| Singapore | 1.0 | 0.8 | 0.7 | 0.1 |
| Solomon Islands | – | 0.5 | 0.4 | * |
| South Korea | 3.1 | 5.3 | 4.9 | 1.4 |
| Sri Lanka | 1.3 | 1.0 | 0.9 | 0.2 |
| Taiwan | 1.9 | 1.5 | 1.4 | 0.3 |
| Thailand | 2.3 | 1.8 | 1.6 | 0.4 |
| Tonga | – | 0.5 | 0.4 | * |
| Vanuatu | – | – | 0.4 | * |
| Vietnam | 1.6 | 1.3 | 0.7 | 0.2 |
| Western Samoa | 0.6 | 0.6 | 0.4 | * |
| *Total developing* | 35.3 | 42.0 | 45.1 | 10.0 |
| Australia | 7.6 | 6.0 | 5.6 | 4.0 |
| Japan | 17.1 | 13.6 | 12.5 | 41.8 |
| New Zealand | 2.5 | 2.0 | 1.8 | 0.5 |
| *Total regional* | 62.5 | 63.6 | 65.0 | 46.3 |
| Austria | 1.0 | 0.8 | 0.7 | 0.7 |
| Belgium | 1.0 | 0.8 | 0.7 | 0.7 |
| Canada | 2.7 | 5.5 | 5.1 | 6.2 |
| Denmark | 1.0 | 0.8 | 0.7 | 0.6 |
| Finland | 1.0 | 0.6 | 0.7 | 0.4 |
| France | – | 2.1 | 2.5 | 2.9 |
| Italy | 2.3 | 1.8 | 1.6 | 2.2 |
| Netherlands | 1.5 | 1.2 | 1.1 | 1.9 |
| Norway | 1.0 | 0.8 | 0.7 | 0.5 |

| | Voting power in 1968 | Voting power in 1976 | Voting power in 1986 | Share of total paid-in financial contributions by 1986 (OCR and SFR) |
|---|---|---|---|---|
| Spain | – | – | 0.7 | 0.4 |
| Sweden | 1.0 | 0.6 | 0.5 | 0.6 |
| Switzerland | 1.0 | 0.8 | 0.9 | 1.1 |
| UK | 3.1 | 2.4 | 2.2 | 2.9 |
| US | 17.1 | 13.6 | 12.3 | 16.1 |
| West Germany | 3.4 | 4.6 | 4.3 | 6.5 |
| Total non-regional | 37.5 | 36.4 | 35.0 | 43.7 |
| Total developed | 64.7 | 58.0 | 54.9 | 90.0 |
| Grand total | 100.0 | 100.0 | 100.0 | 100.0 |

\* Less than five hundredths of one per cent.
*Note*: Figures may not tally due to rounding.

*Source*: ADB, *Annual Report* (1968, 1976 and 1986).

the major donors have taken steps to ensure that their share of votes is not eroded.

Voting power is weighted in favour of the donors, but is inadequate as an indicator of real influence in the Bank for two reasons. First, it is based only on OCR subscriptions and takes no account of special fund contributions. While capital subscriptions constituted the major initial contribution of member countries, over time contributions to the ADF have gained importance and are at present over three times actual paid-in capital. By 1986, member governments' paid-in contributions to the Bank and the ADF totalled $9779 million, of which $2354.4 million (24 per cent) consisted of paid-in capital subscriptions, and $7424.6 million (76 per cent) of ADF contributions received by the Bank.

As ADF contributions have increased, voting power has become less representative of actual financial contributions. For example, by 1986 Japan had contributed $3730.8 million to the ADF, which far exceeded the US contribution of $1222.1 million, although their respective capital subscriptions entitled both countries to virtually identical voting shares of 12.5 and 12.3 per cent respectively. Similarly, based on its capital subscription, of which $150.3 million is paid-in, Australia is entitled to a voting share of 5.6 per cent, compared with Canada's paid-in capital of $135.9 million and voting share of 5.1 per cent, in spite of the fact that by 1986 Canada had contributed $471.8

million to the ADF in contrast to Australia's $243.8 million. Several major ADF donors have drawn attention to this inconsistency, and in the early 1980s some West European countries requested a special capital increase to allow them to raise their voting power, in part to reflect their contribution to the ADF.[10] More recently Japan has pushed for greater voting power, to reflect its very substantial contribution to the ADF.[11]

Special fund contributions do not increase the donors' votes, but their significance in keeping the ADF operational is acknowledged by both member countries and Bank management, and they do increase the donors' leverage over Bank policies. The fact that by 1986, 90 per cent of all financial contributions had been made by the developed countries, with Japan and the US between them accounting for 58 per cent, and the other donors, principally Canada, Australia and West Germany, for 32 per cent, in contrast to the developing countries' share of 10 per cent, mainly from China, India, South Korea and Indonesia, is therefore considerably more indicative of real influence than voting power.

Secondly, financial influence is supported by the implicit, and in some instances explicit, threat that the contributions will not be renewed unless the donors' policy requirements are met. Delays and reductions in subscription to capital increases have been used by member governments and legislatures as a means of expressing dissatisfaction with Bank policies and operations. For example in the early 1970s Sweden and Finland reduced their capital subscriptions, mainly owing to their discontent with the Bank's Vietnam policy and the country allocation of lending. US congressional opposition has caused lengthy delays in the appropriation of US capital subscriptions and resulted in a significant drop in US voting power in 1977, and ADF replenishment negotiations have been used systematically by US administrations to obtain leverage in policy issues.

## Decision-making in the Bank

The Bank's decision-making bodies are the board of governors and the board of directors, while policies and programmes are implemented by the Bank's staff, headed by its president. In principle the powers of the Bank are vested in the board of governors, which is reserved the right, among other things, to decide questions of membership, change the authorised capital stock, amend the charter, and elect the executive directors and president.[12] The board of governors convenes annually for three days in late April or early May and consists of a governor and alternate governor from each member country. In practice, the board of directors, which convenes once or twice a week under the chairmanship of the president, is responsible for directing the operations of the Bank, and takes decisions concerning the approval of loans, technical assistance and other operational activities.[13] The twelve executive directors, six from the donors and six from the DMCs, are elected by voting groups on the board of governors and are full-time Bank officials. The president of the Bank, who is by tradition Japanese, is responsible for the management of Bank staff and operations. While he is in principle responsible to the board of directors, in practice Bank presidents have exercised considerable independence in running the Bank. The organisational structure of the Bank is set out in Figure 2.1.

The number of executive directors on the board and their distribution between regional and non-regional members was a major question of contention in drafting the Bank charter, and was closely linked with the basic vote issue. In the initial discussions, which focused on a ten-member board, the DMCs favoured a division of 7 regional and 3 non-regional directors, while the donors wanted a division of 6 regional and 4 non-regional directors. When the 20 per cent compromise was reached in the basic vote question the DMCs demanded compensation in the form of greater representation on the board of directors. Due to the strongly opposed views of the donors and the DMCs, however, no final settlement was reached, and a compromise was worked out of seven regional and three non-regional directors for the first two years of Bank operations. As part of this arrangement, the Bank charter included the stipulation that after two years of operations the Board of Governors 'shall review the size and composition of the board of directors, and shall increase the number of Directors as appropriate, paying special attention to the desirability, in the circumstances at that time, of increasing representation in the Board of Directors of smaller less developed member countries'.[14] According to Krishnamurti, this was a clear acceptance of the regional countries' demand that their representation on the board should be increased from 7 to 9 after two years.[15] At the 1969 annual meeting, however, Canada and numerous smaller donors were also seeking greater representation on the board, and following considerable pressure by the donors, it was agreed to increase the board by two executive directors, one regional and one non-regional, to be

26

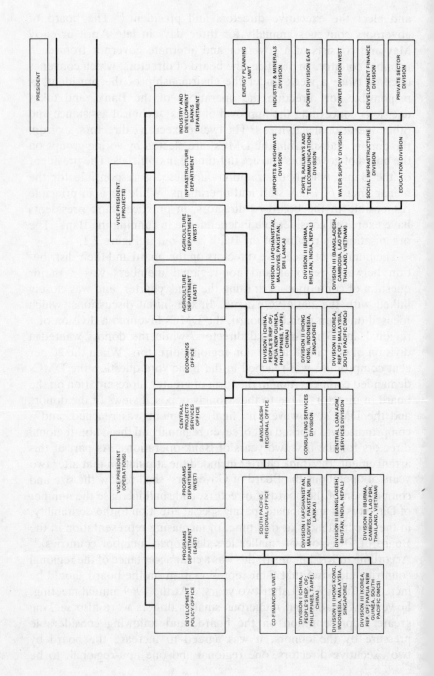

PRESIDENT

VICE PRESIDENT (PROJECTS)

INDUSTRY AND DEVELOPMENT BANKS DEPARTMENT
- ENERGY PLANNING UNIT
- INDUSTRY & MINERALS DIVISION
- POWER DIVISION EAST
- POWER DIVISION WEST
- DEVELOPMENT FINANCE DIVISION
- PRIVATE SECTOR DIVISION

INFRASTRUCTURE DEPARTMENT
- AIRPORTS & HIGHWAYS DIVISION
- PORTS, RAILWAYS AND TELECOMMUNICATIONS DIVISION
- WATER SUPPLY DIVISION
- SOCIAL INFRASTRUCTURE DIVISION
- EDUCATION DIVISION

AGRICULTURE DEPARTMENT (WEST)
- DIVISION I (AFGHANISTAN, MALDIVES, PAKISTAN, SRI LANKA)
- DIVISION II (BURMA, BHUTAN, INDIA, NEPAL)
- DIVISION III (BANGLADESH, CAMBODIA, LAO PDR, THAILAND, VIETNAM)

AGRICULTURE DEPARTMENT (EAST)
- DIVISION I (CHINA, PEOPLE'S REP. OF; PAPUA NEW GUINEA, PHILIPPINES, TAIPEI, CHINA)
- DIVISION II (HONG KONG, INDONESIA, SINGAPORE)
- DIVISION III (KOREA, REP. OF; MALAYSIA, SOUTH PACIFIC DMCs)

ECONOMICS OFFICE

CENTRAL PROJECTS SERVICES OFFICE
- BANGLADESH REGIONAL OFFICE
- CONSULTING SERVICES DIVISION
- CENTRAL LOAN ADM. SERVICES DIVISION

VICE PRESIDENT (OPERATIONS)

PROGRAMS DEPARTMENT (WEST)
- SOUTH PACIFIC REGIONAL OFFICE
- DIVISION I (AFGHANISTAN, MALDIVES, PAKISTAN, SRI LANKA)
- DIVISION II (BANGLADESH, BHUTAN, INDIA, NEPAL)
- DIVISION III (BURMA, CAMBODIA, LAO PDR, THAILAND, VIETNAM)

PROGRAMS DEPARTMENT (EAST)
- CO-FINANCING UNIT
- DIVISION I (CHINA, PEOPLE'S REP. OF; PHILIPPINES, TAIPEI, CHINA)
- DIVISION II (HONG KONG, INDONESIA, MALAYSIA, SINGAPORE)
- DIVISION III (KOREA, REP. OF; PAPUA NEW GUINEA, SOUTH PACIFIC DMCS)

DEVELOPMENT POLICY OFFICE

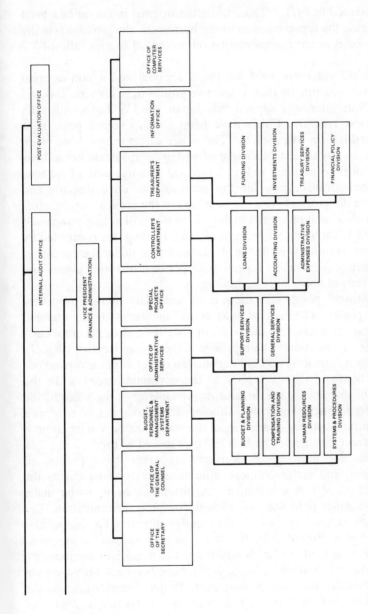

*Figure* 2.1 The organisational structure of the ADB (April 1987)

*Source:* ADB.

implemented in 1971.[16] Thus, while the original intention had been to increase the representation of the borrowers, the increase actually weakened regional representation on the board from a ratio of 7:3 to 8:4.

Separate votes are held for the 8 regional and 4 non-regional executive directors by their respective groups of governors, and due to the voting formula applied only Japan, the US, India, Australia and, most recently, China have been able to secure permanent directorships for themselves. The other directorships have been worked out by the establishment of voting groups along broad lines of political, economic and geographical affinity, and of various rotational arrangements for the posts of executive director and alternate director between the members of the groups. Six director-ships with a total of approximately 55 per cent of voting power and responsible for about 90 per cent of Bank funding, are controlled by the donor countries, while the six directorships under the control of the developing members represent 45 per cent of voting power and 10 per cent of financial contributions.

As Krasner points out, there is no secondary literature on how voting power is translated into actual influence in the regional development banks.[17] In the board of governors, each governor casts the votes of the country he represents. The annual meeting, though, is largely a formality, and the negotiation of key issues is carried out in the board of directors prior to the governors' meeting. In the board of directors, each director in principle casts the votes of the countries in his voting group, although these need not be used as a unit, and if a country dissents from the other members in its group it can instruct the director on how its votes should be used.

In practice most board decisions are taken by a process of consensus, and major political differences are resolved during the preparation of policy initiatives. A distinction needs to be made between policy influence and influence on project formulation. The influence exerted by individual executive directors on the policies adopted and promoted by the Bank has become increasingly im-portant, and tends to be closely related to financial contributions. Consequently, both the US and Japan have been notably successful in introducing their policy initiatives. Project formulation, on the other hand, is carried out by Bank staff and is only subject to control by the executive directors when a project is submitted to the board. In the rare instances when directors have resorted to voting, the

*Table* 2.2 Distribution of ADB staff by nationality (as of May 1983)

| Country | Total professional staff | Per cent | Senior staff | Per cent |
|---|---|---|---|---|
| US | 61 | 11.4 | 11 | 15.1 |
| Japan | 48 | 9.0 | 10 | 13.5 |
| Australia | 38 | 7.1 | 4 | 5.5 |
| Canada | 34 | 6.4 | 4 | 5.5 |
| UK | 27 | 5.0 | 4 | 5.5 |
| West Germany | 19 | 3.6 | 4 | 5.5 |
| France | 14 | 2.6 | 1 | 1.4 |
| New Zealand | 12 | 2.2 | – | – |
| Netherlands | 11 | 2.1 | – | – |
| Sweden | 8 | 1.5 | 1 | 1.4 |
| Denmark | 6 | 1.1 | – | – |
| Finland | 4 | 0.7 | – | – |
| Belgium | 3 | 0.6 | – | – |
| Austria | 2 | 0.4 | – | – |
| Italy | 2 | 0.4 | – | – |
| Norway | 2 | 0.4 | – | – |
| Switzerland | 2 | 0.4 | 1 | 1.4 |
| *Total donors* | 293 | 54.8 | 40 | 54.8 |
| India | 46 | 8.6 | 12 | 16.4 |
| Philippines | 36 | 6.7 | 2 | 2.7 |
| South Korea | 27 | 5.0 | 3 | 4.1 |
| Malaysia | 24 | 4.5 | 3 | 4.1 |
| Pakistan | 19 | 3.6 | 6 | 8.2 |
| Indonesia | 14 | 2.6 | 1 | 1.4 |
| Sri Lanka | 14 | 2.6 | 2 | 2.7 |
| Thailand | 12 | 2.2 | – | – |
| Singapore | 11 | 2.1 | – | – |
| Burma | 10 | 1.9 | – | – |
| Bangladesh | 9 | 1.7 | 1 | 1.4 |
| Nepal | 7 | 1.3 | – | – |
| Taiwan | 7 | 1.3 | 1 | 1.4 |
| Afghanistan | 3 | 0.6 | 2 | 2.7 |
| Hong Kong | 2 | 0.4 | – | – |
| Laos | 1 | 0.2 | – | – |
| Other borrowers* | – | – | – | – |
| *Total borrowers* | 242 | 45.2 | 33 | 45.2 |
| *Total regional* | 340 | 63.6 | 47 | 64.4 |
| *Total non-regional* | 195 | 36.4 | 26 | 35.6 |
| *Total* | 535 | 100.0 | 73 | 100.0 |

* Bhutan, Cambodia, Cook Islands, Fiji, Kiribati, Maldives, PNG, Solomon Islands, Tonga, Vanuatu, Vietnam, Western Samoa.

*Source*: ADB, *Organizational Listing* (31 May 1983).

issues have usually been political and voting has proved to be a relatively ineffective means of influencing Bank decisions.

When the Bank was being established, the question of the presidency and the location of the Bank were closely linked, with Japan initially seeking both. Once it was decided to locate the headquarters in Manila, Japan made an assertive effort to secure the presidency of the Bank. At the inaugural meeting of the board of governors in November 1966, Watanabe Takeshi, the leading Japanese representative in negotiations for the establishment of the Bank, was elected its first president. Since then the presidency has been reserved for Japan. Watanabe was president from 1966 to 1972, followed by Inoue Shiro (1972–6), Yoshida Taroichi (1976–81) and Fujioka Masao since November 1981. With the exception of Inoue, who was from the Bank of Japan, the ADB presidents all made their careers at the Japanese Ministry of Finance.

In contrast to the president, who is formally elected by the board of governors, the vice-presidents are appointed by the board of directors on the recommendation of the president. Since 1978, there has been considerable strengthening of the representation of non-regional countries at the vice-presidential level, reflecting the importance of financial contributions. From 1967 to 1978, the Bank had one vice-president, an Indian national. Upon his retirement in 1978, two vice-presidents were appointed, one from India and the other from the US. In 1983, in response to demands from the smaller donors for greater representation in top management, a third vice-president was appointed, from West Germany.

The distribution of staff by member country, which is set out in Table 2.2, also closely reflects the formal distribution of power in the Bank. The regional countries account for 63.6 per cent of professional staff, compared with voting power of 64.2 per cent, while the corresponding figures for the donor countries are 54.8 and 57.8 per cent. To a certain degree, the division of staff enhances the role in the Bank of the US, India and the major borrowing countries, in contrast to that of Japan. It is noteworthy that India, the US and Japan between them account for 45.2 per cent of senior staff positions, compared with 29 per cent of all staff positions. Five countries – Pakistan, Australia, Canada, West Germany and the UK – account for a further 30.1 per cent of senior staff. On the other hand, some small borrowers, the Indo-Chinese countries and the small island countries have virtually no representation on Bank staff.

# 3 Donor Policies and Interests

Underlying policy formulation in the ADB are the policies and interests of its member countries, in particular the donors. Based on the extent of their influence in the Bank and differences in their policy objectives, the Bank's donors can be divided into three groups: Japan (12.5 per cent of votes and 41.8 per cent of financial contributions), the US (12.3 per cent of votes and 16.1 per cent of financial contributions), and the other donors (30.1 per cent of votes and 32.1 per cent of financial contributions), although the countries in the last group can be subdivided based on policy differences and, for example, their level of financial participation in the Bank. The objectives pursued by the donors in the ADB can also broadly be classified into three categories: political and strategic, economic and commercial, and developmental. Significant differences can be pointed out in the relative importance of these objectives to the different donors.

Owing to Japan's high level of economic reliance on the Asian region, its development policy is closely linked to the pursuit of Japanese economic and commercial interests. At the same time, Japan has an obvious interest in maintaining political stability in Asia and particularly Southeast Asia. US participation in the Bank is derived more directly from the political and strategic importance of the Asian region to US interests, and while it also has clear economic objectives, the US is not very dependent on trade with the ADB countries. In comparison, the Western European donors' and Canada's participation in the Bank is mainly a reflection of their support for multilateral development assistance as a means of meeting recipient needs, on the one hand, and their interest in the trade opportunities offered by the Bank, on the other. Australia and New Zealand have a more direct regional interest in the Bank, but their policy interests are closer to those of the other smaller donors than the two major donors. This chapter compares the donors' policies toward the ADB, with emphasis on four issues: the volume of funds channelled through the Bank and the ADF, the terms of Bank lending, the country allocation of lending, and development priorities, particularly with regard to rural development.

31

## JAPAN

Studies of Japanese aid indicate a closer link between development cooperation and economic and commerical interests than in the case of other major donors, mainly due to the extreme reliance of the Japanese economy on foreign trade.[1] Through its participation in the ADB, Japan has concentrated on pursuing both general economic interests and specific short-term commercial interests. While the ADB also serves long-term Japanese political and security interests, Japan has avoided using the Bank as a forum for specific short-term political issues.

Since 1960 Japanese economic cooperation has been marked by two periods of significant growth in overseas development assistance (ODA) commitments, and by a virtually continuous increase in the share of ODA allocated for multilateral agencies, particularly the World Bank and the ADB. Following an initial increase in ODA between 1965 and 1967 and a slight decline in 1968, at the ADB annual meeting in 1969 Finance Minister Fukuda Takeo announced a target of doubling Japan's assistance to the Asian region within five years.[2] This was followed by an increase in ODA from $435.6 million in 1969 to $1011 million in 1973. After a period of stagnation in 1974–6 in the wake of the first oil crisis, in 1977 the government again announced a target of doubling ODA over the following five years, and in 1978 the target period was reduced to three years. Between 1977 and 1980 Japanese ODA increased from $1424.4 to $3303.7 million. Multilateral aid accounted for an average of 8.5 per cent of ODA in 1960–5, but following the establishment of the ADB and the expansion of other multilateral commitments it rose to an average of 17.4 per cent in 1966–9. During the 1970s Japan's multilateral ODA expanded from $86.5 million or 18.9 per cent of aid commitments in 1970 to $1342.9 million or 40.6 per cent in 1980.[3]

Japan has given particular priority in its multilateral aid to the ADB, due both to its close control over the Bank and to the concentration of ADB lending in South Korea and the large ASEAN countries, which has served to bring commitments to the ADB much more closely in line with Japan's bilateral interests than commitments to other multilateral agencies. To the extent that a Japanese development policy has emerged, it has been derived from Japanese economic interests. The concept of a development policy based on national interests is clearly defined in the Japan External Trade Organization's 1979 report on economic cooperation:

In recent days, the opinion that we should employ economic cooperation more actively for the purpose of gaining economic security has grown in strength. This argument says that because we are dependent on overseas sources for almost all of our energy, natural resources, raw materials and other vital materials and goods that form the foundation of our economic society, we should concentrate various policy tools for securing these essentials and economic cooperation should be orientated in that direction.[4]

The economic objectives pursued by Japan through aid relate both to the Japanese economy's need for expanding markets for exports and foreign investment, and to its dependence on imported natural resources mentioned above. The situation is clearly reflected in the structure of Japan's trade with the Asian region. In 1975, over 95 per cent of Japanese exports to the Bank's DMCs were industrial products, namely machinery and equipment (43.1 per cent), metals (20.4 per cent), chemicals (14.9 per cent) and light industrial products (16.9 per cent), while imports from the ADB countries consisted mainly of mineral fuels (40 per cent), raw materials (21.6 per cent) and foodstuffs (20.3 per cent).[5] Imports have been secured by directing assistance to countries and sectors of importance to Japan, while exports of Japanese capital goods and technology have been promoted through policies which ensure a high level of consultancy and procurement contracts for Japanese companies.

## Japanese Policy in the Bank

The leading role played by Japan in setting up the ADB was one of the main regional initiatives of the outward looking foreign policy of the Sato government.[6] However, as both Yasutomo and Huang have documented, the Japanese idea for the ADB dates back to 1962, and while Japan adopted a low-key position in the initial discussions on the Bank within ECAFE, in fact a Japanese draft along very similar lines to the ADB charter which was eventually adopted was prepared as early as 1963, before the commencement of the ECAFE negotiations on the establishment of the Bank.[7]

Japanese multilateral aid is directed through two government channels. Grants to the UNDP and the UN specialised agencies and other bodies are administered by the Ministry of Foreign Affairs, while funding and policy for the multilateral banks is the responsibility of the Ministry of Finance (MOF). The MOF was directly involved in the establishment of the ADB, and the close liaison between the

Ministry's International Finance Bureau and the ADB has been reinforced by the recruitment of MOF personnel to key positions in the Bank.[8] In addition to three of the Bank's four presidents, the Japanese executive director and the director of the Bank's Administration Department (since 1979 the Budget, Personnel and Management Systems Department) have regularly been recruited from the MOF. In fact, the first director of the Administration Department, Fujioka Masao, in 1981 returned to the Bank as its president. This close relationship, combined with the central role of the MOF in Japanese budgeting, has enabled Japan to become the principal source of finance for the ADB, and has made it possible for the ADB president to rely on the MOF for support in seeking capital increases and replenishments of the ADF. The fact that Japan's ADB policy has centred around maintaining the financial base for Bank operations, and to a much lesser degree focused on questions of development policy, can be attributed to the central role of the MOF.

Japanese policy toward the ADB has remained relatively stable, which can be attributed to the fact that the Liberal Democratic Party has continuously been in power and has followed a constant development cooperation policy, with emphasis on expanding ODA and the role of multilateral institutions. The two issues most actively pursued by Japan in the Bank have been the mobilisation of resources for Bank operations, and the question of agricultural development and food production. Underpinning both issues is a clear concern for Japanese national interests.

From the start of ADB operations, Japan assumed a leading role in mobilising funds for the Bank's concessional lending, and due to the low level of US contributions this role has grown significantly over time. The Bank's charter includes general provisions for the setting up of special funds, but makes no specific arrangements for concessional lending. President Watanabe's initial appeals for contributions, in 1966 and 1967, were also expressed in such general terms that the initiative for proposing the precise conditions of such funds shifted to the donors.[9] Between 1968 and 1973 contributions were made on a bilateral basis, although with considerable pressure among donors to ensure some consistency between contributions, and since the establishment of the ADF in 1974 contributions have been negotiated on a cost-sharing basis, with mutually agreed levels of commitment from each donor.

Starting in 1968 Japan made regular annual contributions to the special funds, increasing from $20 million in 1968 to $45.4 million in 1973. As bilateral contributions governed by various conditions increased in size, and as the inability of successive US administrations to secure appropriations from Congress for special fund contributions became apparent, however, there were increasing calls from other donors for the establishment of a unified mechanism for the mobilisation and administration of concessional funds. At the 1972 board of governors' meeting, in a move precipitating the establishment of the ADF, Japan indicated its support for such a fund and announced that it would be prepared to finance one third of an increase in special funds, provided the cooperation of other developed countries was obtained.[10]

In 1974 Japan contributed one third of the initial funds for the ADF and already the following year called for a replenishment programme, announcing that it would continue to contribute a third of ADF funds.[11] In 1978, due to cutbacks in US commitments to the ADF, the second replenishment of $2150 million was only achieved after Japan, joined by Australia, Austria, West Germany, Switzerland and the UK, made up for the shortfall. In this connection the Japanese contribution increased to 36.8 per cent of the replenishment. In 1982 the negotiations for the fourth replenishment of the fund further pushed up the size of the Japanese contribution. The original replenishment of $4100 million sought by President Fujioka was opposed by the US and the UK, and the Reagan administration made it clear that it would contribute a maximum of $520 million, which according to the prevailing formula for the cost-sharing of ADF contributions among donors would have reduced the replenishment to $2300 million. To achieve the replenishment of $3200 million required to maintain the level of ADF lending, Japan and several other donors increased their contributions, which raised Japan's share to 38 per cent, and Australia's from 5 to 7 per cent, while that of the US declined from 22.5 to 16 per cent.[12]

Table 3.1 gives the breakdown of the donors' cumulative paid-in OCR contributions and contributions actually made available to the ADF. The table demonstrates both the virtually complete reliance of the ADF on donor contributions and the fact that the latter constitute a much larger financial input than paid-in capital subscriptions. Due to its continuously increasing share and to delays in the contributions of some other countries, by 1986 Japan's share of contributions paid in to the ADF had risen to 50.2 per cent. Canada, West Germany, the other West European donors, and, to a

*Table* 3.1 Breakdown of cumulative financial contributions to the ADB and ADF by donor country (as of end of 1986)

| Donor countries by voting group | Paid-in OCR contributions $million(%) | | Paid-in ADF contributions $million (%) | | Total paid-in contributions $million (%) | |
|---|---|---|---|---|---|---|
| Japan | 353.7 | (15.0) | 3730.8 | (50.2) | 4084.6 | (41.8) |
| US | 351.6 | (14.9) | 1222.1 | (16.5) | 1573.7 | (16.1) |
| Canada | 135.9 | (5.8) | 471.8 | (6.4) | 607.7 | (6.2) |
| Netherlands | 19.4 | (0.8) | 163.7 | (2.2) | 183.2 | (1.9) |
| Sweden | 4.6 | (0.2) | 55.9 | (0.8) | 60.5 | (0.6) |
| Denmark | 8.8 | (0.4) | 49.0 | (0.7) | 57.9 | (0.6) |
| Norway | 8.8 | (0.4) | 37.9 | (0.5) | 46.8 | (0.5) |
| Finland | 8.8 | (0.4) | 32.7 | (0.4) | 41.5 | (0.4) |
| Voting group (sub-total) | 186.5 | (7.9) | 811.0 | (10.9) | 997.5 | (10.2) |
| West Germany | 112.4 | (4.8) | 519.4 | (7.0) | 631.8 | (6.5) |
| UK | 53.1 | (2.3) | 232.2 | (3.1) | 285.2 | (2.9) |
| Austria | 8.8 | (0.4) | 58.9 | (0.8) | 67.7 | (0.7) |
| Voting group (sub-total) | 174.3 | (7.4) | 810.5 | (10.9) | 984.8 | (10.1) |
| France | 60.5 | (2.6) | 225.5 | (3.0) | 285.9 | (2.9) |
| Italy | 35.4 | (1.5) | 180.4 | (2.4) | 215.7 | (2.2) |
| Switzerland | 15.2 | (0.6) | 97.0 | (1.3) | 112.2 | (1.1) |
| Belgium | 8.8 | (0.4) | 56.7 | (0.8) | 65.6 | (0.7) |
| Spain | 8.8 | (0.4) | 28.2 | (0.4) | 37.0 | (0.4) |
| Voting group (sub-total) | 128.7 | (5.5) | 587.7 | (7.9) | 716.4 | (7.3) |
| Australia | 150.3 | (6.4) | 243.8 | (3.3) | 394.2 | (4.0) |
| New Zealand | 39.9 | (1.7) | 10.5 | (0.1) | 50.4 | (0.5) |
| Total donor countries | 1385.1 | (58.8) | 7416.4 | (99.9) | 8801.5 | (90.0) |
| Total developing countries | 969.3 | (41.2) | 8.2 | (0.1) | 977.4 | (10.0) |
| Total | 2354.4 | (100.0) | 7424.6 | (100.0) | 9779.0 | (100.0) |

*Note*: Figures may not tally due to rounding.

*Source*: ADB, *Annual Report* (1986).

proportionately lesser extent, Australia, have also played a substantial role in financing the ADF. The table shows how much less than Japan the US has contributed to the ADF, but is still biased towards the US for two reasons. First, it does not include ASF and MPSF contributions and therefore takes no account of the fact that before 1974 the US made no contributions to special funds. Second, while the table reflects the low level of US participation in the ADF, it does not reflect the fact that, in the negotiations to establish the level of commitments, where most other donors were willing to make considerably larger contributions, the limits set by the US brought down the size of other donors' contributions and, effectively, the entire ADF.

In contrast to its financial support for the Bank, Japan's policies concerning the terms of aid are more restrictive than those of most other donors. Japan's concern for its own economic and commercial interests has been particularly apparent in its approach to the question of special funds and procurements, where Japanese policies have aimed at ensuring a large share of contracts for Japanese companies. In the initial discussions on the setting up of special funds in 1967, a divergence emerged between Japan and the US, whose approach reflected the extent to which they considered the Bank an instrument of national policy, and the other donors, whose approach more directly reflected their support for the principle of multilateralism.[13] As White puts it, Japan and the US 'made it plain that they regarded the special funds as little more than a thinly disguised form of bilateral finance, administered for purposes and on conditions which fitted their own national objectives'.[14] Both major donors wanted to tie their special fund contributions to their own goods and services, and Japan in particular wanted to establish several different funds with clearly specified geographical and sectoral limitations, while the other donors and the borrowing countries advocated a single fund with a minimum of conditions on contributions. As a result of Japanese pressure, initially two special capital funds were established, the ASF and the MPSF, with tied contributions, and only when the ADF was set up were procurements under concessional loans opened fully to international competitive bidding.

Japan has given support to a country distribution of lending similar to that of its bilateral programme, but has, in stark contrast to the US, avoided raising sensitive political issues in the Bank. A good example is the relatively neutral position adopted by Japan on Vietnam. In the early 1970s, the Japanese Foreign and Finance

Ministries held informal discussions with ADB Presidents Watanabe and Inoue about the possibility of setting up a special fund for reconstruction in Indo-China under the administration of the ADB. Owing to its political sensitivity, however, the idea was not pursued. In 1976, Japan remained outside the political debates on Vietnam within the Bank. Japan also supported the resumption of ADB lending to Vietnam, but suspended bilateral assistance in 1979 following Vietnam's invasion of Cambodia.[15]

The relatively low-key policy profile maintained by Japan in the Bank, both by the executive director and at annual meetings, can largely be attributed to a desire to support the policies and initiatives of the president, and an implicit assumption that initiatives taken by the president will in any case reflect Japanese policy interests. Where Japan has indicated policy priorities they have been in support of the Bank's president, in contrast to relatively critical positions taken by several member countries. For example in 1982 and 1983 the Japanese governors in their speeches drew attention to the need to mobilise additional private sector funding, particularly through co-financing with private banks, to increase the efficiency of ADB lending and to expand the Bank's capacity to provide economic advice and expertise to borrowing countries.[16] All three issues were new to Japanese policy statements, but all three were also being given particular priority by President Fujioka.

At the Bank's 1987 annual meeting, President Fujioka was criticised for placing excessive emphasis on increasing annual lending and was urged by several donors, particularly the US, Canada and Australia, to pay more attention to the quality of lending. Japan responded to this criticism by indicating its support for Fujioka's policies, and at the same time advocated various means of expanding ADB lending. In addition to announcing a substantial increase in its ODA over the next three years, Japan indicated its willingness to establish a special facility to support ADB lending and, against US opposition, pushed for a special capital increase and increase in its voting power.[17]

## The Rural Sector

Alongside Japan's central role in funding the ADB, the single most consistent theme in Japan's policy toward the Bank has been her support for the agricultural sector, in particular for efforts to increase food production in Southeast Asia. This interest stems from Japan's almost complete dependence on imports of livestock fodder and certain staple foods, particularly wheat, maize, soya beans and sugar. In 1974 Japan imported 95.9 per cent of its wheat and 99.6 per cent of its maize, and the corresponding figures in 1972 for soya beans and sugar were 97 per cent and 81 per cent.[18] Moreover, due to trends in Japanese food consumption, dependence on food imports has been increasing rather than declining. According to Sanderson's calculations, while Japan was 80 per cent self-sufficient in food in 1955, by 1972 this figure had dropped to 51 per cent, with projections indicating possible further decline.[19] Due to this increasing dependence, and to the fact that a large proportion of food imports comes from a few principal suppliers, the Japanese government has very actively been seeking to stabilise and deconcentrate sources of imports.

The concern for food security has led to a two-tiered approach to agriculture in Japanese development assistance, based on the promotion of cash crop production in developing countries in an effort to diversify Japan's import sources, and on the promotion of rice production in Asian countries with a view to their achieving food self-sufficiency and thus contributing to regional and global food security.[20] Particularly in the 1960s the concept of 'development imports', the overseas production and development of commodities important to the Japanese economy, gained legitimacy as an official justification for aid programmes, contributing to the stability of supplies of primary products and food. Within this context, in the 1970s both Japanese bilateral aid and private investment in Asian agriculture were notably directed towards diversifying Japan's agricultural imports.[21]

At the same time, the objective of substantially increasing rice production in Asia, along the lines of Japanese agricultural development, has dominated Japanese thinking about Asian agricultural development and has played an important role in the formulation of programmes for economic cooperation. The first major Japanese efforts to develop Asian agriculture, in the mid-1960s, were based on investment in rice production in Southeast Asia, and the global crop failure in 1972, which resulted in widespread grain shortages and soaring food prices, heightened Japan's awareness of its food security situation and served to intensify Japanese efforts to promote food production through bilateral and multilateral programmes. As Okita aptly observes, 'If other Asian countries increase food production and reduce their grain imports, this will indirectly contribute to Japan's food security.'[22]

The relationship between food security and development assistance is highlighted by the fact that Japan's development aid has placed the most emphasis on agriculture following international foodgrain shortages and escalated food prices. Agriculture was a relatively neglected area in Japan's foreign economic policies in the 1950s, but the grain shortages of the early 1960s led to a significant increase in the role of the agricultural sector in Japanese aid in the mid- and late 1960s. This was marked by a number of policy measures, including the introduction of the concept of a fund to finance agricultural development in Southeast Asia, the organising in Japan of a Conference for Agricultural Development in Southeast Asia in 1966, and the founding of a Tropical Agricultural Research Center in 1970. The emphasis placed by the ADB on agricultural development from the start of its operations, including the undertaking of the *Asian Agricultural Survey* in 1967–8 and the establishment of the Bank's ASF in 1968, to which Japan was the first and largest contributor, was also a result of Japanese policy initiative.

The idea for the establishment of a fund to promote agricultural development in Southeast Asia was introduced by Japanese Foreign Minister Miki Takeo in 1965, but was subsequently set aside for lack of a suitable forum.[23] The concept resurfaced at the first Ministerial Conference for Economic Development in Southeast Asia held in Tokyo in April 1966, which was another of the Sato government's major regional initiatives. The conference reaffirmed the importance of promoting agricultural development in Southeast Asia, and led to the convening in Tokyo in December 1966 of the Conference for Agricultural Development in Southeast Asia,[24] which was conveniently timed only two weeks after the inaugural meeting of the ADB, also held in Tokyo.

The agricultural conference confirmed that expanding food production was the most pressing task confronting the participating countries in the agricultural sector. Specifically, it emphasised that rice yields should be increased by introducing improved foodgrain varieties, fertilisers, better cultivation methods and pest control, combined with large-scale investments in irrigation and drainage.[25] The Miki proposal was one of the main matters discussed at the conference and formed the basis for the resulting joint communiqué, which proposed the establishment of a fund to provide long-term low-interest loans for agricultural development in Southeast Asia, as a special fund of the ADB.[26] While delegates from the Philippines, Thailand, Indonesia and other countries proposed to entrust the management of the fund to a committee made up of participants at the conference, at the insistence of the Japanese delegation the conference recommended that the fund be put under the ADB.[27] This gave Japan considerable control over the fund, but also increased Japan's responsibility to ensure adequate financing. The Bank's board of directors accepted the idea of establishing an agricultural special fund, but stressed that lending needed to be based on a coherent and well-documented programme of action, and it was mainly to meet this need that the *Asian Agricultural Survey* was started, in July 1967.[28]

In April 1968 the ASF became operational with the announcement by Japan that a $20 million contribution was included in its 1968–9 budget as the first instalment of a $100 million contribution over a four-year period.[29] The letter from the Japanese government to the Bank concerning the contribution attached several conditions to its use, mainly that it should be used only for agricultural development, that it should be used mainly in Southeast Asia, that the maturity period for loans should not be longer than 25 years (including a grace period of 7 years or less) and the interest rate at least 3 per cent, and that procurement would be tied to goods and services supplied by Japan.[30] The conditions attached to the contribution, particularly the limitation to the agricultural sector and to Southeast Asia, reflect the origin of the ASF and Japan's specific interest in developing agriculture in Southeast Asia.[31]

The stringent conditions aroused criticism among both other donors and the borrowers, particularly at the 1969 annual meeting, and led to strong pressure on Japan to expand the sectoral and geographical coverage of the contribution and soften the loan terms to bring them in line with those of the IDA. Japan's following contribution of $20 million in 1969 was made on the same terms, but in late 1969 the conditions were moderated and the subsequent Japanese contributions of $30 million in 1970 and 1971 were made to the MPSF, on softer terms, and with procurements open to the developing member countries and other donors contributing to special funds.[32]

The foodgrain shortages of the early 1970s were followed by a second period of emphasis on agriculture in Japanese aid. While most donors and international agencies were moving towards broader strategies for rural development, in which increasing agricultural production was seen as one of a number of interrelated objectives,

Japanese initiatives continued to focus on foodgrain production. In addition to continued support for multilateral institutions, which included substantial financial support for the newly established International Fund for Agricultural Development (IFAD), in 1976–7 the Japanese Overseas Economic Cooperation Fund (OECF) introduced a proposal for extensive investment in Asian irrigation as a means of expanding food production (the proposal is discussed in Chapter 4). This was followed in 1977 by the introduction of a bilateral grant aid programme, 'New Assistance for the Promotion of Food Production', which received allocations of $20 million in 1977, $50 million in 1978 and $100 million in 1979, mainly for the Asian countries.[33]

In terms of Bank staffing, it is also interesting to note that Japan has consistently maintained a senior official in the department responsible for agricultural projects. From 1970 to 1973 Sakatani Yoshinao was deputy director of the Project Department, from 1974 to 1977 Suma Kazuaki was deputy director of Projects Department I, and from 1978 to 1982 Takase Kunio was deputy director of the Agriculture and Rural Development Department. In 1983, Takase, who had formerly worked for the Japanese Ministry of Agriculture and Forestry and the OECF, and participated in drafting both the *Asian Agricultural Survey*'s section on irrigation and drainage and the OECF's proposal for large-scale investment in Asian irrigation, became director of the Bank's newly established Irrigation and Rural Development Department. With Takase's retirement the agricultural departments were once again reorganised, in early 1987.

## THE UNITED STATES

The objectives pursued by the US through its participation in the multilateral banks have been classified both in official reports and by researchers into three groups: political and strategic, developmental, and economic.[34] According to the Treasury Department's 1982 report on US participation in development banks, the political and strategic objectives are 'based on the US foreign policy role as a leader of the non-Communist world', and can be pursued in the banks by the promotion of steady economic growth and lending to countries of political and strategic importance.[35] The development policy promoted by the US through the banks is described by the Treasury Department as a combination of 'humanitarian concern with alleviating poverty and improving the material well-being of the poor in developing countries', and 'the preservation and growth of a free, open and stable economic and financial system'.[36] In economic terms, the US has been concerned with both developing export opportunities for American companies and protecting the interests of its private sector.

The US has placed notable emphasis in its policy to the ADB on long-term and short-term political objectives. US initiatives in the Bank have concentrated on ensuring a high level of lending to countries of political and strategic importance to the US, and on promoting policies and projects developing market economies and promoting the role of the private sector. The US has also used the Bank as an instrument of national policy in specific issues, particularly the legitimisation of US-supported regimes in South Vietnam and Taiwan, opposition to the Socialist Republic of Vietnam, and the question of human rights. Compared with Japan's stable, economically oriented policy, US policy in the Bank has been more openly political and subject to change following changes in US administrations.

**US Policy in the Bank**

The single most important factor in understanding US policy toward the multilateral banks is the relationship between successive administrations and Congress with regard to the banks. The Treasury Department formulates US policy toward the ADB, negotiates US participation in capital increases and replenishments of the ADF, and instructs the US executive director on the approval of projects. However, while administrations negotiate and agree on financial contributions covering periods of several years, the appropriation of individual instalments is subject to annual approval by Congress. This has given Congress, and particularly congressional opponents of multilateral aid, substantial leverage over the policies formulated by the administration. More importantly, the appropriation process has given the US leverage over the Bank and enabled US representatives to bring up policy issues in connection with funding negotiations, with the implicit threat of endangering not only the US contribution but the linked contributions of other donors. Rowley puts it more bluntly:

Washington's way of bringing the ADB to heel, as with the World Bank, is to drag its feet over contributions to their soft-loan windows, causing a delay in the linked contributions from the institutions' other member-countries, thereby gaining leverage to force its own policy prescriptions.[37]

US policy toward the ADB has reflected the policies and interests of different administrations. The US decision in 1965 to participate in the Bank was closely related to the administration's policy of counterbalancing the escalation of the Vietnam war by providing large-scale economic assistance to Southeast Asia, which was first announced by President Johnson in April 1965.[38] Following this shift in its Asia policy, the US played an active role in setting up the Bank, and the administration planned to match Japan's contribution of $100 million with a $200 million contribution to the Bank's special funds. The administration's request for special funds, however, was turned down by Congress, largely as an expression of Congress's concern about the administration's Vietnam policy.[39] Despite regular requests from the Johnson and Nixon administrations, the first US contribution of $50 million to the Bank's special funds was appropriated by Congress only in 1974. Thus, from the outset the US played a much more limited role in funding the Bank than was originally envisaged.

In discussions on appropriations for the ADB, particularly from the early 1970s onwards, congressional criticism of the Bank has focused on a broad range of issues, including whether Bank operations conform with US political priorities, the economic costs and benefits of US participation, and the relative merits of bilateral and multilateral aid from the point of view of US political interests.[40] Pointing to the need to respond to this criticism in order to secure funding from Congress, the US pursued a number of political and administrative issues in the Bank, mainly the allocation of loans to countries of political importance to the US, increased procurement from the US, and the introduction of improved monitoring and evaluation systems for Bank projects. However, congressional opposition to multilateral aid grew during the 1970s, and appropriations for both capital increases and special fund contributions were subject to lengthy delays, which reduced US voting power from an initial 17.1 per cent to a temporary low of 7.5 per cent in 1974, and resulted in Japan taking the lead in financing the ADF.

The Carter administration brought a significant change in US development priorities, which in the ADB took the form of a stronger emphasis on poverty alleviation, low-income groups and the rural sector, and a more direct introduction of various political issues, particularly the question of human rights.[41] In spite of its undertakings to expand multilateral assistance, the administration continued to encounter opposition in Congress and was unable to raise US participation in the ADF to either the level requested by the Bank or the level other donors were willing to share the cost of. During the Carter administration the US expanded the criteria for its executive directors in multilateral banks to vote against loans to include human rights and trade protectionism.

The advent of the Reagan administration in 1981 marked another shift in US aid policy, with major cuts in public spending and greater emphasis on bilateral, politically oriented assistance, the policy conditionality of multilateral aid, and the role of the private sector.[42] At the 1981 annual meeting, the US representative stressed the Bank's role 'in helping the Asian region to adopt sound market-oriented policies and development strategies' and announced that lower US contributions to the Bank could be expected.[43] The same year the Treasury Department undertook a comprehensive study of the US role in multilateral development banks, which recommended increasing the banks' co-financing with the private sector, stricter enforcement of policy conditionality, and reduced participation in the banks' concessional windows, combined with revised 'maturation' and 'graduation' policies to ensure that concessional loans concentrated on the poorest borrowers.[44] The US policy changes were announced at the 1982 annual meeting, and, largely in response to US pressure the same year, President Fujioka initiated an effort to expand co-financing with the private sector. In the 1980s the Reagan administration's influence has been evident in the strong emphasis in Bank lending on privatisation. The administration's initial policy of reducing funding was evident in the March 1983 general capital increase, which was 105 per cent instead of the 125 originally planned, and the fourth ADF replenishment, which was reduced from $4.1 to $3.2 billion, with some other donors assuming a larger proportion than in previous replenishments.

The US position on the conditions of Bank lending reflects American economic objectives, and must be examined in the light of the relatively low share of procurement contracts awarded to American companies in relation to US financial contributions (see Tables 6.3 and 6.4). In the negotiations for the establishment of special funds, both the US and Japan wanted procurements from their contributions to be tied, and the first US contribution in 1974 was tied. While ADF lending is open to ICB and later contributions were therefore untied, the US did not advocate untying, has been very critical of the high level of contracts going to Japanese companies, and has been the principal opponent of measures to favour increased procurement from the borrowing countries.

American country priorities, again, reflect a concern with lending to low-income countries, on the one hand, and US political interests, on the other. Interestingly, the concentration of ADF lending in Bangladesh and Pakistan and OCR lending in Indonesia, the Philippines, South Korea and Thailand is closely in line with US bilateral priorities (see Table 6.2). At the same time, the US has taken very specific measures in the question of lending to Vietnam. In the early 1970s the US supported ADB lending to South Vietnam, but after the Socialist Republic of Vietnam took over the Vietnamese seat in both the World Bank and the ADB, in 1977 Congress proposed an amendment to the foreign assistance appropriations bill prohibiting the use of US funds in a number of countries, including Vietnam, Laos and Cambodia. As such restrictions on contributions would have conflicted with the banks' charters, a compromise was reached under which the administration instructed its executive directors to vote against loans to these countries.[45] Consequently in 1978 the US voted against the resumption of ADB lending to Vietnam, for which it was strongly criticised by a number of member countries. In spite of US opposition, the World Bank approved one loan and the ADB two technical assistance grants for Vietnam in 1978, but following the Vietnamese invasion of Cambodia in 1979, both the World Bank and the ADB imposed a freeze on their operations in Vietnam. With the World Bank, Congress took the additional measure of securing the personal written assurance of its President Robert McNamara that lending would not be resumed to Vietnam.[46]

While projects are generally approved by the board of directors through a process of consensus, the US stands out as the one member that has systematically used voting against projects as an instrument of policy. Compared with the relative autonomy and flexibility exercised by the executive directors of other countries and voting groups, the US executive director receives regular policy instructions, including when to approve or oppose loans.[47] During the 1970s, US policy in development banks was marked by a shift from reliance on behind-the-scenes pressure to abstention on or voting against loans on specific policy grounds. Between 1968 and 1980 the US executive director at the ADB voted against or abstained on approximately 40 loan or technical assistance proposals mainly during the Carter administration.[48] An examination of US voting criteria indicates five policy priorities: cost-effectiveness of lending, protection of the US private sector, human rights, opposition to lending to Indo-China, and support for privatisation in the borrowing countries.

Projects were opposed on grounds of cost-effectiveness either because of cost overruns on earlier parts of the projects or because the projects were considered too expensive or unsuitable for concessional financing. Two projects were opposed on broader economic criteria. In the case of an integrated rural development loan to Nepal in 1978, the US questioned the absorptive capacity of the Nepalese economy, and the same year the US opposed a loan to Pakistan for the manufacturing of automotive components, on the grounds that it encouraged an inappropriate development strategy.[49]

Protection of the US private sector has taken two forms, voting against projects which compete with the interests of specific US producers, and voting against countries which have expropriated the property of US-based transnational corporations without compensation. In 1977 Congress refused to authorise increased US partici- pation in development banks until the Carter administration accepted an amendment requiring US directors to oppose loans for the production for export of palm oil, sugar or citrus crops if the loan would cause injury to US producers of the same or competing agricultural commodities.[50] The restriction on palm oil was a reflection of the farm lobby's concern over growing palm oil exports from Malaysia and Indonesia,[51] although the extent to which such exports actually harm the domestic sales and exports of US soya bean oil producers can seriously be questioned. These criteria did not lead to negative US voting in the ADB when they were applied in 1977–8, but in 1986 the US opposed lending for palm oil production in Indonesia on similar grounds.

The question of human rights was introduced into decision-making in development banks by Congress in 1976, but it was only under the Carter administration that US executive directors were systematically instructed to vote against loans to governments considered to be violating human rights, unless the loan proceeds were deemed directly to benefit needy people.[52] In 1977–80 the US director at the ADB voted against or abstained on numerous projects on human rights grounds in Afghanistan, Laos, the Philippines, South Korea and Vietnam. In the cases of South Korea and the Philippines, the votes met the specified criteria and opposed mainly power projects and industrial projects. Voting against projects in Vietnam and Laos, however, was a reflection of American opposition to lending to a socialist Indo-China, and as the loans voted against were mostly for agriculture and rural development, it could be said that they did not strictly meet the administration's human rights criteria. The Reagan administration initially moved from voting to exercising increased financial leverage over Bank policy, but since 1985 it has included both protection of the US private sector and the promotion of privatisation as voting criteria, voting against loans for public sector corporations.

## The Rural Sector

The role of the rural sector in US development aid is shaped by both developmental and politico-strategic considerations. While a large share of American bilateral assistance has gone to low-income countries, particularly India and Bangladesh, a large proportion has also gone to countries of specific political and strategic significance. Similarly, USAID projects for the rural sector have been planned within the context of both developmental and strategic priorities. For example, in Thailand USAID rural development projects are concentrated almost entirely in the Northeast, which is the country's poorest region, but also an area of particular strategic significance in containing any conflict in Indo-China.[53]

In the ADB the US has consistently supported lending for agriculture and rural development, but unlike Japan it did not give particular priority to the rural sector until the worldwide food shortages in 1972–3 forced international attention on the problems of agriculture. Under the Nixon–Ford administration the US encouraged the Bank to shift lending from infrastructure to agriculture and education, but it was the Carter administration that placed particular emphasis on increasing lending for agriculture and pushed for policy changes in the Bank's approach to rural lending. Once the Reagan administration took office, the priority of the rural sector declined.

The first indication of increased US support for the agricultural sector was in the statement of the US governor at the 1975 annual meeting, which drew attention to the world food problem, commended the Bank for expanding agricultural lending to 25 per cent of all projects, and expressed specific support for fertiliser and feeder road projects.[54] The following year the American statement endorsed the further expansion of agricultural lending to 37 per cent, and urged the Bank to increase the use of intermediate technology in projects.[55]

The most significant change in US development policy, and in US concern with the rural sector, came with the Carter administration, which adopted a strategy incorporating the objectives of growth, equity and employment, and emphasised a number of new approaches, including appropriate technology, integrated rural development projects, and the satisfaction of 'basic human needs'. An indication of this shift was given already at the annual meeting in April 1977, at which the US governor recommended that the Bank pay greater attention to lower-income groups by emphasising 'employment and other social purposes particularly in the rural areas'.[56] As a follow-up to a report prepared by the Bank on appropriate technology, the US called for technical assistance to explore appropriate technology for both road construction and semi-arid agriculture.[57] The policy change was clearly announced in 1978, with the introduction of the concept of 'growth with equity' into US policy, and a call for various changes in the Bank's lending policies:

> Within the tenets of multilateralism, the United States – like all other member countries – has a responsibility to seek to ensure that the development banks remain responsive to new directions in development policy. To this end we have encouraged the development banks to pay close attention to the technology employed in their loan projects, so that the resulting resource utilization reflects underlying factor availabilities. We have encouraged the banks to target project benefits so as to better aid the most disadvantaged of a country's population. We have urged that the sector distribution of lending be modified to focus the bank's resources more on meeting basic human needs.[58]

During the Carter administration, the US approved the second Asian agricultural survey, *Rural Asia: Challenge and Opportunity*, as a basis for modifying the design and implementation of Bank projects, and endorsed the sector paper on agriculture and rural development, which the US in 1979 commended for recognising 'that the proper distribution of the benefits of agricultural output is as important as the increase in output'.[59]

Paradoxically, while US policies have in principle favoured low-income groups and the rural sector, the continuous cutbacks and delays in the appropriation of special fund contributions have impaired the Bank's ability to provide concessional funds, precisely for low-income countries and the rural sector. In several instances, the delays in US appropriations, and the resulting delays in the contributions of other donors, have virtually halted ADF lending. The Reagan administration's policy toward the multilateral banks has reduced the emphasis on the rural sector in two ways. First, both the administration and congressional opponents of multilateral aid have questioned whether the shift from infrastructure to agriculture and projects incorporating 'soft' objectives in the banks during the 1970s is compatible with the administration's 'sound market-oriented policies'.[60] Such criticism, however, must also be seen within the broader context of US farm-belt opposition to agricultural lending by the multilateral banks on the grounds that it will harm US exports.[61] Second, particularly during its early years, the Reagan administration – as opposed previously only to Congress – adopted a policy of cutting back financial support for the banks' concessional 'windows', which, while not directly based on a criticism of rural lending, restricted ADF operations and, consequently, rural lending.

## THE OTHER DONORS

Compared with Japan's high level of economic dependence on Southeast Asia and with the strategic importance of a number of ADB countries to the US, the Western European donors and Canada have somewhat more limited political and economic interests in the Bank's DMCs. The Asian region and the Pacific are of strategic significance to Australia and New Zealand, but their economic and commerical ties with the region's developing countries continue to be limited.[62] Research on donor policies also indicates a distinction between 'large state donors', defined as donors with a population of over about 24 million (in the Bank: France, Italy, Spain, the UK, and West Germany, in addition to Japan and the US) and 'small state donors' (Australia, Austria, Belgium, Canada, Denmark, Finland, the Netherlands, New Zealand, Norway, Sweden and Switzerland), with the policies of the former derived more from national interests and those of the latter from a perception of the needs of the developing countries.[63] While the Bank's smaller donors, defined in this study as all donors other than Japan and the US, have narrower political and economic interests in the Bank, suggesting that their participation is based on their support for multilateral assistance, this difference in the premise of their aid policies should also be considered. Of the smaller donors' voting groups in the Bank, those of Canada, the Netherlands and the Nordic countries, and Australia represent countries classified as small donors, while the two others are dominated by large donors (see Table 3.1).

Small donors in general channel a larger proportion of their assistance through multilateral agencies, partly because of the limited implementation capacity of the field structures of their bilateral programmes and partly due to their support for multilateralism. Research also indicates that their policies differ significantly from those of large donors. Hoadley, for example, concludes that small donors give proportionately more aid, conform more closely with international targets on aid volume and ease of terms, and focus more on the poorest countries, and that in general their policies are less directly self-interested and more oriented toward recipient need.[64] These conclusions are confirmed by the policies of most of the smaller donors in the ADB, which indicate that the Bank has served primarily as a channel for their multilateral ODA, guided by their development assistance policies, and secondly as a means of promoting their economic and commercial interests in the region, but has had less importance as an instrument for issues not directly related to aid policy.

## Policy Issues

The first major issue on which the smaller donors took an independent stand in the Bank concerned the proportion of resources to be allocated to special funds, and the conditions for granting these resources. Within the context of policies for providing low-income countries with assistance on concessional terms, the smaller donors attached considerable importance to establishing the Bank's capacity for concessional lending. Together with Japan they have provided the bulk of the resources for the ADF, in contrast to the severely constrained participation of the US (see Table 3.1). From the outset, most of the smaller donors advocated more liberal policies than either Japan or the US on the conditions attached to special funds, such as geographical or sectoral limitations, the tying of procurements, and the interest rates and maturity of loans.

In the negotiations on the setting up of special funds, the smaller donors, led by Canada and including the UK, the Netherlands, West Germany and the Nordic countries, opposed the restrictive approach

of Japan and the US and supported the establishment of one fund
with a minimum of conditions on contributions. This was justified
not only in terms of enhancing the Bank's operational effectiveness
and efficiency but as a means of guaranteeing the multilateral nature
of the Bank. At the 1968 annual meeting, the Canadian governor
pointed out the 'danger that if the Bank is used to too great an extent
as an umbrella for what are essentially bilateral aid operations, it
might detract from its basic role as a multilateral institution'.[65] In the
same speech, Canada's support for a unified fund and opposition to
restrictions were explained as follows:

> In this context, it would be in order to point to specific issues and the
> choices open to us. For instance, consideration is now being given to the
> establishment of a Special Fund for agriculture, another for transport, a
> third for technical assistance and a fourth which is called multipurpose
> fund. Within these funds, there would be other limitations, such as
> geographical or sectoral restrictions on the use of contributions. If
> implemented, these arrangements would reflect the view of individual
> members of development priorities within the region. As a result, there
> would be, almost inevitably, less cohesion in the thrust of the Bank's
> developmental activities. It would make the Bank less of a focal point for
> concerting priorities and it might have adverse implications in terms of
> administrative efficiency and simplicity. It would certainly be desirable
> that no restrictions be placed on the flow of resources between funds if
> required to finance worthwhile projects. It follows that the use of
> contributions to Special Funds should be subject to the general objectives
> and priorities of the Bank rather than those of individual contributors.
> For our part, we will follow these precepts and make available the entire
> Canadian contribution for general purposes.[66]

Owing largely to the prevalence of Japan, however, two special
capital funds were established, both with varying restrictions on the
independent contributions of different donors. Many of the smaller
donors, including Canada, Australia, the UK, West Germany,
the Netherlands and some of the Nordic countries made initial
contributions to the funds, in particular the MPSF, between 1968
and 1971, while at the same time continuing to advocate the reciprocal
untying of contributions and the establishment of a unified fund. The
untying of contributions, however, was constrained both by the
precedent of tied contributions set by Japan and by the large number
of procurement contracts from the Bank's ordinary loans being
awarded to Japan under ICB, and led to most other donors tying
their contributions. In an exceptional step towards untying, the
Netherlands, followed later by the UK and a number of other smaller

donors, stipulated that its contribution could also be used for procurement from DMCs and any other donors contributing to the special funds on at least equally liberal terms.[67]

The initially high level of procurements from Japan aroused particular criticism among the donors with few procurement contracts, and highlighted the donors' commercial interest in participating in the Bank and its bearing on the question of untying. The statement of the Finnish governor at the Bank's annual meeting in 1973, for example, alludes to the question of lending efficiency, but also clearly links the question of continued or increased funding for the Bank with that of increased procurement contracts:

> . . . we believe that it is in the interest of the borrowing countries to have a more balanced procurement pattern than has been the case in the past. I might also add that a more equitable distribution of procurement among member countries, naturally derived through international competitive bidding, would help in persuading national legislators to continue to grant financial support to the Bank. After all, for each developed country this institution is only one of the potential recipients of resources destined for multilateral development assistance.[68]

The smaller donors, together with Japan, were instrumental in the establishment of the ADF in 1974, which not only met their demands for an administratively unified concessional fund but also allowed contributions to be reciprocally untied, and have since played a central role in enabling the ADF to maintain and expand its lending. Negotiations for ADF replenishments have focused on the establishment of a replenishment figure, which has been split among donors based on a specific formula for cost-sharing, and have regularly been restricted by the insistence of the US on replenishments lower than either those requested by ADB management or those supported by most other donors. The ADF replenishments in 1978 and 1982 were achieved only after significant increases in the proportion of the Japanese contribution, supported by additional contributions by many of the smaller donors, to compensate for the drop in the US share. The shortfalls in US contributions, and their detrimental impact on ADF lending, have been the subject of criticism by both other donors and the Bank's borrowers, and some donors have also drawn attention to the fact that US voting rights are not affected by cutbacks in its ADF contributions.

Many smaller donors have also expressed divergent views concerning the country allocation of lending (see Chapter 6). While

Japan and the US have clear economic and political interests underlying their country preferences, bilateral interests have been much less prevalent in the smaller donors' policies, which have in general stressed that resources should be channelled to the poorest countries. The smaller donors' strong support for special funds, and for the concentration of concessional lending in the lowest income countries is derived from this principle, and several donors have criticised both the application of political criteria by the US and the concentration of the Bank's OCR lending in the higher income borrowing countries.

During the initial years of the Bank's lending, OCR and SFR loans were granted without significant regard to the borrowing countries' income level, leading numerous donors, mainly Canada, the UK, West Germany, Australia, Italy, the Netherlands and the Nordic countries to call for the application of criteria to ensure that concessional loans went to the least developed countries. As a result, in 1972 the Bank established country criteria limiting concessional lending to countries with relatively low per capita GNP and debt repayment capacity, and with the setting up of the ADF a system was initiated for the 'maturation' of borrowers from soft to hard loans and eventual 'graduation' from borrower status. However, in 1978, largely due to political pressure from the US, this differential treatment was eroded by the introduction of a category of countries with 'marginal eligibility' for concessional loans, to provide the middle-income Indonesia, Thailand and the Philippines with access to soft loans. The move was opposed by numerous other donors, and particularly strongly by France, the Netherlands and the Nordic countries.[69]

The question of lending in Indo-China has also aroused political controversy in the Bank, mainly between the US, on the one hand, and France, Sweden and several other donors, on the other. Between 1970 and 1974 the Bank gave a number of loans to both South Vietnam and Laos. However, as the war in Indo-China drew to a close, numerous Western European donors as well as Australia and New Zealand indicated that they wanted the Bank to lend for post-war reconstruction in Vietnam, Laos and Cambodia.[70] A stronger position was taken by Sweden, which not only called for lending to Indo-China but openly criticised the Bank for its 'one-sided support of South Vietnam'.[71] Despite consistent calls from numerous smaller donors for the Bank to provide loans to the Socialist Republic of Vietnam and Lao People's Democratic Republic, the ADB was slow to resume operations in either country, due mainly to US opposition. In 1978, the Bank initiated lending to Laos, but since 1979 the Bank has not lent to Vietnam.

## Rural Development

Alongside the policy shift in the World Bank, the strongest impulse for a change in ADB policies and the incorporation of economic growth with social objectives and a greater emphasis on rural development came from the smaller donors, many of which substantially revised their development policies in the early 1970s. Policy statements by Canada and Sweden in 1971–2 already stressed that development was not only a question of economic growth but also one of equity, and pointed out the role they expected the Bank to play in combating poverty and promoting social justice. As tangible steps towards policy change, in 1973 Canada indicated its support for new lending modalities and project types, including 'integrated area development schemes',[72] while the Swedish governor suggested that the Bank's project identification criteria be expanded:

> It might seem from what I have said so far that awareness of social factors is mainly a theoretical stance. Application of these ideas could, however, have very practical consequences for the Bank's lending policy. I would like to suggest briefly a few of such possible consequences. For every project, the effect on employment and income distribution should be studied. The project appraisal should thus pay due attention to social costs and benefits. Greater efforts should be made to seek projects not only in the least developed countries but also for the benefit of the poorer part of the population.[73]

These were followed in 1974–5 by similar indications of policy change by many of the other smaller donors, including Australia, the Netherlands and the Nordic countries, as well as several of the larger West European donors. At the Bank's 1974 annual meeting Australia outlined a change in its development policy:

> Since assuming office in December 1972 our Government has taken a fresh look at Australia's aid policies and programs with the aim of making them more responsive to the needs of the developing countries. In particular, we intend to pay greater attention to the social aspects of development and to the welfare and distributive effects of aid. Consistent with this approach we, for our part, would like to see greater emphasis being placed

in the distributive and employment effects of Bank financed projects. The Bank's operations would thus assist in raising the living standards of the poor majority in developing countries, in the creation of wider employment opportunities, the strengthening of the rural sector and in promoting greater diversification of the economic structure.[74]

The same year, the UK reiterated its concern for poverty alleviation and its emphasis on lending for agriculture and education, and in 1975 the Netherlands pointed out that it would like the Bank's project selection criteria to be brought more closely in line with those applied in Dutch bilateral aid:

In the last few years our national aid policies have undergone some changes. In the selection of projects to be financed great care is being taken that these projects benefit the lower strata of the population. Therefore not only economic criteria are applied but also social criteria. Of course the Netherlands Government would like to see that these criteria which it applies itself in its bilateral aid programs will also govern the multilateral part of its aid.[75]

In the mid- and late 1970s most of the Bank's donors were in favour of increasing the poverty-orientation of the Bank's lending, particularly in the rural sector. In their policy statements, many donors called for greater emphasis on income distribution, employment creation and 'basic human needs', for revised project identification criteria and an appraisal methodology incorporating social cost-benefit analysis, and for innovative lending modalities, particularly integrated rural development projects and projects incorporating labour-intensive, intermediate or appropriate technology. The consensus which emerged in the Bank on the importance of the rural and social infrastructure sectors, and, following the first oil crisis, of the energy sector, is clearly demonstrated by the fact that since the mid-1970s these are the three sectors of consistent growth in ADB lending (see Tables 1.1 and 1.2).

At the same time, however, differences in the general emphasis and specific priorities of the smaller donors have also been evident, reflecting divergent development policies and, in some instances, changes of government. For example, while Canada and numerous other small donors have emphatically supported the borrowers' demands for increased financing of local costs, West Germany, the UK, France and Australia have taken a more cautious position on the issue. In the beginning of the 1980s, economic recession in many countries and changes of government in the US and UK led to a resurgence of bilateralism in aid policies which tended to enhance differences among the Bank's donors on the relative priority of poverty-oriented rural lending, and differences on questions of operational policy and loan conditions.[76] Broadly, this split follows the more conventional division between large and small donors, with the large European Community (EC) countries supporting stricter loan conditions and policy conditionality and the small Western donors, mainly Canada, the Netherlands and the Nordic countries, advocating more spending on low-income groups and projects with a direct social impact.

Alongside changes in their development policies, the donors' economic and commercial interest in securing contracts for Bank projects has remained relatively constant, moulding the Bank's procurement and consultancy policies, and is to some extent reflected in the donors' sectoral priorities. It is significant that in providing funds for the TASF, donors have retained control over the use made of their contributions, including varying degrees of tying to their own technical expertise. The fact that the UK, Canada, Australia and New Zealand have particularly strongly advocated education and vocational training projects is a reflection of their concern with social development, but is also clearly linked with the prevalence of their consultancy companies and contractors in the educational sector. Similarly the emphasis placed by Canada, Finland and Sweden on forestry is obviously an outgrowth not only of their concern for environmental considerations and the rural poor but of their technical dominance in this field.

# 4 The Bank's Rural Development Policy

The ADB's development policy for the rural sector can be divided into two periods, each of which was guided by a major survey of the rural sector undertaken by the Bank. From the Bank's establishment until the early 1970s, its development strategy was one of economic growth, which in agriculture entailed increasing output by modernising production methods. In the mid-1970s the Bank gradually moved to a strategy of rural development with simultaneous emphasis on increasing production, creating employment and raising rural incomes, which has with slight modification remained valid in the 1980s. This policy change should be seen within the context of the broader shift in the donor community from aid policies based on growth towards poverty-oriented rural development policies, which took place in the mid-1970s largely following the initiative of the World Bank. Two features, however, set the ADB's policy apart from that of the World Bank and other aid agencies. First, the ADB's initial policy was strongly influenced by an irrigation-based model derived from the precedent of agricultural development in Japan. This model, and its strong focus on foodgrain production, was also shaped by Japan's concern with its own foodgrain security, and has continued to influence Bank policy into the 1980s. Second, in the ADB the shift to a policy of rural development was gradual and cautious, particularly compared with the strong emphasis placed on rural development by McNamara in the World Bank.

## MODERNISING AGRICULTURAL PRODUCTION

From the start of Bank operations in 1967 until approximately 1974, the Bank's policy for the rural sector centred around modernising production methods through the widespread application of the technology of the green revolution, specifically through the introduction of improved high-yielding varieties (HYVs) of seeds, the improvement of water control, and the increased use of fertilisers and pesticides. The adoption by the Bank of a technological, growth-oriented strategy was influenced by the ongoing programmes of leading aid agencies such as the World Bank and USAID, which in the late 1950s and 1960s were instrumental in introducing the green revolution in Asia. The Bank's strategy was also closely linked to a school of economic thought emphasising the relationship between investment in irrigation and in agricultural inputs and increased yields. The *Asian Agricultural Survey* which was undertaken by the Bank in 1967 and published in 1968, guided the Bank's rural lending policy until the early 1970s.[1]

## The Asian Agricultural Survey

Following the Japanese initiative for the establishment of a fund to provide development finance for Southeast Asian agriculture in the mid-1960s, the first operational decision taken by the ADB board of directors was to initiate a survey of Asian agriculture. The purpose of the survey was to identify investment opportunities for and constraints on increasing agricultural production, as a basis for both national investment decisions and ADB lending operations. The terms of reference for the survey were prepared by and the survey work guided by a consultative committee of internationally known agricultural experts, co-chaired by Ohkawa Kazushi of Hitotsubashi University and Theodore W. Schultz of the University of Chicago. The technical and economic work was carried out by a team of ADB staff and experts from various institutions, led by Chung Nam Kyu of the National Agricultural Cooperative Federation of South Korea, with W. David Hopper, at the time working for the Rockefeller Foundation, as deputy team leader. The survey itself consisted of a regional economic report, which set out the basic assumptions, development model and policy recommendations of the team, and subsectoral reports on different aspects of agricultural development prepared by various team members, of which the most important were the reports on rice production, and irrigation and drainage. The reports were submitted to the members of the consultative committee, whose comments were included in the survey as a separate review report which served to place the survey's strategy within the context of a policy debate.

The survey was undertaken in the wake of a slump in rice production in many Asian countries in 1965–6, which had markedly raised the international price of rice and led to an increased focus in Asian countries on raising agricultural growth rates and attaining a greater degree of food self-sufficiency. The survey was also under-taken at a time when the World Bank, USAID and the Ford and Rockefeller Foundations were providing extensive support for the green revolution in Asia, both by funding programmes for the development of new varieties of wheat and rice, particularly by the International Rice Research Institute (IRRI), and by providing funds for national programmes to introduce new foodgrain production technologies. Based largely on agricultural development in the industrialised countries and the increases in rice production achieved in the East Asian countries, in the late 1960s there was widespread optimism among both aid agencies and the national governments of the ADB countries concerning the prospects for overcoming food deficits through the introduction of HYVs and improved fertilisers and pesticides. This optimism was reflected in President Watanabe's speech at the Bank's first annual meeting in 1968, which included a lengthy discussion of the survey, the new agricultural technologies, and 'the brilliant promise for the future of Asian agriculture'.[2]

The survey's main policy objective was the rapid expansion of food production, and its development strategy was one of modernising agricultural production by replacing traditional farming practices with science-based technology, supported by improved water control and prices and costs geared to provide an incentive for farmers to adopt technological innovations. In the regional economic report the survey team acknowledged that focusing on food production and selecting an approach based on the application of science and technology restricted the survey to recommending a single development strategy, with numerous implications, but expressed the unanimous view that 'the only valid route to sustained rural development is a movement toward a farming based on applied science'.[3] The secondary position assigned to social and political issues, particularly the question of poverty, was explicitly stated in the basic assumptions of the survey's development model:

The model approaches regional problems by making four assumptions: (a) that foods, especially rice, have a first priority in development; (b) that an expansion of production is the priority goal, i.e. matters of equity, backwardness and poverty are acknowledged, but given lower priority to production growth; (c) that programs should aim at developing a 'modern' national agriculture, i.e. an agriculture based on the application of the latest findings of science and technology, adapted to the physical and cultural environment of the countryside; and (d) that farm prices relative to the costs of using new production technologies provide an incentive for the adoption by farmers of the new techniques.[4]

The survey recommended an investment strategy based on the improvement of field infrastructure, the introduction of a broad range of technological inputs, particularly with a view to promoting the double cropping of rice and, ultimately, the mechanisation of agricultural production. The key areas identified for capital investment and technical assistance were rural infrastructure, the fertiliser industry, agricultural processing industries, the development of crop protection, and the development of improved seed varieties.[5] Allowing for differences between countries, the survey envisaged a division of responsibility in which national public sector investment, supported with loans from international agencies including the ADB, would focus on infrastructure, particularly irrigation and drainage, land settlement, transportation and rural extension. The production of fertiliser, other chemical inputs and agricultural machinery, as well as agro-processing, again, was considered the prerogative of the private sector, with a significant role envisaged for foreign investment. The development of seed varieties and crop protection was seen primarily as the responsibility of national and international research institutions, particularly the IRRI.

The survey examined a broad range of rural institutions, including land tenure arrangements, agricultural credit and marketing, agricultural education and extension and farmers' organisations. Its main concern, however, was with the role of rural institutions in supporting the adoption of new technologies, and its recommendations for areas of technical assistance and investment consequently focused on agricultural extension, credit and farmers' organisations. Questions of land tenure and ownership, when they were discussed at all, were examined in relation to raising yields rather than in the context of equity. Land reform was seen as inevitable in the long term, but was not considered essential for agricultural development as defined in the survey and was not included among the survey's priorities:

> The Survey Team did find instances where there was serious need for tenure reform to provide tenants with a secure interest in the land they farm, but in most of the region there seems little validity in the general argument that land reform is a necessary precondition for further agricultural development, although in the long run many countries will not be able to escape the need for major tenurial reforms . . . From the recent experience of many regional countries there seems little doubt that programs addressed to an expansion of production by overcoming present technical constraints will not falter because of absence of reform in the relation between landlord and tenant.[6]

Among the individual members of the consultative committee there was considerable disagreement with the team's report, and their comments, in the separate review report, anticipated the distributional and social problems to which the green revolution gave rise. First, the committee drew attention to the bias in farmers' access to support systems, and, consequently, in their ability to make use of technological inputs, and underscored the need to ensure that small farms benefit from resources channelled into increasing productivity.[7] Similar observations were made by Ishikawa, who was commissioned by the Bank in 1968 to prepare a study on the potential for implementing the survey strategy in the Philippines and Thailand.[8]

Second, the committee expressed some reservations about the strong emphasis placed by the survey team on agricultural inputs compared with organisational and structural factors. The committee members drew particular attention to the subordinate position assigned to the question of land tenure, and pointed out that while the ADB might, due to the political and social overtones of the question, wish to avoid involvement, it would inevitably need to have some regard to 'problems of the distribution of benefit from development'.[9] Two members of the committee were particularly sceptical of the applicability to Asian peasants and smallholders of a production-oriented approach which they saw as better suited to the economies of industrialised countries. They also felt that the unequal response elicited by the incentives of the strategy recommended by the survey would seriously exacerbate social and political tensions in the rural sector:

> In many regions a hard and desperate fight may begin between peasants and smallholders on the one hand and landlords, merchants, moneylenders, etc. on the other. The latter are quickly aware of the new possibilities. They must do what they can (in legal and illegal ways) by using political influence, relations and power to maintain their dominant position and to obtain a maximum of profit from the new situation for their own pockets. They may feel that if they allow the so far highly dependent smallholder to gain economic freedom and independence by increasing production, productivity and income, the foundations of their wealth and their social and economic role may be in danger.[10]

The above, however, reflected two dissenting opinions rather than the consensus of the committee, and stood in sharp contrast to the general view of the survey team.

Following the survey the Bank took steps to facilitate the implementation of its recommendations. In 1968 two policy papers based on the survey were submitted to and received the general endorsement of the board of directors. The first discussed the central role of research into new seed varieties in the survey's strategy, and recommended that the Bank support regional research institutions and programmes, particularly the IRRI.[11] The second set out policy guidelines and identified broad priority areas for Bank lending.[12] In April 1969, in connection with its annual meeting, the Bank organised a regional seminar on agriculture to discuss with its borrowers the practical implications of the survey. There was general agreement at the seminar that within the framework of the survey the Bank should concentrate on water management, irrigation and drainage, agricultural product processing, agricultural research and education, agricultural credit, and fisheries development.[13]

## The Japanese 'Model' for Agricultural Development

The agricultural development strategy of the survey is firmly rooted in the work of a school of agricultural economics concerned primarily with the relationship between investment in agricultural inputs, human resources and irrigation, on the one hand, and increasing agricultural output, on the other. The two chairmen of the consultative committee, Schultz – who in 1979 was awarded a Nobel prize for his work in economics – and Ohkawa, as well as Vernon Ruttan – who together with Ohkawa in 1976 chaired the consultative committee for the Bank's second survey – are among the leading representatives of this school. The analytical framework of the survey's regional economic report, and the entire survey, is based on the concept of agricultural development as a sequential process from traditional to modern, and bears a strong resemblance to the framework for modernising agricultural production in Schultz's *Transforming Traditional Agriculture*.[14] Within this framework, the survey's model is based mainly on an analogy with the historical experience of agricultural development in Japan, Taiwan and South Korea, a central theme in Ohkawa's work.[15]

Compared with Schultz's classification of agricultures into three types – traditional, transitional and modern – the survey places the Asian countries on a development continuum, on the assumption that 'as each of the regional countries moves along the continuum, from traditional agriculture to modern agriculture, it will confront problems faced by those who have preceded them along the same path'.[16] In defining this course of development, extensive reference is made to agricultural development in Japan, Taiwan and South Korea. The analogy is based on a comparison of variables related to the survey's strategy for increasing production, particularly the area and percentage of rice land under irrigation, rice yield per hectare, and the type of seed varieties, fertilisers and other chemical inputs being used. Rural institutions are considered of secondary importance in explaining or guiding agricultural development, but are discussed in the light of their potential role in the introduction of technological innovations.

Both the survey's regional economic report and various subsectoral reports, particularly that on irrigation and drainage, are based on Japan's model of agricultural development. As a background to its discussion of the stages on its modernisation continuum, the survey divided Japanese agricultural development into four phases, based on the level of water control, the type of agricultural technology and inputs being used and yield per hectare. During the first phase, before the year 645, rice was grown on the land under rain-fed conditions; from 645 to 1868 water control (irrigation, drainage and flood control) was adopted, particularly around 1600 when the Edo Shogunate was established; from the Meiji Restoration in 1868 until 1950 yield was increased through the adoption of improved technology (fertilisers, new varieties of grain, and pesticides); and from 1950 onwards cultivation methods have been improved and production diversified and mechanised. According to the survey, the success of the model is indicated by the fact that between its first and fourth stages, rice output, the model's indicator of development, increased from one ton to over five tons per hectare.[17]

In support of the model, the survey refers to the yield increases achieved through a similar sequence of resource programming in Taiwan and South Korea. Further support is provided in a paper by Hsieh – who from 1967 until 1980 headed the Bank's various departments responsible for agricultural and rural projects – and Ruttan comparing rice production strategies in Taiwan, where growth in production was rapid, and the Philippines and Thailand, where agricultural growth was comparatively slow. Hsieh and Ruttan note that while Taiwan started from irrigation development and effective water control and went on to adopt new rice varieties and the related inputs, the sequence in the Philippines and Thailand was the reverse, and they explain the slow growth in production in these two countries as being due to new inputs being introduced without the requisite improvements in water control.[18]

Based on the average rice yield per hectare in 1964–7, the survey classifies the ADB countries into four stages corresponding to the Japanese model: the land development stage, with yields of below 1 ton per hectare (Laos); the water control stage, with yields of from 1 to 2.5 tons per hectare (Afghanistan, Cambodia, Ceylon, India, Indonesia, Nepal, Pakistan, the Philippines, South Vietnam and Thailand); the inputs stage, with yields of from 2.5 to 3.5 tons per hectare (Malaysia); and the cultivation methods stage, with yields of above 3.5 tons per hectare (South Korea and Taiwan). The stages also serve as the basis for the distribution of investment resources recommended by the survey. The main areas of investment are divided into three categories: water control, inputs (seed varieties, fertilisers and pesticides) and cultivation methods (mainly mechanisation), with the relative share of irrigation declining and that of inputs and mechanisation progressively increasing. At the first stage the survey suggests that 70 per cent of resources be invested in water control, 30 per cent in inputs and none in cultivation methods, at the second stage the corresponding figures are 60, 30, and 10 per cent, at the third stage 50, 30 and 20 per cent, and at the fourth stage 40, 30 and 30 per cent, respectively.[19]

The Japanese model deserves critical scrutiny from two points of view. The first relates to its general validity. There is considerable danger in drawing close analogies between the development process in countries with as widely divergent economic, political and social systems as Japan, Taiwan and South Korea, on the one hand, and the countries of Southeast and South Asia, on the other. The model's concern with the question of agricultural productivity, and its assumption that agricultural development is a relatively uniform sequence of events, leads to a focus on a few readily quantifiable economic variables and to the virtual omission of less tangible variables, and largely divorces the discussion of agricultural development from its broader socio-political context.

The low priority assigned to land tenure as an explanatory variable and to land reform as an objective of the development process is based on the survey's implicit assumption that governments will undertake tenurial reforms in the wake of increased productivity. Little attention is paid to the serious obstacle to land reform and agricultural development posed by the close linkages between the distribution of land ownership and local power structures. It is particularly important to note that in the three model countries land reforms were to a large extent implemented by external élites, bypassing the vested interests of local power structures. The first phase of Japanese land reform was carried out in connection with the Meiji Restoration, but the process was carried to completion under US military occupation after the Second World War. In South Korea, the US similarly implemented extensive land reform, while in Taiwan tenurial reform was carried out by the Nationalists from the mainland, with financial and technical support from the US.[20] The unique circumstances under which these reforms were carried out provide little justification for the survey's assumption that land reform does not require specific policy measures and cast considerable doubt on the applicability of the model.

Second, the model should be seen within the context of the policies of the Bank and its borrowers. Particularly in the first years of its operations the Bank placed strong emphasis on adhering to the principles of 'sound' banking, with a view to establishing its reputation and credit rating on international financial markets. This argument was frequently used to justify what has been termed the 'cautious' lending policy of ADB President Watanabe, which included avoiding politically controversial issues.[21] Similarly, and for politically obvious reasons, the Bank's major borrowers expressed little interest in including the question of land reform among the Bank's lending priorities. Seen in this light, the production-oriented approach of the Japanese model was one of considerable political expedience.

## RURAL DEVELOPMENT

The mid-1970s marked a significant rise in the priority of the agricultural and rural sector in ADB lending, accompanied by a gradual shift by the Bank towards a strategy of poverty-oriented rural development encompassing three main objectives – economic growth, employment and income distribution. In contrast to the modernisation strategy, the rural development strategy placed emphasis on increasing the agricultural output of low-income groups in rural areas and ensuring that jobs created in agricultural production were supplemented with substantial off-farm employment in other sectors. While the green revolution had been initially successful in accelerating Asian rice production in the late 1960s, by 1970 it was evident that the success had been limited mainly to relatively large holdings and that a further expansion of rice production would require fundamental changes in both domestic policies and aid policies. The stagnation of Asian rice production in 1971–2 and decline in 1972–3, which contributed to a worldwide food shortage, highlighted the acuteness of the problems of the rural sector.[22]

## The World Bank and Rural Development

In the early 1970s, the World Bank and its President Robert McNamara played a leading role in reorienting the policies of the aid community to incorporate economic growth with employment creation and income distribution and in increasing financial flows to the rural sector. McNamara's speech at the World Bank annual meeting in September 1971 centred around the population problem, but also drew attention to the related problems of malnutrition and unemployment.[23] In 1972 two of McNamara's major policy statements pointed out the highly unequal distribution of the benefits of economic growth in developing countries and emphasised the need to reorient aid policies to ensure a more equitable distribution of incomes to the poorest groups in society.[24] The policy change was also evident in a 1972 outline of the World Bank's policies for the agricultural sector.[25]

McNamara's speech at the World Bank's annual meeting in September 1973 in Nairobi, however, is usually considered the turning point in the World Bank's shift from a development policy based on growth to one of rural development.[26] The speech started out from the question of rural poverty and the observation that development policies and programmes aimed at accelerating economic growth had in most developing countries benefited mainly relatively high-income groups and reinforced the unequal distribution of incomes. In the speech, McNamara coined the term 'absolute' poverty, which he described as 'a condition of life so degraded by disease, illiteracy, malnutrition and squalor as to deny its victims human necessities', as distinct from the 'relative' poverty existing in numerous countries, including major donors. McNamara went on to identify increasing the productivity of small-scale subsistence agriculture as the principal solution to rural poverty, and called both for developing countries to adopt national policies directed towards a more equitable distribution of the benefits of growth and for donor countries to reorient and substantially increase ODA for the rural sector.[27]

As a framework for national policies and World Bank operations,

McNamara outlined the elements of what he termed a strategy for rural development. Compared with the World Bank's lending policies in the 1960s, which emphasised investment in industry and infrastructure and, in the agricultural sector, mainly in irrigation, McNamara's rural development strategy stressed the need to implement a broad range of programmes to increase production on small farms and ensure a more equitable distribution of rural incomes. Central importance was attached to the need for changes in the organisational structure for supporting smallholder agriculture and the need for structural changes in the rural sector, particularly land and tenancy reform. In discussing the elements for increasing agricultural output – credit, irrigation, extension services, applied research and public services – McNamara's emphasis was not simply on investment but on taking appropriate measures to ensure that the elements were accessible to small farmers.[28]

McNamara's Nairobi speech was followed by specific measures to redirect World Bank lending operations and a significant increase in lending for the agricultural sector. In 1974 the World Bank's Development Research Center, together with the Institute of Development Studies (IDS) at the University of Sussex, produced a report entitled *Redistribution with Growth*, which gained semi-official status as an outline of the World Bank's revised development strategy.[29] This was followed in 1975 by the publication of sector policy papers on rural development, land reform and agricultural credit.[30]

In connection with the policy changes, World Bank lending for agriculture more than doubled, from $436.3 million in 1972 to $937.7 million in 1973, and the sector's share of total lending increased from 14.8 per cent in 1972 to 27.5 per cent in 1973. In 1974 agricultural lending increased slightly, to $955.9 million, and in 1975 it increased by 94 per cent to $1857.5 million or 31.5 per cent of all loans.[31] Since 1975, World Bank lending for agriculture and rural development has remained at approximately one third of all lending. The expansion of agricultural and rural lending was accompanied by the emergence of various types of 'new style' projects, which according to the Bank were designed to ensure that at least half the beneficiaries fall 'within the poverty group constituting the bottom 40 per cent of the population'.[32]

While the ADB was strongly influenced by the World Bank's rural development strategy, the shift in the ADB's development policy was gradual, taking place between 1973 and 1977, and cannot be connected with any single event or specific policy statement such as

McNamara's Nairobi speech. The first indications of change come in the early 1970s. In his speech at the Bank's 1972 annual meeting, President Watanabe referred to the problem of unemployment, and to the attention drawn to the question of unemployment and underemployment by McNamara.[33] The following year, in his first speech to the board of governors, President Inoue observed that unequal income distribution in many developing countries had kept the gains of growth from being shared among 'the poorest two-thirds of their populations', and indicated that the ADB was discussing a framework for more effectively aiding its least developed members.[34]

In November 1973, six weeks after McNamara's Nairobi speech, in what was a clear response to the World Bank's policy initiative, the ADB board of directors discussed a paper prepared by the Project Department on incorporating land reform into Bank operations.[35] The board paper's approach to rural development was based on the observation that the success of the technological approach to agriculture had been confined mainly to large farms and suggested a development strategy based on land and tenancy reform. The paper's analysis of the problems of the rural sector bore a marked resemblance to the rural development strategy set out by McNamara and differed fundamentally from that of the *Asian Agricultural Survey*:

> While the technological breakthrough has led to higher production, it has been largely confined to a limited number of farmers with larger farm sizes and ample financial and managerial resources and it has failed to reach the vast majority of small farmers, whether owners or tenants. The higher yields have pushed up land values and made the cultivation of farmland through hired labour and machinery more profitable. For the big farmers it has been easier to adopt the new technology since the financial risk has been small due to the size of their farming operations and to their better management skills. When adopted, the doubling or trebling of yields has meant a corresponding increase in their incomes. On the other hand, the small farm owners and tenants, due to the risk and uncertainties involved and to their financial and managerial constraints, have generally failed to participate in the tempo of the 'green revolution'. This phenomenon has led to polarization in the levels of production and income and thereby to massive problems of welfare and disparity in income distribution. In addition, it has resulted in the eviction of tenants and increased unemployment in the rural sector and has brought about adverse changes in the man-land relationship.[36]

The paper recommended that the Bank examine the possibility of assisting member governments with the planning and implementation of land reform, combined with policies to increase absorption of the rural labour force and the distribution of rural incomes. Reference was made both to the central role given to land and tenancy reform in McNamara's Nairobi speech and to the measures to promote land reform incorporated in ongoing World Bank, IDB and USAID projects.[37] The paper was submitted by the Project Department to the board for discussion, but did not directly lead to changes in operational policies. It was significant, however, as a sign of the changing approach of Project Department staff to the rural sector, and of the direct impact of changes in World Bank policy on the policy debate within the ADB.

## The Second Asian Agricultural Survey

In 1974 there were clear indications of the growing importance attached by the ADB to the rural sector. Lending for agriculture and agro-industry increased by 70 per cent, and the Project Department was restructured into two departments, one of which handled mainly agricultural and rural development projects. In his speech to the board of governors in April 1974, President Inoue underscored the critical nature of the food problem in Asia and the need to increase investment in agriculture substantially to ensure adequate availability of rice.[38] However, compared with both McNamara's speech and the board paper on land reform, the emphasis in the president's address was on stepping up Bank support for agricultural production rather than shifting the emphasis of lending towards poverty alleviation.

As a basis for a review of its operational policies for agriculture and rural development, in 1975 the Bank initiated a second survey of Asian agriculture, which was prepared in 1976 and published in 1977.[39] The terms of reference for the second survey were prepared jointly by the Bank and a consultative committee of international experts co-chaired by Ohkawa Kazushi, at the time working for the International Development Center of Japan, and Vernon Ruttan of the US Agricultural Development Council. The shift in political orientation is indicated by the fact that the committee also included, for example, Michael Lipton of the IDS. The preparation of the survey was carried out by a task force consisting of ADB staff and experts from various institutions.

The second survey's recommendations for the rural sector differ in many key respects from those of the first survey, and are closely in line with the World Bank's strategy for rural development.[40]

President Yoshida's foreword to the second survey notes that 'the severity of food shortages in many Asian countries during the early 1970s and the continued presence of widespread rural poverty and un(der)employment suggest that the expectations implicit in the [*Asian Agricultural Survey*] have for various reasons not been realised'.[41] This is a clear acknowledgement of the need for a change in Bank policy. A commentary in the *Far Eastern Economic Review* is less sympathetic in its description of the second survey as an admission of the failure of the rural-sector policies promoted by the Bank in the 1960s.[42]

The second survey is broadly divided into four parts – a review of progress in the rural sector since the first survey, a discussion of the main tasks to be tackled, an outline of the elements of a strategy for rural development, and a discussion of the ways in which foreign aid needs to be adapted to facilitate the implementation of a programme for rural development. In contrast to the first survey, which identified food production as the main problem, the second survey identifies three principal problems: food production, unemployment and poverty. Along similar lines to the World Bank's analysis of the rural sector, the second survey notes that, while improved agricultural technologies have increased output, this has barely kept pace with population growth and has been accompanied by increased unemployment and poverty. Consequently the second survey recommends a two-tiered approach to rural development aimed simultaneously at raising food production and increasing rural employment, the latter as the strategy's principal means of distributing incomes. The second survey sets out a rural development strategy consisting of four elements: land reform, agricultural growth through the development and application of technology, the provision of support services, particularly credit, and the provision of extensive off-farm employment.[43]

Like the Project Department's 1973 paper, the second survey singles out land reform as the main institutional prerequisite for rural change. Land reform is justified mainly in terms of productivity and labour absorption, but also in terms of its 'social levelling' effect. In comparing the productivity increases brought about by the application of HYVs and agricultural inputs on small and large holdings, the second survey notes that 'where discriminative support systems could be organised, there appeared to be no perceptible difference in productivity between various size groups of holdings'. Having thus identified access to support systems rather than the size of holdings as the major obstacle to raising production, the second survey goes on to observe that, as cropping intensities are generally higher on smallholdings, greater increases in output would be achieved on smallholdings, in addition to which production on smallholdings would entail a higher use of labour. At the same time, the second survey points out the considerable political opposition land reform could be expected to encounter in numerous borrowing countries, and the need to supplement land reform with a reform of credit institutions, increased public spending on supportive infrastructure and improved agricultural extension and research.[44]

The second survey's discussion of agricultural production starts from a critical examination of the green revolution:

> The means for achieving a rapid transformation appeared to be at hand in the 1960s with the development of the modern varieties of rice and wheat. But the record of performance shows that, while food production has kept pace with population growth for the region as a whole, we seem to be no nearer to solving the food problem than we were a decade ago. In fact there is a growing concern that the 'green revolution' is slowing down.[45]

Due to the limited prospects in most of Asia for bringing new land under cultivation for foodgrain production, the second survey notes that increasing food production will, by necessity, centre around the question of raising output through the adoption of yield-increasing inputs and technology. However, in contrast to the first survey, the second survey stresses the need to adopt a technological approach based on maximising both output and the employment of unskilled labour. The second survey argues that appropriate technologies – which it defines as those suitable for adoption on small farms, with a tendency to enhance the use of available local resources, particularly labour – could play a key role in ensuring that increases in production were accompanied by the mitigation rather than aggravation of income disparities, unemployment and underemployment.[46]

Thirdly, the survey discusses the role of supportive measures, particularly credit. Within the Asian context of land scarcity, access to cash inputs – mainly fertiliser and other chemicals – is of key importance in ensuring that farmers can take advantage of the potential for increasing yields offered by the introduction of HYVs and improved water control. According to the second survey, one of the major reasons for the unequal distribution of the benefits of the green revolution was the fact that existing credit arrangements – both government credit institutions and informal credit – were not readily accessible to small farmers. Consequently, the second survey under-scores the need to develop flexible lending institutions to provide credit to small farmers, supplemented by government efforts to regulate existing informal credit arrangements.[47]

The fourth element of the strategy consists of promoting large-scale programmes for off-farm employment. While the second survey's recommendations for increasing agricultural production are intended to raise on-farm employment, a fundamental assumption is that the jobs created in agricultural production will be inadequate to absorb the rapidly expanding rural labour force and will need to be supplemented with extensive off-farm employment opportunities. As the main component of its rural employment programme, the second survey calls for the massive allocation of public resources for labour-intensive rural works, particularly the construction of farm-to-market roads, irrigation works, drainage and flood control facilities, bridges and other public facilities. As a second employment-creating measure the survey recommends investment in rural-based, small-scale manu-facturing industries.[48]

Finally, the second survey assesses the past role of foreign assistance in promoting agricultural and rural development and makes a number of recommendations on how aid could be reoriented and made more flexible, to facilitate the implementation of an employment-oriented rural development strategy. While intended primarily as a background for a review of the Bank's operational policies, the recommendations are also directed at foreign assistance in general and cover a broad range of relatively controversial issues. The main recommendations include a substantial increase in ODA for the rural sector, a reduction in the cost of aid to recipients through increased concessional lending, increased programme lending, increased local cost financing, the untying of bilateral aid and the modification of the operational procedures of multilateral aid to facilitate the use of domestic consultants and labour-intensive technology, and a modification of procurement procedures in favour or regional and domestic procurement.[49]

## Changes in Bank Policy

At the 1977 annual meeting President Yoshida announced that the second survey would serve as a basis for changes in ADB policy, and, in his address to the 1978 annual meeting, his lengthy discussion of economic growth and the distribution of the benefits of growth as the two primary objectives of development was a concrete endorsement of many of the survey's recommendations.[50] At the same meetings numerous member countries, particularly the borrowers, the smaller donors and the US, endorsed the survey as a basis for modifying Bank lending policy. In the late 1970s lending for agriculture and rural development continued to increase, and in 1978 a reorganisation of the Bank's projects departments resulted in the establishment of a separate Agriculture and Rural Development Department.

However, it is important to note that while the second survey served as the basis for a review of Bank policy, it cannot, in itself, be considered a policy document. It reflected the thinking of a large segment of staff and management, and many member countries, but was also the subject of considerable policy debate and was toned down and modified substantially in the process of being translated into Bank policy. In the wake of the second survey, a number of papers were prepared by Bank staff to facilitate the policy changes it recommended. A paper on economic and financial project appraisal discussed changing project analysis to reflect a broader concern for social objectives, while papers on the Bank's role in promoting appropriate technology and small-scale industries reflected the survey's recommendations concerning employment creation.[51] These papers, however, have had little practical significance.

Of considerably more importance was the Bank's sector paper on agriculture and rural development, which was prepared by Bank staff in 1977–8, based on the second survey but concerned primarily with outlining priorities for Bank operations. The sector paper was reviewed by the board of directors in a series of meetings in early 1979 and led to the formal approval of a board paper setting out its consensus on the Bank's role in agriculture and rural development.[52] At the same time, the board decided that the Bank should aim to increase the level of lending for agriculture and rural development by 20 per cent each year during the period 1979–82.

The sector and board papers are both based on the second survey's analysis of the rural sector. However, a comparison between the second survey and the two policy papers, and particularly the survey's recommendations on controversial issues which have been modified in or omitted from the policy papers, provides considerable insight into the political nature of policy formulation in the Bank. The second survey identifies land reform as a prerequisite for much of its rural development strategy, but the sector paper is much less emphatic about the necessity of land reform, and the board paper makes no direct reference to land reform but simply points out that 'Rural institutions and structures need to be modified to achieve a more efficient allocation of inputs and a more equitable distribution of outputs and incomes'.[53] While institutional reform is identified as a priority area for initiatives by the developing countries, in clear deference to the borrowing governments reluctant to undertake extensive tenurial reforms, it is not singled out as suitable for incorporation in ADB projects. Compared with the second survey's numerous recommendations for modifying foreign aid, the sector and board papers discuss the modification of ADB operational policies in only three areas: local cost financing, which the board paper considers adequate, programme lending and the incorporation of 'social' components in rural development projects. It is particularly interesting to note that while the survey recommends significant amendments to the Bank's consultancy and procurement policies, as these would have conflicted with the donors' economic interests, the recommendations are not included in the sector and board papers.

The above changes notwithstanding, the sector and board papers maintain the general thrust of the survey's strategy, with simultaneous emphasis on increasing agricultural production and raising rural employment and incomes. Both papers single out four main problem areas for the coming decade:

a) the continuing lack of rural employment opportunities;
b) the unsatisfactory performance of production and distribution systems for food and other rural products;
c) inadequate project and programme implementation capacities in the developing countries at both the national government and local levels; and
d) the increasingly serious degradation or destruction of vital ecosystems.

Correspondingly, four priority areas for Bank action are discussed:

a) providing more and better rural employment;
b) improving production and distribution systems for rural products;
c) training managers for rural development programmes; and
d) protecting ecosystems.

Emphasis is on the first two areas.

To meet these needs, the board paper recommends a substantial broadening of the Bank's project priorities to include not only established areas such as irrigation and water control, agro-industries and fisheries, but new activities such as feeder road construction, labour-intensive rural works, the provision of more support services, agricultural and non-agricultural training, livestock development and the maintenance of forests and watersheds.[54]

The broadening of the bank's rural investment priorities was favoured by many borrowers and most of the donors. In addition to receiving the strong support of the smaller donors, it is significant that the policy changes being discussed in the Bank were in line with the development priorities of the Carter administration, which gave its specific endorsement to both the second survey and the sector paper as a basis for redirecting the Bank's rural lending.

At the same time the Japanese government supported a line of thinking more closely related to the first *Asian Agricultural Survey*, concerned primarily with the question of food security, and recommending large-scale investment in irrigation schemes, with much less emphasis on employment creation and poverty alleviation. The Japanese statements at the annual meetings between 1976 and 1979 stressed the importance of increasing food production in the region, and in 1977 the Japanese government introduced a new bilateral grant programme entitled 'New Assistance for the Promotion of Food Production', under which $170 million was channelled into the Asian region between 1977 and 1979.

The most significant Japanese effort to influence foreign aid for the Asian rural sector, however, was a grandiose proposal aimed at doubling rice production in Asia through massive investment in irrigation over a period of 15 years. The idea was initiated by the then President of the Japanese Overseas Economic Cooperation Fund (OECF), Okita Saburo, and the Director of the Fund's Economic Research and Appraisal Department, Takase Kunio – who served as Manager of the ADB's Irrigation Division from 1967 to 1974, and in 1983 was appointed as Director of the Bank's newly established Irrigation and Rural Development Department – and was first made public by the OECF in 1976.[55] Subsequently a more detailed proposal was prepared by a task force of specialists under the auspices of the Trilateral Commission, and was submitted in October 1977 for discussion to the World Bank, the FAO and the ADB.[56]

Starting from projections of steep growth in rice deficits in South and Southeast Asia, and a resulting increase in the region's dependence on cereal imports in the 1980s, the Trilateral task force report considers the expansion of food production an overriding priority for both national investment and foreign assistance. The selection of strategy is summarised in the report as follows:

> There are a variety of means of reducing the deficit in food – slowing the rate of population growth, achieving a more equal distribution of food and income, [or] increasing food production and reducing wastes. Strategies to increase food production and reduce waste can be most readily implemented and are the ones that shall be stressed in this report.[57]

Irrigation, particularly the improvement of existing irrigation schemes, is considered by the report the most cost-effective way to increase rice production, and forms the backbone of the report's strategy, which entails investing approximately $54 billion in Asian irrigation between 1978 and 1993.[58]

The strategy bears a marked resemblance to that of the first *Asian Agricultural Survey*, due to the emphasis given to the relationship between irrigation and agricultural output, because it refers to Japan, Taiwan and South Korea as successful examples of agricultural development, and due to its lack of concern with land reform.[59] In justifying its recommendations, the Trilateral report makes specific reference to the four-step Japanese model, the first survey and the research of Okita and Takase.[60] The similarity between the first survey and the Trilateral task force proposal is demonstrated in an article by Okita summarising the rationale behind the latter:

> According to Takese's research, a close relationship in rice production exists between irrigation and yield per hectare. In Japan, 98% of all rice fields are irrigated and their per hectare yield is six tons. In South Korea and Taiwan, 70% and 80% of all fields are irrigated and the per hectare yield is five tons, while the proportion of irrigated fields is 30% to 40% in South and Southeast Asia, where the per hectare yield is about two tons. Therefore, if the irrigation rate in South and Southeast Asia were doubled, it would be possible to double the yield per unit area.[61]

In the same article, which discusses different aspects of Japanese food policy, Okita – who has also served as Japanese Foreign Minister – links the origins of the Trilateral proposal to Japan's concern about the implications of food security in Asia for the Japanese economy.[62]

Owing to the enormity of the funding requirements of the proposal and the lack of coordinated support, it was not as such adopted for implementation. At a follow-up meeting held in February 1978 the

ADB was the most supportive of the proposed implementing agencies, and expressed its willingness to cooperate with the Japanese government in organising a regional meeting on the matter.[63] In contrast, the World Bank indicated that it could not serve as the centre for such a programme but would consider being actively involved in its implementation, and the FAO indicated that it was 'cautiously supportive'.[64] Although the scheme was not implemented, in the context of the debate on rural investment within the ADB the proposal did serve to shift attention from broad-based rural development following the example of the World Bank back to the question of food production and irrigation. Moreover, there are clear indications that the Japanese model has continued to influence Bank thinking into the 1980s.[65]

## Rural Development Policy Since 1980

While the rural sector has remained a priority area for the donor community, in the early 1980s a number of significant changes took place in donor policies. Following the global economic recession there was a general tightening of aid policies, including substantial reductions in ODA and a growing emphasis on bilateral and commercially oriented assistance. This tendency was clearest in the changes in aid policy introduced by the Reagan administration, which included giving priority to bilateral, politically directed aid, increasing the conditionality of multilateral aid, and stepping up pressure for multilateral agencies to adopt policies in line with the administration's political and economic priorities. The retirement in 1981 of World Bank President Robert McNamara, who was arguably the aid community's strongest proponent for the rural sector and under whom the World Bank adopted numerous policies in relative independence from congressional pressure, marked the beginning of a shift in the World Bank's policies. Under A. W. Clausen, who succeeded McNamara in July 1981, and, more recently, Barber Conable who took over from Clausen in 1986, major changes in World Bank policies, including greater emphasis on the role of the private sector and stricter policy conditionality, have been closely in line with the policies being promoted by Congress and the administration. In the ADB, a similarly accommodating line has been adopted by Fujioka since his assumption of the presidency in 1981.

In the early 1980s, the rural sector and energy remained the two priority areas for ADB lending, with the former accounting continuously for one third of all lending (34.3 per cent between 1980 and 1986). In policy statements, however, a decline in the official emphasis on poverty-oriented rural development is discernible. In 1980 and 1981, President Yoshida referred to four major challenges facing the developing countries of the region in the 1980s: the world energy situation, agricultural production, providing employment and ensuring that the poor benefit equitably from growth. In his first speech to the board of governors in 1982 President Fujioka had narrowed these down to three: foodgrain production, energy and the structural adjustment of the borrowers' economies to ease balance of payments difficulties.[66]

In the early 1980s no broad sectoral study comparable with the first and second surveys was undertaken, and only relatively minor changes took place in the Bank's rural development strategy. In 1981, the Bank initiated a study of its operational plans and priorities for the 1980s, in which connection a number of sector profiles were prepared. The sector profile for agriculture and rural development was subsequently expanded and circulated in 1983 as a staff paper discussing the performance of the rural sector in the 1970s and its development and investment needs in the 1980s.[67] After being endorsed by the board, the working paper was further revised, published and circulated in the region in 1985, for the guidance of both the Bank and its borrowers.[68]

Underlying the priorities set out in the staff working paper are the same policy objectives as in the sector policy paper of 1979 – increasing food production and expanding rural employment, as a means of increasing rural incomes. The paper discusses the differences in agricultural performance between the Southeast Asian countries, in which relatively strong economic growth was accompanied by increased per capita food production in the 1970s, and the South Asian countries, in which, with the exception of Sri Lanka, per capita food production either stagnated or declined, and emphasises that a country-specific approach will be required in determining strategies for raising output. At the same time, the paper observes that in absolute terms the rural labour force in both Southeast and South Asia will continue to increase in the 1980s and will require a large number of new jobs. The fundamental similarity between the paper's approach and that set out in the sector policy paper in 1979 is evident from the following:

Overcoming hunger and malnutrition is only partly a problem of accelerating food production. Equally important is the need to provide productive employment to the ever-increasing labor force which has to be enabled to produce or earn its food rather than rely on welfare measures. This means that programs and projects to increase food production have to be complemented by measures specifically aimed at ensuring the participation of small farmers and creating additional employment in agricultural and non-agricultural activities.[69]

That the Bank continues at the policy level to emphasise broad-based rural development is also indicated by the fact that it organised a regional seminar on rural development in October 1984, to discuss ways of enhancing its role in rural development, followed in November 1986 by an ADB–ILO regional workshop on rural employment creation.[70]

# 5 Organisational Constraints

A major contention of this study is that organisational and institutional factors are a key constraint on the implementation of policy change through project change. The changing development priorities of the donor community, which reflect both changing perceptions of development needs and political changes in the donor countries, have led to a variety of pressures on the Bank for project innovation. At the same time, however, the Bank's organisational concern with efficiently mobilising, committing and disbursing resources has given rise to institutional pressures and operational procedures which constrain rather than encourage project change. While changing development policies in the rural sector have called, for example, for smaller innovative, multi-component projects, with specific target groups and incorporating experimental technologies, the continuously increasing resources at the Bank's disposal have led the Bank's management to focus on the efficient – rather than the innovative – commitment of these resources. This, in turn, has led to a tendency towards large-scale, uniform projects with a minimum of implementation difficulties, which has worked counter to many of the operational changes called for in rural lending. This chapter discusses the impact of the Bank's organisational concern with channelling funds to its borrowers, and other organisational factors, on project formulation and content.

## Fund-Channelling

Tendler's study on foreign aid makes the important observation that the scarcity or abundance of aid resources depends on the context within which aid programmes are examined. In an aggregate context aid resources are scarce, but seen within the organisational context of a funding agency they are relatively abundant. Once resources have been committed to an aid agency, Tendler points out, the organisation and its staff are under pressure to move these resources, both because aid agencies tend to define their outputs in terms of how much money they move, and because only be effectively committing resources will the organisation be able to justify requests to its donors for further – and usually increased – funds. Tendler concludes that aid agencies' concern with moving money to a large extent determines organisational objectives and the allocation of staff resources, and is crucial in shaping the content of aid programmes and projects.[1] Payer is more blunt in her assessment of the impact of fund-channelling on World Bank projects:

> The World Bank is in the business of lending money. Its officers gain promotion on the basis of how well they are able to fill the quota (they call it the 'pipeline') for the area or country under their charge, in order to meet McNamara's massively expanding lending goals. As a result, they fund projects that are dubious by their own standards of cost-effectiveness, and lend large sums to projects that could have been funded at much less cost. The result is projects which are top-heavy with money spent on overpriced inputs, including an army of expensive foreign consultants.[2]

The organisational objectives pursued by the ADB's management have been built around fund-channelling, although a close examination suggests a somewhat more complex set of objectives than that originally outlined by Tendler. Broadly the function can be broken down into three components: a concern with mobilising resources, including funds for hard lending on international financial markets and funds for soft lending directly from donors; a concern with committing resources, in the form of new loan approvals; and a concern with the rapid disbursement of resources. Together these comprise the fund-channelling cycle, although varying emphasis has been placed on different elements at different times.

In the initial years of the Bank's existence, particularly during the presidency of Watanabe Takeshi between 1966 and 1972, there was a strong emphasis on establishing the ADB's reputation and credit rating on international financial markets, and the Bank's reputation with its major donors as a suitable channel for ODA. This concern is reflected in Watanabe's speech accepting his appointment as President at the Bank's inaugural meeting in 1966:

> It behooves us therefore, in our infancy, to step cautiously, exerting every effort toward establishing a high credit standing, and proving the worthiness of this institution. In this way, and only in this way, will the necessary additional resources, in all the various forms, be made available to the Bank. It is my ardent desire that all developed countries, in every corner of the world, who are concerned with the welfare of Asia, will appreciate our efforts and continue to contribute generously to our common endeavour.[3]

The priority given by Watanabe to the different aspects of resource mobilisation led him to adopt a cautious lending policy, focusing on traditional 'bankable' sectors and projects. As he noted in an article published soon after the Bank's establishment:

> There is only one basic policy to which I firmly adhere, namely, to ensure that each loan conforms to the principles of sound banking, and that each project is based upon valid economic precepts. This is the only way to establish the good credit of the Bank, and to thereby assure the continuous flow of funds through our organization.[4]

The same concern with establishing the Bank's financial reputation and credit rating, and its close linkage with the selection of infrastructure and industry projects and production-oriented agricultural projects, is also evident throughout Watanabe's memoirs.[5]

By the first half of the 1970s regular increases in the Bank's ordinary capital and a more or less regular flow of concessional funds from the donors had been established, as had the Bank's credit rating. The latter was indicated by the fact that in the early 1970s the Bank's bond issues were accorded a triple-A credit rating on international financial markets. Management's concern consequently shifted to ensuring that projects departments were preparing an adequate number of projects for approval each year, and that the disbursement of funds increased correspondingly. As a result the Bank was able to expand loan commitments at an average annual rate of approximately 20 per cent throughout the 1970s (see Table 5.1). Due to the rapid increase of loan approvals, however, increasing concern was caused to management by the disbursement problem, that is ensuring that funds were being spent at the same pace as new loans were approved and more funds were requested and received from donors. President Inoue first drew attention to the low disbursement rate at the 1973 annual meeting,[6] and subsequently initiated a number of measures to streamline loan administration. In his speech the following year, he noted that the problem required changes in the Bank's operational approach, including more emphasis on 'quicker-yielding more directly productive projects'.[7]

Following these measures the disbursement rate increase significantly in 1973–5, but declined again in 1976 (see Table 5.1), leading President Yoshida to take further steps to speed up project implementation. These included allocating more staff time for loan administration, streamlining and simplifying procedures, conducting training courses for counterpart staff in borrowing countries, and introducing annual disbursement targets.[8] Yoshida's address at the 1977 annual meeting indicates the significance of disbursements not only from the borrowers' viewpoint but from the point of view of mobilising additional funds from the donors:

> I submit that [the low disbursement rate] is a matter which needs our serious consideration. Unless we can show to capital-exporting countries, and indeed also the tax-payers in developing countries, that projects once started will be expeditiously implemented, we will be inviting disillusionment. It would raise understandable doubts among the donors whether the demand for aid is commensurate with the capacity to utilize aid. Moreover, every investment that is delayed in implementation means a substantial economic loss to the developing country concerned; our developing member countries cannot afford such avoidable losses.[9]

At the beginning of the 1980s, emphasis shifted from raising disbursements to stepping up loan commitments, mainly due to a significant drop in demand for ADB loans in the region, but also as one of a number of ambitious undertakings initiated by President Fujioka, who assumed office in 1981. Loan approvals increased at a substantial rate in the 1970s, but following the global recession and cutbacks in government spending in many Asian countries, in 1982 ADB lending increased by only 3.2 per cent over lending in 1981.[10] Fujioka expressed considerable concern over this in his 1983 address to the board of governors,[11] and subsequently announced a target of annually increasing lending by 15 per cent during the next five years, and introduced measures 'to speed up project processing and other stages of the project cycle'.[12] When lending in 1983, in spite of extensive pressure on Bank staff by Fujioka, increased by only 9 per cent, the target for 1984 was raised from 15 to 21 per cent to make up for the shortfall of the previous year.[13] In 1984 lending increased by 18 per cent, but in 1985 it declined by 15 per cent and in 1986 it increased by only 5 per cent (see Table 5.1), indicating that demand for ADB loans continues to stagnate. It has also been pointed out that the Bank will soon be confronted with a 'backwash' of repayments of earlier loans,[14] which it can be assumed will further increase organisational pressure to expand lending.

According to Bank staff annual lending targets have been translated by Fujioka into lending quotas for projects divisions, against which professional performance is measured and on whose achievement career prospects hinge. In an interview with the *Far Eastern Economic Review*, however, Fujioka denied imposing lending quotas and said that he has sought merely to 'push staff hard and make them work more efficiently'.[15] In addition to the annual expansion of lending, Fujioka has placed emphasis on the Bank's 'operational efficiency', defined as maintaining low staff and administrative costs in relation to the volume of lending and disbursements.

The emphasis on annual approval and disbursement targets and staff 'efficiency' has led to considerable pressures on Bank staff, particularly in projects departments. The need to expand annual loan commitments has placed pressure on staff to prepare and process loans for approval before the end of the Bank's fiscal year, in some cases with disregard for technical, institutional, economic or financial considerations, and has led to a phenomenon known as 'bunching', the rushed submission of large numbers of projects for board approval during the last months of the year. Recently there have been substantiated allegations that projects departments and management have, in a number of instances, ignored or played down the importance of technical and economic considerations which might have slowed down project processing and even of the suppression and falsification of data, in order to push projects through for board approval within the context of annual loan targets.[16]

Organisational concern with approvals and disbursement rates also has clear implications for decisions in the Bank related to the distribution of loans by sector and country. With regard to lending by sector, loans for physical infrastructure, industry and energy are relatively straightforward to plan and implement, and in general have a higher disbursement rate and less implementation problems than loans for the rural sector. As the *Asian Agricultural Survey* put it:

> If the ADB so chooses it could spend its entire capital fund and all its income for the next several decades on regional infrastructure development. The task is attractively simple. Civil engineering projects are clean and orderly (although construction may present a few headaches) and the payoffs can usually be calculated with at least an economist's precision.[17]

In a similar vein, loans for irrigation construction and to directly support agricultural production are easier to administer and have a higher disbursement rate than integrated rural development projects and other types of lending for poverty alleviation. Consequently there has been a degree of conflict between management's concern with smooth implementation and high disbursements, on the one hand, and the Bank's developmental objectives and political pressure on the Bank to undertake more innovative rural sector projects, on the other.[18] There is a similar conflict in the fact that project implementation tends to be easier and disbursements higher in the relatively high-income countries, while increased lending to the poorer countries, although in line with the Bank's developmental concerns, complicates loan implementation and brings down disbursements.[19]

The most important question is that of the relationship between quantitative lending targets and project quality. While the stress on annual lending targets has led to streamlined project planning and implementation, it has also forced staff to prepare projects within the confines of tight deadlines and administrative criteria. In this context it can be assumed to have enhanced tendencies towards the preparation of large projects, easily manageable projects, projects with a high disbursement rate, projects with a relatively short cycle, 'repeater' projects in which similar loans are given to a country at regular intervals, 'sector' loans, and standardised projects in which a similar design is applied in different countries. There are arguments for and against each of the above tendencies, but in several significant respects they conflict with the changes in the Bank's rural policy, and to this extent they work against project innovation and change.

There is also evidence of conflict between the prolonged implementation periods and correct sequencing of project components which rural development projects may require, on the one hand, and organisational pressure for adherence to lending targets, on the other. This point, which has been the subject of contention between the Bank's top management and projects departments, is made in a recent paper by Satish Jha, at the time a division manager in the Bank's Irrigation and Rural Development Department:

Most of the Bank-financed rural/area development projects are based on feasibility studies which provide for a complete package of development components without much consideration for appropriate phasing and sequential arrangements. This can be attributable to the [technical assistance] budget limitation and time constraints, as well as to the expressed desire of the concerned governments to expedite loan processing. The Bank's own loan targets also require speedy processing of loans for such projects after completion of the feasibility studies. The general assumption used is that all project components are inter-linked and can proceed simultaneously in terms of implementation. The available information does not confirm this. In the majority of cases, construction of the physical infrastructure components has moved faster than the direct production-related and social components. This suggests that there is ample scope for phased development and sequential arrangements in the implementation of different project components.[20]

Management pressure for departments to meet annual targets has aroused strong objections not only among Bank staff but also on the board of directors. Many donors, in particular, have criticised annual lending targets for detracting from the quality of individual projects. The variance between management and donors on this issue is exemplified by the fact that in the early 1980s, at the same time as Fujioka was placing increasing emphasis on annual targets, at the insistence of numerous donors the Bank introduced three-year planning figures in its annual reports in an effort to alleviate pressure on projects departments to meet annual targets at the possible expense of project quality. Donor concern with deteriorating project quality culminated in 1986 in a delay in the approval of a $35 million edible oil project in Burma and the abstention of two executive directors on the approval of an $11 million aquaculture loan to Nepal, the latter a highly exceptional measure in the context of the board's consensus-oriented decision-making process.[21] More recently further projects have been criticised by the board, and at the Bank's 1987 annual meeting several donors, notably the US, Canada and Australia, voiced their concern over the low quality of selected projects.

It is difficult to establish a clear relationship between adherence to lending targets and loan quality, defined, for example, by the extent of difficulties encountered in project implementation or the achievement of project objectives. However, it is interesting to note that the US Treasury Department's 1983 report on multilateral banks concludes that in the case of the World Bank emphasis on lending targets has had an adverse impact on loan quality, while the recent study commissioned by the Development Committee's Task Force on Concessional Flows also notes that agencies' fund-channelling function often conflicts with the quality of lending.[22]

Table 5.1 sets out annual loan approval and disbursements and clearly shows the reasons behind the ADB's changing emphasis on moving money.[23] As new approvals increased steadily in the early 1970s, disbursements did not keep pace and only levelled out at what seems to have been established by the Bank as an acceptable level of 40 per cent of new approvals in the latter half of the 1970s.

Table 5.1 Annual loan approvals, annual loan disbursements and average size of loans by the ADB, 1968–86

| | Annual loan approvals ($ million) | Increase over previous year (per cent) | Annual loan disbursements ($ million) | Increase over previous year (per cent) | Disbursements as proportion of new approvals (per cent) | Number of new loans | Average loan size ($ million) | Increase over previous year (per cent) |
|---|---|---|---|---|---|---|---|---|
| 1968 | 41.6 | – | 1.8 | – | 4 | 7 | 5.9 | – |
| 1969 | 98.1 | 136 | 7.5 | 317 | 8 | 19 | 5.2 | –12 |
| 1970 | 245.6 | 150 | 17.1 | 128 | 7 | 30 | 8.2 | 58 |
| 1971 | 254.0 | 3 | 48.7 | 185 | 19 | 26 | 9.4 | 15 |
| 1972 | 316.1 | 24 | 61.1 | 25 | 19 | 32 | 9.9 | 5 |
| 1973 | 421.5 | 33 | 146.5 | 140 | 35 | 39 | 10.8 | 9 |
| 1974 | 547.7 | 30 | 187.5 | 28 | 34 | 39 | 14.0 | 30 |
| 1975 | 660.3 | 21 | 361.9 | 93 | 55 | 40 | 16.5 | 18 |
| 1976 | 775.9 | 18 | 326.6 | –10 | 42 | 36 | 21.6 | 31 |
| 1977 | 886.5 | 14 | 356.2 | 30 | 40 | 45 | 19.7 | –9 |
| 1978 | 1158.7 | 31 | 462.2 | 30 | 40 | 52 | 22.3 | 13 |
| 1979 | 1251.6 | 8 | 486.3 | 5 | 39 | 57 | 22.0 | –1 |
| 1980 | 1435.7 | 15 | 579.0 | 19 | 40 | 58 | 24.8 | 13 |
| 1981 | 1677.6 | 17 | 667.1 | 15 | 40 | 54 | 31.1 | 25 |
| 1982* | 1730.6 | 3 | 795.1 | 19 | 46 | 56 | 30.9 | –1 |
| 1983 | 1893.2 | 9 | 936.9 | 18 | 49 | 53 | 35.7 | 16 |
| 1984 | 2234.3 | 18 | 1000.5 | 7 | 45 | 47 | 47.5 | 33 |
| 1985 | 1908.1 | –15 | 1010.1 | 1 | 53 | 46 | 41.5 | –13 |
| 1986 | 2001.3 | 5 | 1024.3 | 1 | 51 | 48 | 41.7 | 0 |

* In the 1982 *Annual Report* loan approvals are given as $1730.6 million, but in annual reports since 1984 the 1982 figure is given as $1683.6 million, due to cancellations.

*Source:* ADB, *Annual Report* (1968–86).

Disbursements have not increased as significantly in the 1980s, although in proportion to new approvals they have increased, due to the slow increase in 1982–3 and decline in 1985 of new approvals.

As a rough indicator of loan content, the table also examines loan size, which increased from an average of $5.9 million in 1968 to $41.7 million in 1986. Increases in loan size have to some extent followed periods of emphasis on increasing lending, both in 1973–6 and in 1982–4, and support the assumption that pressure to expand lending leads staff to prepare larger projects, possibly at the expense of project content in terms of development objectives. It is particularly noteworthy that between 1982 and 1984, when Fujioka was pressing strongly for increased lending, annual lending did increase but the number of new loans declined, while average loan size in two years increased by over 50 per cent, from $30.9 to $47.5 million.

In discussing loan size it is also interesting to note that the IDB, following international pressure for innovative lending modalities, introduced a programme in 1978 for financing small projects, to provide concessional credit to 'groups who, due to their financing conditions and lack of credit experience, fail to qualify for conventional sources of public and commerical credit'.[24] According to the IDB these credits have benefited 'low-income farmers, small-scale entrepreneurs, craftspersons, and other members of the region's labor force'.[25] Between 1978 and 1986 the IDB granted 149 credits worth a total of $63.8 million under this programme, with an average credit size of slightly over $0.4 million. The ADB does not have a comparable programme.

**Project Formulation**

The ADB's project cycle is based on that of the World Bank and consists of six stages.[26] The entire formulation process, before loan negotiations between the Bank and the borrower and the submission of a project to the board for formal approval, consists of three stages: identification, preparation and appraisal. Project identification is mainly the responsibility of the two Programs Departments (until 1987 the Country Department), which carry out country programming missions tentatively to identify projects for possible Bank financing within the context of national and sectoral plans. Project preparation and appraisal, again, are carried out under the supervision of the responsible projects departments. Once a potential project has been identified, the concerned projects department will conduct fact-finding, which is usually followed by the preparation of a feasibility study on the project. Project preparation is in principle the responsibility of the borrower, but in practice Bank staff play a very active role, and feasibility studies are typically prepared by outside consultants funded by the ADB under a technical assistance grant. Project appraisal is the responsibility of the concerned projects department, and is usually to a large extent based on the feasibility study. The appraisal includes an assessment of the technical, economic, institutional and financial aspects of a project, with particular emphasis on a detailed economic and financial analysis. The appraisal report forms the basis for loan negotiations between the Bank and the borrower, is submitted to the board for formal approval, and is an integral part of the loan agreement.

To gain a realistic appreciation of the circumstances which guide project formulation by the Bank, however, the process must be seen within the context of management's quantitative lending targets and the organisational abundance of resources which need to be committed each year. The three first stages of the project cycle are based on the theoretical assumption that there are a large number of investment possibilities and alternative approaches to projects and only limited resources. Consequently, the three stages are in principle intended as a means of indentifying investment possibilities, defining the relative priority of projects, selecting the most viable projects, assessing the alternative approaches to implementing a particular project, and, finally, selecting the most economically viable and technically appropriate solutions for project implementation.

Conditions in practice are very different. The constant expansion of the Bank's resources available for lending and the pressure to meet annual lending targets have had little direct relation to changes in the demand for ADB loans among the borrowing countries. Moreover, according to a report prepared for the Economics Office by an external consultant, in practice the thrust of project formulation by the Bank has been on the second stage of the cycle – technical project preparation by projects departments – rather than the first stage – the systematic identification of a broad range of investment alternatives as a basis for selection.[27] Consequently, in contrast to theory, the first stages of the cycle have to a large extent taken place within the context of a limited number of identified investment alternatives or low demand for Bank loans, on the other hand,

and relatively abundant Bank resources, on the other. This has substantially detracted from the role of the first three stages of the cycle as a means of selecting priority projects and assessing alternative approaches, and has reduced their role to that of finding projects to finance and preparing and processing them with a view to securing their approval. That this has taken place at the possible expense of technical and developmental considerations, is summed up by the consultant's report:

Under the present system [of project formulation], the emphasis is given to pushing loan packages through the pipeline once they have been identified. Not surprisingly then, neither procedures nor guidelines can be said to exist for the specification and periodic review of alternative project modes and designs.[28]

The economic analysis of projects at the appraisal stage plays a particularly important role in determining the criteria for project selection and approval. However, as economic appraisal follows lengthy project preparation, both Payer and Ayres point out that in the World Bank it has to a large extent assumed the role of an *ex post facto* justification for projects already selected on a variety of other grounds.[29] In its assessment of the ADB's appraisal methodology, the above-cited consultant's report draws attention to a similar shortcoming, noting that the general impression conveyed by the Bank's appraisal guidelines is that appraisal is 'a discrete activity that commences after a loan package has been determined and its project components have been designed'.[30] Consequently the staff conducting the appraisal may, as the consultant rather cautiously puts it, 'be placed under pressure to present a project proposal in its most favourable light' or 'be tempted to give a positive bias to the figures contained in the economic appraisal'.[31] Recent reports in fact indicate considerably more serious malpractices in economic analysis.[32]

Both project formulation criteria and the type of economic analysis used in project appraisal were the subject of extensive debate in connection with the growing emphasis placed by the donor community on incorporating income distribution and employment considerations into development programmes. Starting in the early 1970s attention was drawn to the possibility of using income distribution and poverty alleviation as pre-selection criteria, mainly by identifying projects designed to benefit rural areas, low-income areas and groups, and specific target groups. At the same time various methodologies were developed to supplement conventional calculations of projects' economic internal rate of return (EIRR) and financial rate of return with the calculation of a social rate of return.

Under McNamara in the early 1970s the World Bank began to consider a project's anticipated impact on poverty in rural areas as a broad pre-selection criterion for many of its rural projects, and assumed a central role in developing methodologies for social cost-benefit analysis. Taking into consideration the impact of rural projects on low-income groups and specific target groups had by the mid-1970s become a relatively institutionalised feature of project identification, and the World Bank's operational manual, issued in 1980, incorporated the consideration of income distribution into the bank's appraisal methodology.[33] According to Ayres, however, the World Bank's economic analysis has in practice continued to focus on economic and financial rates of return, and social rates of return are rarely used, even for poverty-oriented projects.[34] Similarly, in the early 1970s the IDB took initiatives to broaden the scope of its project selection criteria and economic analysis.[35] This was followed by what Howe considers the most positive step taken by an aid agency to incorporate analysis of the distributional effects of projects into the formulation process. In 1979, one of the conditions attached to the replenishment of the IDB's resources was that a low-income level be defined for each borrower and that, in addition to normal economic, financial and technical criteria, the criterion be applied that at least 50 per cent of the IDB's resources must benefit low-income individuals.[36]

In comparison, the ADB has been slow to initiate change in either its economic appraisal methodology or broader project formulation criteria. Following the lead of the World Bank, in 1977–8 the Bank's Economics Office prepared a paper recommending a number of changes in the Bank's appraisal methodology, of which the most significant were the conducting of preparatory work for the adoption of social cost-benefit analysis and the incorporation of income distribution into project appraisal.[37] However, these recommendations have not been reflected in the Bank's most recent guidelines for economic analysis of projects, issued to staff in 1983, which continue to stress economic efficiency and the objective of maximising output, and give equal weight to both incomes accruing to different income groups and the end-users of incomes.[38] The Bank's cautious approach to modifying its appraisal methodology is summarised in the guidelines as follows:

In recent years, the methodological framework for economic analysis has been extended explicitly to incorporate income distribution criteria, reflecting the concern for the alleviation of poverty and the need for greater savings in developing countries. While this approach is conceptually more refined, its use has been limited because of the complexity of analysis and problems involved in giving social weights to income and saving accruing to different income groups. It is therefore proposed that incorporating of these social considerations in the methodology for appraisal of Bank-assisted projects be deferred until a comprehensive assessment of application and practicability can be made.[39]

However, the guidelines do propose that efficiency analysis be supplemented by analysis of project impact on 'other socioeconomic objectives' with particular reference to low-income groups and target groups.[40] While this is ostensibly reflected in the increased orientation of irrigation and rural development projects, and some infrastructure projects, toward low-income groups, this study argues that in practice the focus and impact of projects on such groups has continued to be negligible (see Chapters 7 and 8). The Bank's continuing concern with the formulation and appraisal process as a means of implementing more effectively poverty-oriented lending is reflected by the fact that it commissioned the above-cited assessment of its appraisal methodology in the early 1980s. However, the implementation of the recommendations of the study, which amount to a substantial revision of the project formulation process, has yet to be evidenced.

At the same time, it should be noted that the debate on the economic analysis of projects also has a political dimension. In connection with demands for changes in the Bank's development policy in the early 1970s, expanding the criteria for project selection was one of the operational changes most frequently called for by the smaller donors. Subsequently the work undertaken by the Economics Office to revise and expand the Bank's appraisal methodology received particular praise from these donors. On the other hand, the fact that few concrete steps have been taken to implement any changes must also be seen in the light of the more recent changes in the policies advocated by some donors. The opponents of multilateral aid in the US Congress, for example, have been particularly critical of the introduction of 'vague' economic and social criteria in the multilateral banks' economic analysis.[41]

**Organisational Structure**

A number of features of the ADB's organisational structure can also
be related to the Bank's difficulties in reorienting its lending activities.
The first is the Bank's centralised structure. In his study of the World
Bank, Ayres draws attention to the World Bank's high degree of
centralisation, with 94 per cent of its staff in Washington, relying
mainly on relatively short field missions to maintain contact with
borrowing countries, as a constraint on implementing a poverty-
oriented lending programme.[42] While the ADB is geographically
much closer to most of its borrowers than the World Bank, it has
adopted a similar centralised organisational structure, relying on
field visits from its Manila headquarters for project formulation,
supervision and evaluation. There are only three exceptions to this
centralisation. In 1981 the Bank established a resident office in
Dhaka, mainly in an effort to remedy extensive problems in loan
implementation in Bangladesh. In 1984 a regional office was established in Vanuatu to cover projects in the South Pacific, where, due
to the small size of loans and high staff travel costs, the Bank's
centralised administration was not considered cost-effective. Third,
in 1987 the Bank opened an office in Jakarta, to facilitate project
implementation and speed up the disbursement of loans in Indonesia.
While the experience of these offices will be evaluated and may
eventually lead to further decentralisation, at present the ADB
continues to be more centralised than the World Bank. In comparison,
it is interesting to note that the IDB is relatively decentralised, with
offices in almost all borrowing countries.

Second, while the division and structure of the Bank's departments to a certain extent reflect the changes in the Bank's lending
priorities, they have also served to constrain lending within a definite
framework. An examination of the changes which have taken place
in the projects departments indicates the degree to which the ADB
has or has not restructured its bureaucracy in response to policy
changes. Initially the Bank had one department responsible for
preparing and implementing projects. The first major restructuring
took place in 1974, when the Project Department was split into
Projects Department I (with five divisions: Fisheries and Livestock;
Development Banks; Industry, including education; Irrigation; and
General Agriculture) and Projects Department II (with four divisions:
Highways and Airports; Power; Ports, Railways and Telecommunications; and Water Supply and Urban Development).

The second major restructuring, in 1978, acknowledged the leading position of agriculture and rural development, which had reached an annual average of over 28 per cent of all lending. In the restructuring, three separate projects departments were established, the Agriculture and Rural Development Department (with five divisions: General Agriculture; Rural Development and Agricultural Credit; Irrigation I, covering East Asia, Southeast Asia and the South Pacific; Irrigation II, covering South Asia and Indo-China; and Fisheries and Livestock), the Infrastructure Department (with four divisions: Airports and Highways; Ports, Railways and Telecommunications; Water Supply; and Social Infrastructure, including education, health and urban development – in 1982 the latter was split into the Social Infrastructure Division, covering health, population and urban development, and the Education Division), and the Industry and Development Banks Department (with four divisions: Industry and Minerals; Power; Development Banks I; and Development Banks II; in 1981, due to expanding lending, the Power Division was split into Power Division East and Power Division West; at the same time, due to reduced lending, the Development Banks divisions were merged).

When rural lending reached 35 per cent of all lending in 1983 the Agriculture and Rural Development Department was divided in two, the Agriculture Department (with three divisions: Agro-Industry and Forestry; Fisheries and Livestock; and Agricultural Support Services) and the Irrigation and Rural Development Department (with three divisions, covering different groups of countries).

From the point of view of the rural sector, the significant changes are those which have taken place in the Agriculture and Rural Development and the Infrastructure Departments. In the former, between 1974 and 1983 the number of divisions concerned with agriculture and rural development expanded from three to six, reflecting the ADB's growing concern with irrigation, credit, inputs and support services. The General Agriculture Division (renamed the Agro-Industry and Forestry Division in 1983) and Fisheries and Livestock Division have remained fundamentally unchanged, but Irrigation expanded from a division in 1974 to a department comprising three divisions in 1983, and the importance of support services was acknowledged through the establishment of a Rural Development and Agricultural Credit Division in 1978 (which became the Agricultural Support Services Division in 1983).

However, the establishment of two departments, one with responsibility for irrigation and integrated rural development projects and the other covering agricultural projects and support services, may also have served to reinforce rather than break down conventional project boundaries. As the provision of various support services is the key element in moving from construction-oriented irrigation projects towards integrated irrigation and rural development projects, it can be argued that the separation of the division responsible for support services from the Irrigation and Rural Development Department has contributed to the very limited degree to which irrigation projects have in fact become integrated (see Chapter 7).

In the Infrastructure Department the increasing emphasis on social aspects of development led to the establishment of the Social Infrastructure Division in 1974 and the Education Division in 1982. Both have implemented a number of projects in rural areas, in the fields of health, population and vocational and technical education. On the other hand, no significant changes have taken place in the Infrastructure Department's Airports and Highways Division or within the Industry Department to reflect a growing emphasis on employment creation in rural areas through labour-intensive construction and the development of small-scale industries. This can be related to the fact that the policy recommendations concerning road construction and small-scale industries were made by the Agriculture and Rural Development Department, and suggests that the Bank's departmental structure has served to contain concern with rural development mainly to within that department.

At the beginning of 1987, the Bank underwent another restructuring. The Country Department was split into Programs Department (East) and Programs Department (West), while the entire agricultural sector was restructured based on country groups, in contrast to its previous subsectoral structure. Thus the Agriculture Department and Irrigation and Rural Development Department became Agriculture Department (East) and Agriculture Department (West), with a total of six divisions for different groups of countries and with specialists responsible for different subsectors in each division (see Figure 2.1). The restructuring was partly a response to the declining economic viability of investing in irrigation in Asia, and may be connected with a gradual shift away from irrigation in the subsectoral emphasis of the Bank's rural lending. It was also intended to strengthen the country emphasis of rural lending and may help to reduce subsectoral barriers. However, Bank staff have also pointed out that having projects staff specialise in one or a few countries will detract from the departments' ability to facilitate the region-wide transfer and exchange of experience in different subsectors, which was one of the advantages of the previous subsectoral structure.

In addition, there are considerable differences in the approaches to rural development advocated by Bank staff. While some staff members have favoured innovative types of projects, many others have supported more familiar or conventional approaches, pointing out the administrative and technical difficulties involved in planning and implementing new project types. In the rural sector, staff resistance to innovation has been particularly evident with regard to two issues: the degree to which the Bank should become involved in integrated rural development projects, and the question of labour-intensive construction technology. Parallels can be drawn with World Bank staff, whose differences regarding rural development Ayres reports as being described by staff members themselves as the conflict between the 'agricultural development boys' and the 'rural poverty boys'.[43]

More directly relevant to the ADB is Ascher's observation regarding the essential difference between programme and projects staff. Programme staff are usually generalists and are responsible for the development of country programmes and loan portfolios, and may in this role support policy change. Projects staff, again, are specialists with direct responsibility for project design and implementation, which is why Ascher argues that they are particularly 'role-conservative' and resistant to change.[44] The strong emphasis placed by the ADB on project preparation and appraisal by projects staff, as opposed to identification by programme staff in the Programs Departments, lends considerable validity to Ascher's argument. It is also related to management's emphasis on annual lending targets, and brings us back to the constraining influence of organisational factors.

# 6 Operational Policies and Practices

The ADB's operational policies and lending practices are formulated within the context of the Bank's political debate on development policy and the organisational constraints discussed in the preceding chapter. Underlying operational policies and practices are two conflicts. The first is between the Bank's developmental objectives and the interests of the borrowing countries, on the one hand, and the political and economic interests of the donors, on the other. While changes in the Bank's rural development policy have called for changes in operational policies such as increased lending to low-income countries, more financing of local costs, greater procurement from developing countries, greater use of domestic consultants, more emphasis on appropriate technologies, and more flexible loan terms, many of these go counter to questions of commercial or political interest to the Bank's donors. The second conflict is between the Bank's development objectives and considerations of operational and organisational efficiency. Several of the above changes in operational policies, while facilitating the achievement of development objectives, may also complicate or slow down project planning and implementation, thus conflicting with concerns related to fund-channelling. This chapter examines these questions in the light of four central operational issues: the country allocation of lending, project procurements, consulting services and local cost financing.

## The Country Allocation of Lending

The extent to which the country allocation of development bank lending is or is not governed by political criteria is a question of some contention among researchers. Please argues that World Bank lending is, with few exceptions, allocated on a non-political basis, but presents no empirical evidence to support his case.[1] Numerous other authors, again, convincingly link country selection with political factors, including Ayres, who demonstrates how closely World Bank lending is in line with US interests, Wall, who links World Bank lending with political stability, and Krasner, who correlates the allocation of lending by regional development banks with indicators of the economic interests of the major developed countries.[2]

In a manner similar to the World Bank, the ADB charter specifies that the Bank shall not be influenced in its decisions by political factors, and that only economic considerations should be relevant to Bank decisions.[3] For purposes of loan allocation, based on GNP per capita, the ADB divides the borrowing countries into three groups. Group A countries are fully eligible for ADF loans, and include the Pacific island countries and countries with very low GNP per capita (Afghanistan, Bangladesh, Bhutan, Burma, Cambodia, Laos, the Maldives, Nepal, Pakistan, Sri Lanka and Vietnam). In addition some group A countries, mainly Pakistan, Burma and Sri Lanka, are eligible for a 'blend' of ordinary and ADF loans. Of the group B countries, Papua New Guinea (PNG) is eligible for ordinary and ADF loans and the Philippines, Thailand and Indonesia were marginally eligible until the early 1980s. Thailand last received an ADF loan in 1981 and Indonesia in 1979, while the Philippines received a 'blended' loan in 1986. In recognition of their economic difficulties, in 1987 Indonesia and the Philippines were granted limited eligibility for ADF lending. Group C countries (Fiji, Hong Kong, Malaysia, Singapore, South Korea and Taiwan) are only eligible for normal loans, although Taiwan has not borrowed since 1971, nor Hong Kong and Singapore since 1980. In the Bank, loan allocation is formally viewed as the process of a country 'maturing' from ADF eligibility through 'blend' status to hard loan status and, finally, 'graduating' to become a non-borrower, in principle based on GNP per capita and debt repayment capacity.[4]

This section examines the respective roles of three groups of factors – developmental considerations, political considerations, and borrowers' economic performance – in explaining the Bank's allocation of lending by country. Table 6.1 gives the country allocation of OCR and SFR lending in relation to GNP per capita and population, and indicates a clear tendency for Bank lending to concentrate on the borrowing countries with relatively high GNP.[5] Per capita lending in 1967–86 for group C is $46.1 and the corresponding figure for group B is $29.9, while per capita lending in group A countries is only $19.8. The concentration of lending in South Korea, Malaysia, Indonesia, the Philippines and Thailand is particularly marked. While these countries account for 45.9 per cent of the borrowing countries' total population, they have received 58.4 per cent of all loans. The group A countries, with a per capita GNP in 1980 of less than $300,

Table 6.1 Country allocation of lending in relation to the GNP per capita and population (cumulative as of December 1986)

| Borrowing country | GNP per capita in 1985 (US $) | Share of total lending (%) | Total loan approvals ($ million) | OCR loans ($ million) | ADF loans ($ million) | Population in 1985 (million) | Share of population of borrowing countries (%) | Cumulative Bank lending per capita ($) |
|---|---|---|---|---|---|---|---|---|
| *Group C* | | | | | | | | |
| South Korea | 2180 | 11.13 | 2169.5 | 2165.8 | 3.7 | 41.06 | 5.75 | 52.8 |
| Malaysia | 2050 | 6.58 | 1282.6 | 1279.3 | 3.3 | 15.68 | 2.19 | 81.8 |
| Singapore | 7420 | 0.93 | 181.1 | 178.1 | 3.0 | 2.56 | 0.36 | 70.7 |
| Hong Kong | 6220 | 0.52 | 101.5 | 101.5 | – | 5.42 | 0.76 | 18.7 |
| Taiwan | n.a. | 0.51 | 100.4 | 100.4 | – | 19.11 | 2.67 | 5.3 |
| Fiji | 1700 | 0.31 | 60.5 | 60.5 | – | 0.70 | 0.10 | 86.4 |
| *Total Group C* | | 19.98 | 3895.6 | 3885.6 | 10.0 | 84.53 | 11.83 | 46.1 |
| *Group B* | | | | | | | | |
| Indonesia | 530 | 19.36 | 3773.1 | 3610.8 | 162.3 | 165.15 | 23.11 | 22.8 |
| Philippines | 600 | 12.45 | 2427.8 | 2298.5 | 129.3 | 54.67 | 7.65 | 44.4 |
| Thailand | 830 | 8.87 | 1728.4 | 1656.3 | 72.1 | 51.30 | 7.18 | 33.7 |
| PNG | 710 | 1.40 | 272.6 | 137.3 | 135.3 | 3.37 | 0.47 | 80.9 |
| *Total Group B* | | 42.08 | 8201.9 | 7702.8 | 499.1 | 274.49 | 38.41 | 29.9 |
| *Group A* | | | | | | | | |
| Pakistan | 380 | 16.56 | 3228.0 | 1440.2 | 1787.9 | 96.18 | 13.46 | 33.6 |
| Bangladesh | 150 | 9.87 | 1924.3 | 11.4 | 1912.9 | 98.69 | 13.81 | 19.5 |
| Sri Lanka | 370 | 2.92 | 568.5 | 14.1 | 554.3 | 15.84 | 2.22 | 35.9 |
| Nepal | 160 | 2.82 | 549.6 | 2.0 | 547.6 | 16.68 | 2.33 | 32.9 |
| Burma | 190 | 2.72 | 530.9 | 6.6 | 524.3 | 36.58 | 5.12 | 14.5 |
| Afghanistan | n.a. | 0.49 | 95.1 | – | 95.1 | 18.16 | 2.54 | 5.2 |
| Laos | n.a. | 0.37 | 72.1 | – | 72.1 | 4.44 | 0.62 | 16.2 |
| Vietnam | n.a. | 0.23 | 44.6 | 3.9 | 40.7 | 59.46 | 8.32 | 0.8 |
| Bhutan | 160 | 0.13 | 24.7 | – | 24.7 | 1.28 | 0.18 | 19.3 |
| Maldives | 290 | 0.02 | 3.4 | – | 3.4 | 0.18 | 0.03 | 18.9 |
| Cambodia | n.a. | 0.01 | 1.7 | – | 1.7 | 7.42 | 1.04 | 0.2 |
| *Total Group A* | | 36.14 | 7042.8 | 1478.2 | 5564.6 | 354.91 | 49.66 | 19.8 |
| India | 250 | 1.28 | 250.0 | 250.0 | – | * | * | * |

| | | | | | | | | |
|---|---|---|---|---|---|---|---|---|
| *Pacific Islands* | | | | | | | | |
| Western Samoa | 660 | 0.26 | 50.4 | — | 0.16 | 50.4 | 0.02 | 315.0 |
| Solomon Islands | 510 | 0.15 | 28.8 | — | 0.27 | 28.8 | 0.04 | 106.7 |
| Tonga | 730 | 0.06 | 11.3 | — | 0.10 | 11.3 | 0.01 | 113.0 |
| Cook Islands | n.a. | 0.01 | 2.5 | — | 0.02 | 2.5 | ** | 125.0 |
| Vanuatu | n.a. | 0.03 | 5.1 | — | 0.14 | 5.1 | 0.02 | 36.4 |
| Kiribati | 450 | 0.01 | 3.0 | — | 0.06 | 3.0 | 0.01 | 50.0 |
| *Total Pacific Islands* | | 0.52 | 101.0 | — | 0.75 | 101.0 | 0.10 | 134.7 |
| Total | 100.00 | 100.00 | 19491.4 | 13316.7 | 6174.7 | 714.67 | 100.00 | 27.3 |

*Note:* Figures may not tally due to rounding.

\* Due to its recent and exceptional status as a borrower, India is not included in these calculations.

\*\* Less than one hundredth of one per cent.

*Sources:* ADB, *Annual Report* (1986), ADB, *Key Indicators of Developing Member Countries of ADB* (July 1986), and *The World Bank Atlas* (1987).

which account for 49.7 per cent of the borrowers' population, again, have received only 36.1 per cent of all loans. The distribution of per capita lending is largely explained by the fact that ADF lending to the poorest borrowers has been limited by the fund's resource constraints, while the relatively more abundant OCR loans have been earmarked mainly for countries with higher debt repayment capacity.

Table 6.2 compares the principal recipients of ADB loans with the political priorities of the different donor voting groups in the Bank as reflected by their bilateral ODA commitments in the Asian region in 1980–1. Country allocation is closest in line with Japan's priorities, particularly the fact that 57.6 per cent of Japanese aid to Asia – in comparison with 54.9 per cent of ADB lending – goes to Indonesia, Thailand, South Korea and the Philippines, all countries of particular trade and investment interest to Japan. Country allocation is also closely in line with US political priorities, although US bilateral aid has tended to concentrate more on low-income countries, particularly India and Bangladesh. The main difference between ADB country allocation and the bilateral priorities of the other donor voting groups is the greater priority given by the smaller donors to low-income countries and the much lower priority given to middle-income countries, particularly South Korea, Thailand, the Philippines and Indonesia. Many of the smaller donors have mentioned their preference for increased lending to the low-income borrowers in their statements at the Bank's annual meetings. Tables 6.1 and 6.2 suggest that political factors, borrowers' economic performance and their debt absorption capacity play an important role, alongside borrowers' income levels, in determining the allocation of the Bank's lending.

Political factors have also determined various country-specific decisions. The fact that Vietnam has received no loans since 1974 and that Cambodia has only received one loan, in 1971, and the relatively low level of lending to Laos are all a result of US opposition to lending to a socialist Indo-China. Following the Soviet intervention in 1979, the Bank halted both disbursements and new commitments to the Afghan government. It is also interesting to note that while Taiwan has not borrowed since 1971, the year the People's Republic took over the Chinese seat at the UN and the year before the Nixon administration normalised US relations with China, on the other hand there was a long delay before the ADB in 1986 accepted the People's Republic as a Bank member, purportedly due to the increased financial burden this would entail on Bank resources, but also partly due to strong congressional opposition to such a move.

Table 6.2 Comparison between the country allocation of ADB lending and the bilateral ODA of the Bank's donor voting groups (per cent going to 8 major recipient countries)*

| | ADB/ADF | Japan | US | Canada, Netherlands & Nordic countries | Australia | Austria, West Germany & UK | Belgium, France, Italy & Switzerland |
|---|---|---|---|---|---|---|---|
| | Indonesia 17.7 | Indonesia 28.1 | India 23.1 | India 28.2 | PNG 26.7 | India 64.3 | Indonesia 34.4 |
| | Philippines 13.7 | India 26.8 | Bangladesh 12.6 | Bangladesh 17.8 | Indonesia 18.9 | Bangladesh 9.8 | India 19.3 |
| | South Korea 13.3 | Bangladesh 12.6 | Indonesia 12.1 | Vietnam 15.3 | Bangladesh 13.0 | Indonesia 3.8 | Bangladesh 10.7 |
| | Pakistan 13.2 | Pakistan 8.0 | Pakistan 10.3 | Sri Lanka 10.8 | Burma 11.4 | Sri Lanka 3.4 | Pakistan 8.1 |
| | Thailand 10.2 | Nepal 4.9 | Philippines 9.8 | Indonesia 9.5 | Philippines 10.9 | Pakistan 3.1 | Nepal 4.5 |
| | Bangladesh 9.9 | Burma 4.0 | Sri Lanka 9.4 | Pakistan 7.0 | Thailand 8.5 | Burma 2.8 | Vanuatu 4.1 |
| | Malaysia 6.6 | Philippines 3.0 | South Korea 5.0 | Laos 4.2 | Fiji 2.4 | Philippines 2.5 | Philippines 4.0 |
| | Burma 3.6 | South Korea 2.0 | Thailand 4.7 | Nepal 3.5 | Pakistan 1.7 | South Korea 2.4 | Burma 3.8 |
| Total of 8 major recipients | 88.1 | 89.4 | 86.9 | 96.2 | 93.5 | 92.1 | 88.9 |
| Total ODA to ADB countries ($ million) | | 4556.8 | 1868.0 | 2211.0 | 899.1 | 3103.2 | 750.3 |

* The figures for Bank lending are cumulative as of December 1983, while the figures for the donor groups are based on total ODA commitments made in 1980 and 1981.

Sources: ADB, Loan, Technical Assistance and Equity Approvals (August 1984), and OECD, Geographical Distribution of Financial Flows to Developing Countries (Paris, 1984).

The halt in lending to Taiwan cannot be explained by GNP per capita alone, as both Hong Kong and Singapore continued to borrow once they reached the GNP level at which Taiwan stopped borrowing. Finally, the inclusion of Indonesia, the Philippines and Thailand as group B countries with marginal eligibility for soft loans, which enabled these countries to get $117 million in ADF loans between 1978 and 1981 was largely undertaken as a result of political pressure from the US. Prior to this, the three countries had not been eligible for concessional loans since 1974.

**Procurement Policy**

One of the main reasons for the donors' participating in the ADB – and one of the issues most actively pursued by these countries in the Bank – is the opportunity the ADB offers them for promoting their exports to Asia. When the ADB charter was drawn up, a provision similar to that of the World Bank, limiting the use of the Bank's loan proceeds to member countries, was included. The primary intention of this clause was to provide the donors with more incentive to join the Bank.[6] ADB advertising has also stressed the opportunity provided by Bank procurement contracts for export promotion:

> The proceeds of Bank loans are generally ear-marked to finance the foreign exchange cost of the projects and this means that the goods and services to be procured will be supplied from sources outside of the borrowing countries. Furthermore, as a project goes on stream, or becomes operational, there will be recurring requirements for materials, spare parts, and supplies which may not be available locally and have to be imported. It is obvious, therefore, that the trade opportunities created by the provision of Bank financing could lead to new or bigger markets for the supplier countries.[7]

In contrast, the borrowers have been critical of the high degree of procurement from the industrialised countries and have called for measures to promote both domestic procurements and procurements from the DMCs in general.

As the functional model for the regional development banks, the World Bank provided the precedent for the procurement and consultancy policy of the ADB. Immediately after the Second World War the US was virtually the only source of capital goods, and therefore competing for procurements was irrelevant. By the early 1950s, however, new potential suppliers of goods and services had emerged, which led to the introduction in 1951 of ICB for contracts for IBRD projects. ICB is based on international notification of an opportunity to bid for a contract of clear specifications, which is awarded to the lowest bid meeting the specifications. This was intended to give all members of the World Bank, mainly, of course, the Western industrialised nations, a chance to compete as suppliers of goods and services. From the borrower's point of view, ICB was based on the principles of efficiency and economy and was intended to ensure that the borrower got a contract of specified technical standards at the most favourable price.[8]

Since 1951 several amendments have been made to the World Bank system of ICB with a view to promoting procurements from developing countries. On the one hand, these amendments represented the recognition that procurements can play a significant role in fostering industries in developing countries, alongside the principles of efficiency and economy. On the other hand, the changes were introduced at the demand of the developing countries, whose share of procurements had remained low. In 1962 the World Bank granted developing countries' domestic procurements of goods and equipment a preferential margin (15 per cent of the CIF price of foreign goods, or the difference in tariffs, whichever is the lowest) over foreign procurements. In 1974 the World Bank further expanded this principle by granting the domestic civil works contractors of the 40 poorest countries a 7.5 per cent margin of preference in contract bids.[9]

Since the 1970s many other channels of multilateral aid have applied the same principle. The Lomé Convention between the EC and the African, Caribbean and Pacific countries has, since 1975, granted the national firms of the recipients of loans from the EDF a 15 per cent margin of preference in tendering for contracts. The IDB and AFDB as well as the UNDP also grant domestic suppliers a 15 per cent preferential margin.

In examining the provision of goods and services for ADB projects, a distinction must be made first between regular loans, concessional loans and technical assistance grants, and second between procurements and consultants. Contracts for the procurement of goods, related services and civil works are awarded through a process of ICB similar to that of the World Bank. A contract is given wide publicity in *Development Business*, in the press of the borrowing country and through member countries' foreign ministries and trade promotion organisations. On this basis firms bid for the contract, which is awarded to 'the bidder whose bid has been determined to be the lowest evaluated bid and who meets the appropriate standards of capability and financial responsibility'.[10] Once specified technical standards have been met, the decisive factor is the price.

The eligibility of firms to bid for ADB procurement contracts depends on the source of funds in question. Companies from all member countries can tender for contracts under OCR loans, but the practice applied to special funds has been more complex. In the late 1960s and early 1970s, when the ADB had three special funds, the degree to which procurements from these funds were tied varied according to the individual agreements between the contributors and the ADB. In general, procurements with a country's contribution had to be made from the donor, although in certain cases (Belgium, Denmark, the Netherlands, the UK and West Germany) other countries contributing to the fund in question were eligible as well as DMCs.[11] With the establishment of the ADF in 1974, most special fund resources, with the exception of the TASF, were transferred to the ADF, in practice making it the Bank's only source of concessional loans and open to procurement from all Bank members. At present only technical assistance grants are often tied.

Within the debate on operational policies in the ADB, the need to promote procurements from the DMCs as well as domestic procurements, has been regularly pointed out both by the DMCs and in various Bank reports, including the second Asian agricultural survey. In calling for preferential margins, the DMCs have cited not only their potential role in fostering domestic producers, but the fact that in areas such as agriculture and rural development local expertise might actually be more appropriate than foreign expertise. In 1979, for example, Sri Lanka justified its demand for a review of procurement policies as follows:

> In the light of the explicit support for policies which seek to promote the use of appropriate technology and labour intensive methods, we should consider the grant of domestic preference. The time is particularly opportune for this in the light of the Bank's strategy of placing emphasis on an integrated approach to rural development, land utilisation, water management and expansion of rural employment. These are areas where local talent and local skills could have a decisive edge over foreign ones while the qualitative benefits are not easily quantifiable in project evaluation. Such action should be deemed a necessary incentive to improve the very capability of developing countries to avail themselves of such preference.[13]

The ADB's study of operational priorities and plans for the 1980s, which was published in 1983, also drew attention to the fact that procurement practices provide very limited opportunities for domestic producers, and suggested that these practices be changed with a view to building up domestic and regional capabilities. However, even in recommending a preferential margin the report conceded that it will have limited practical significance:

> To compensate for this disadvantage [of local suppliers in international competitive bidding] and to provide an incentive to domestic manufacturers, the World Bank provides local suppliers with a preferential margin of 15 per cent in bid comparison and the [Asian Development] Bank has been urged by the DMCs to do the same. There is no hard evidence, except perhaps in India, that the margin has made a significant difference to the volume of World Bank-financed contracts awarded locally, but in using this margin, even if only symbolic in nature, the World Bank appears as a more liberal institution and it is therefore recommended that the [Asian Development] Bank consider granting a similar preferential margin.[14]

Following intense pressure from the DMCs, in August 1986 the board approved a scheme to discount domestic suppliers' quotations by 15 per cent in evaluating competitive bids to offset the burden of various taxes and duties on domestic suppliers. In taking its decision the board resorted to voting on the proposal, which received 65 per cent of the votes, including those of Japan and some West European donors, but was opposed by the US and several smaller donors. The DMCs, on the other hand, have criticised the scheme, which has various restrictions, as modest and inadequate compared with the margins granted by other multilateral agencies.[15] It is difficult to dissociate the Bank's reluctance to undertake reforms in procurement policy from the commercial interests of many of the donors.

**Procurement Practice**

ICB is sometimes referred to as the principle of untied aid.[16] While competitive bidding is not tied to procurements from a specific country, in practice it stongly favours industrialised countries, countries in a favourable geographical position, and large, established companies with international linkages which enable them to monitor closely the procurement process. In the case of the ADB, Japan's dominance in the region and in the Bank, combined with strong informal ties between Japanese staff members and Japanese commerical interests, has given Japan an edge in bidding for Bank contracts.

Table 6.3 Cumulative procurement by member country as a result of Bank operations (as of 1974, 1979, and 1986; OCR and SFR combined)

| Member country | Goods, related services and civil works | | | | Consultancy services | | | |
|---|---|---|---|---|---|---|---|---|
| | 1974 (%) | 1979 (%) | 1986 (%) | 1986 ($ million) | 1974 (%) | 1979 (%) | 1986 (%) | 1986 ($ million) |
| Japan | 44.3 | 35.4 | 26.5 | 2351.6 | 15.6 | 14.3 | 13.1 | 75.4 |
| US | 9.1 | 6.8 | 7.4 | 659.5 | 22.7 | 24.4 | 21.4 | 123.4 |
| West Germany | 6.9 | 8.6 | 5.5 | 489.5 | 17.1 | 11.2 | 5.2 | 29.9 |
| UK | 6.3 | 6.1 | 4.1 | 360.4 | 2.6 | 9.6 | 12.5 | 72.2 |
| Italy | 4.3 | 3.7 | 2.1 | 188.6 | 12.3 | 9.1 | 4.1 | 23.4 |
| France | 1.9 | 3.0 | 2.0 | 178.4 | 4.0 | 3.5 | 3.1 | 17.7 |
| Switzerland | 1.1 | 2.0 | 1.8 | 163.2 | 0.8 | 1.8 | 5.1 | 29.5 |
| Australia | 2.1 | 2.2 | 1.3 | 117.8 | 5.7 | 4.7 | 3.2 | 18.1 |
| Netherlands | 0.9 | 2.6 | 1.2 | 104.7 | 4.0 | 2.6 | 2.6 | 15.0 |
| Canada | 1.9 | 1.4 | 1.0 | 84.9 | 6.4 | 6.0 | 7.0 | 40.3 |
| Sweden | 0.6 | 0.4 | 0.8 | 73.8 | 0.2 | 0.1 | 0.1 | 0.3 |
| Other developed countries | 3.2 | 2.5 | 2.2 | 193.6 | 2.5 | 6.4 | 4.8 | 27.4 |
| Total developed countries | 82.6 | 74.5 | 56.0 | 4966.0 | 93.8 | 93.8 | 82.1 | 472.7 |
| South Korea | 4.5 | 4.2 | 5.9 | 520.1 | 4.5 | 1.1 | 2.7 | 15.5 |
| India | 2.5 | 2.9 | 2.4 | 216.1 | 0.2 | 2.1 | 3.2 | 18.2 |
| Taiwan | 0.8 | 0.6 | 1.2 | 102.6 | – | 0.1 | 1.8 | 10.6 |
| Singapore | 1.4 | 0.8 | 1.1 | 100.9 | – | – | 0.2 | 1.2 |
| Thailand | 0.1 | 1.3 | 0.9 | 76.3 | – | * | * | 0.2 |
| Philippines | * | 0.3 | 0.8 | 71.3 | 0.4 | 0.9 | 1.4 | 7.9 |

| | | | | | | | |
|---|---|---|---|---|---|---|---|
| Other developing countries | 0.7 | 0.9 | 100.6 | 1.1 | 0.8 | 0.9 | 0.7 | 3.9 |
| Total developing countries | 10.0 | 10.9 | 1187.9 | 13.4 | 5.9 | 5.0 | 10.0 | 57.6 |
| Undetermined | 7.5 | 14.5 | 2713.1 | 30.6 | 0.3 | 1.2 | 8.0 | 45.8 |
| Total | 100.0 | 100.0 | 8,867.0 | 100.0 | 100.0 | 100.0 | 100.0 | 576.1 |

* Less than one tenth of one per cent.

Note: Figures may not tally due to rounding.

Source: ADB, Quarterly Procurement Statistics and Annual Report (1986).

As Clad points out, non-Japanese staff sometimes allege that their Japanese colleagues use their seconded terms at the Bank 'to feed technical data back to their companies in Tokyo, including information about contracts which have not yet been opened for international bidding'.[17] Local supplies, again, have until recently been at a disadvantage, as foreign goods are valued on a CIF basis while local goods are valued at ex-factory price and therefore include duties on raw material imports.[18] This has to some extent been offset by the recent preferential margins, which cover local suppliers but not construction contractors.

Table 6.3 provides a breakdown of cumulative procurements for ADB projects from the main supplier countries. Of the seven leading suppliers, five are developed (Japan, the US, West Germany, the UK and Italy) and two developing (South Korea and India). Procurement of goods, related services and civil works from the DMCs has increased slightly, from 10 per cent in 1974 to over 13 per cent in 1986, but virtually no procurements have been made from Afghanistan, Burma, Bhutan, Laos, the Pacific island countries, PNG, or Sri Lanka, and very few from Bangladesh, Indonesia, Nepal and Pakistan. In addition to India and South Korea, six countries – Taiwan, Singapore, Thailand, the Philippines, and to a lesser degree Hong Kong (0.5 per cent) and Malaysia (0.3 per cent) – account for almost all procurements from the DMCs.

Over time there has been a decline in the concentration of procurements. In 1974, 78 per cent of cumulative procurements were from the seven major suppliers; in 1979 the corresponding figure was 68 per cent; and by 1986 it had declined to 56 per cent. One reason is the increasing proportion of 'undetermined' procurements, which include small contracts and awards to domestic suppliers and contractors.[19] The most marked change is the decline in procurements from Japan, although Japan continues to dominate as by far the largest supplier for Bank projects. While procurements from other developed countries including the US, West Germany, Great Britain, Italy and Australia have shown slight decline, the share of South Korea and Taiwan has increased. The fact that Japan's initial contributions to the Bank's special funds were tied, while contributions to the ADF have been untied, helps to explain the decline in Japanese procurements. The distribution of procurements should also be examined in the light of the sectoral distribution of lending. Japanese procurement reached a peak of 67 per cent in 1972,[20] when infrastructure lending was at its highest, while the Bank's growing emphasis on agricultural projects since 1974 at least partially explains changing procurement patterns. It has also been pointed out that in the late 1960s and early 1970s many Bank projects were in South Korea and Taiwan, giving Japan an advantage in shipping rates over other competitors, while more recently lending has shifted to Southeast Asia, depriving Japan of this benefit.[21]

An issue of particular concern to developed member governments financing the Bank, not only from the commercial viewpoint but also from the point of view of justifying participation in the ADB to their political constituents, is the relationship between costs incurred in and economic benefits derived from ADB operations. In his study on the IDB, De Witt demonstrates the extent to which participating in multilateral development banks is economically beneficial for the US. Based on figures of total US payments to the multilateral banks, on the one hand, and the banks' payments to the US, on the other, De Witt concludes that participating in the banks is advantageous for the US balance of payments.[22]

Table 6.4 examines ADB operations from the point of view of member countries' balance of payments.[23] The total contributions of member countries are compared with their total procurements, placing the members in two categories, those with 'net costs' and those with 'net earnings'. Column A gives each country's paid-in share of subscribed capital, column B gives cumulative contributions to the ADF, column C gives cumulative contributions to the TASF, and these are added up in column D to give the total financial contribution of each country to the Bank. Column E lists cumulative procurements from each member country, from OCR and ADF lending and technical assistance grants. Based on this, the figures in columns F and G indicate whether or not, and to what extent, each country has incurred 'costs' as a member of the Bank. In examining the figures it should be borne in mind that no account is taken of the grant element of loans, which actually places many borrowers in the category of 'net earners'. For the borrowing countries the figures are merely indicative of some countries deriving more benefit than others from ADB operations. It should also be pointed out that the calculations take no account of the impact of procurements on follow-up demand for spare parts and supplies, or further commercial contracts.

Table 6.4 indicates that of the DMCs South Korea, Singapore, Taiwan, India, Thailand, Hong Kong and the Philippines derive a clear commercial benefit from Bank operations. Of the donors,

Table 6.4 Total contributions to and 'earnings' from the ADB by member country (as of December 1986 $000)

| Member country | A Paid-in capital | B Contributions to ADF | C Contributions to TASF | D Total contributions | E Cumulative procurements* | F 'Net costs' | G 'Net earnings' |
|---|---|---|---|---|---|---|---|
| Afghanistan | 4673 | – | – | 4673 | – | 4673 | – |
| Bangladesh | 26531 | – | 47 | 26578 | 6270 | 20308 | – |
| Bhutan | 257 | – | – | 257 | – | 257 | – |
| Burma | 14152 | – | – | 14152 | 25 | 14127 | – |
| Cambodia | 3425 | – | – | 3425 | – | 3425 | – |
| China | 167467 | – | – | 167467 | 48 | 167419 | – |
| Cook Islands | 61 | – | – | 61 | 12 | 49 | – |
| Fiji | 1774 | – | – | 1774 | 1771 | 3 | – |
| Hong Kong | 14152 | 860 | 100 | 15122 | 47833 | – | 32721 |
| India | 164482 | – | 1529 | 166011 | 244042 | – | 78031 |
| Indonesia | 141487 | 2580 | 250 | 144317 | 14297 | 130020 | – |
| Kiribati | 110 | – | – | 110 | – | 110 | – |
| Laos | 587 | – | – | 587 | 43 | 544 | – |
| Malaysia | 70749 | – | 906 | 71655 | 27702 | 43953 | – |
| Maldives | 110 | – | – | 110 | 12 | 98 | – |
| Nepal | 3829 | – | – | 3829 | 5162 | – | 1333 |
| Pakistan | 56597 | – | 565 | 57162 | 4519 | 52643 | – |
| PNG | 2422 | – | – | 2422 | 313 | 2109 | – |
| Philippines | 61893 | – | – | 61893 | 88984 | – | 27091 |
| Singapore | 8844 | – | 100 | 8944 | 103670 | – | 94726 |
| Solomon Islands | 171 | – | – | 171 | – | 171 | – |
| South Korea | 130869 | 3010 | 1450 | 135329 | 537499 | – | 402170 |
| Sri Lanka | 15070 | – | 6 | 15076 | 2285 | 12791 | – |
| Taiwan | 28292 | 1720 | 200 | 30212 | 113562 | – | 83350 |
| Thailand | 35375 | – | – | 35375 | 77151 | – | 41776 |
| Tonga | 110 | – | – | 110 | 29 | 81 | – |
| Vanuatu | 171 | – | – | 171 | – | 171 | – |
| Vietnam | 15461 | – | – | 15461 | 3 | 15458 | – |
| | 135 | – | – | 135 | 18 | 117 | – |

| | | | | | | |
|---|---|---|---|---|---|---|
| Australia | 150 342 | 243 808 | 2 484 | 149 369 | 396 634 | 247 265 |
| Austria | 8 844 | 58 874 | 139 | 66 006 | 67 857 | 1 851 |
| Belgium | 8 844 | 56 733 | 1 273 | 43 314 | 66 850 | 23 536 |
| Canada | 135 896 | 471 839 | 3 346 | 137 192 | 611 081 | 473 899 |
| Denmark | 8 844 | 49 021 | 1 962 | 50 061 | 59 827 | 9 766 |
| Finland | 8 844 | 32 678 | 237 | 9 299 | 41 759 | 32 460 |
| France | 60 474 | 225 450 | 1 655 | 202 213 | 287 579 | 85 366 |
| Italy | 35 374 | 180 369 | 774 | 214 650 | 216 517 | 1 867 |
| Japan | 353 734 | 3 730 838 | 47 045 | 2 438 542 | 4 131 617 | 1 693 075 |
| Netherlands | 19 449 | 163 706 | 1 168 | 124 774 | 184 323 | 59 549 |
| New Zealand | 39 901 | 10 460 | 1 096 | 59 531 | 51 457 | 8 074 |
| Norway | 8 844 | 37 910 | 3 053 | 6 899 | 49 807 | 42 908 |
| Spain | 8 844 | 28 153 | 164 | 137 | 37 161 | 37 024 |
| Sweden | 4 636 | 55 869 | 822 | 75 462 | 61 327 | |
| Switzerland | 15 167 | 96 987 | 1 035 | 196 586 | 113 189 | 14 135 |
| UK | 53 050 | 232 189 | 5 477 | 469 863 | 290 716 | 83 397 |
| US | 351 630 | 1 222 106 | 1 500 | 820 232 | 1 575 236 | 755 004 | 179 147 |
| West Germany | 112 399 | 519 425 | 3 250 | 525 419 | 635 074 | 109 655 |

* OCR, ADF and technical assistance grants combined.

*Source:* Calculated from ADB, *Annual Report* (1986).

the UK, Switzerland, Sweden and New Zealand have benefited substantially, while procurements from Austria, Italy and Denmark were marginally lower than contributions. The other Western European donors' procurements were lower than contributions, although this can mainly be attributed to the stagnation of disbursements in 1984–6, which has kept procurement figures down in relation to contributions. In general procurements from Western European countries have at least equalled contributions, with the exception of Denmark, Finland and Norway. The largest financial 'burden' is borne by the US, Canada and Australia, whose procurement contracts have been substantially lower than contributions. China and Spain only joined the Bank in the mid-1980s, and it is premature to examine their share of procurements.

Procurements from Japan are high, but recently Japan's financial contributions have been higher. From the start of Bank operations until the end of the 1970s Japan was a 'net earner' from Bank operations, a fact which helps explain its central role in funding the Bank. However, its growing share of ADF replenishments in the 1980s has gradually shifted Japan into the 'net costs' category. Following the very high concentration of procurement contracts with Japanese companies in the late 1960s and early 1970s, many of the donors with low procurement shares voiced criticism and demanded stricter enforcement of ICB and the broader international advertising of Bank contracts. The US in particular has periodically expressed concern over the question of procurements. At the 1972 annual meeting the US representative drew attention to his country's low share of procurements, and pointed out the difficulty this entailed in obtaining congressional and public support for participation in the Bank.[24] The following year the US took the argument a step further by stating that 'there is a special responsibility on the part of international institutions to ensure that the benefits of the business generated by the development process do not accrue disproportionately to some while the burdens fall disproportionately on others', and recommended that administrative measures be adopted based on an approach 'of achieving absolute fairness among supplier nations'.[25] This notion of supplier nations apparently has not included the DMCs.

The procurement process has been the subject of close scrutiny by member countries and the centre of several controversies which reflect their conflicting interests in being awarded project contracts. In the early 1970s there was considerable disagreement about procurement under a fisheries loan to South Korea, and the Bank's post-evaluation of the project noted that the diesel engine specifications were written around a type of Japanese engine and concluded that procurement procedures were not followed.[26]

One of the most recent disputes on the procurement issue concerned the award of a $15 million contract to supply 12 rice mills under the Bank's second rice-processing industries loan to Burma. In the first round of bidding for the contract in 1981, the bid of a Japanese company was lowest, but deviated substantially from specified requirements, while a West German company had a bid considerably higher than the figure budgeted by the Bank. Due to extensive imprecisions in the tender documents prepared by the Burmese government, the first round was deemed invalid. For the second round of bidding, in 1982, the Burmese government still did not meet the Bank's requirements in clarifying how the bids would be evaluated, and neither bid perfectly matched the tender requirements. Consequently the ADB's procurement committee had to recalculate the two firms' bids, and concluded that the German bid was lower and should, according to Bank rules, be recommended. The Burmese government, however, favoured the Japanese firm, which was connected with the fact that Burma had recently bilaterally awarded another rice mill contract to Japan. At this point, the Japanese government, through former Finance Minister and former ADB governor Watanabe Michio and the Japanese executive director, applied considerable pressure on the ADB to allow the contract to be awarded to Japan. In a move without procedural precedent President Fujioka established a special committee to review the issue, and the contract was subsequently awarded to the Japanese firm. The departure from established procedure, to the benefit of a Japanese company, was strongly criticised by the US and the other developed countries.[27]

## Consulting Services

Finding technically appropriate solutions, transferring technology and training counterpart institutions and staff in the borrowing countries are among the most important tasks of Bank projects, and of key significance from the point of view of achieving sustainable project impact. The responsibility for the transfer of technical knowledge and skills on ADB projects is largely passed on to consultants hired directly by the Bank, in the case of technical assistance grants, and by the borrowing country in accordance with Bank procedures, in the case of loans. While consultants account for only 6 per cent of total project costs, with the lion's share of loan funds being used for the procurement of capital goods and related services, they play a crucial role in determining the technical content of projects.

The debate within the Bank on the question of consultants has centred around many of the same issues as that on procurements. For the donors, consultancy contracts represent a significant economic return on their contributions to the Bank, and are in some cases directly connected to further contracts. The DMCs, again, have been critical of the large proportion of contracts awarded to consulting firms from the donors. Particularly the low-income countries have criticised consultants from industrialised countries for introducing unnecessarily advanced or capital-intensive technology, and for escalating project costs, both in terms of their high consultancy fees compared with consultants recruited domestically or from other developing countries, and indirectly due to the relatively high cost of the capital-intensive technology used or proposed by the consultants. This position is set out clearly in the statement by the Indian governor at the Bank's annual meeting in 1979:

> There is continued preponderance of firms and individuals from the developed countries, even though it is well known that such a preponderance carries with it the risk of distorting technological choices in favour of excessive capital intensity unrelated to basic factor endowments of developing countries. This policy also leads to ever-escalating costs of consulting services and thereby reduces the real value of funds earmarked for these services. We are convinced that in order to promote employment oriented programs of development there is a need to have a still further look at the Bank's policies for employment of consultants. We are also convinced that in the interest of both efficiency and cost effectiveness, we cannot continue indefinitely to operate a system in which costs play no role whatsoever in the choice of consultancy firms.[28]

Equally important is the fact that one of the main functions of projects is to help to develop a domestic managerial and technical capacity to enable borrowing countries to prepare and implement projects themselves rather than rely continuously on foreign consultants. This can only be achieved by making increasing use of domestic consultants, encouraging cooperation between foreign and domestic consultants, and incorporating suitable training components in projects. On the other hand, from the point of view of smooth project implementation, Bank staff often prefer to work with foreign consultants who are familiar with Bank procedures rather than become involved in the complexities of using and fostering local consultants.

The procedures for the selection of consultants for Bank projects differ in several ways from ICB. Following the drafting of the terms of reference for a job, a list of firms with expertise in the required field is prepared, by the Bank in the case of technical assistance grants, and by the borrower in the case of loans, although in practice in close cooperation with Bank staff. This is narrowed down to a shortlist of the five to seven 'most qualified and suitable' companies, which are invited to submit proposals for the job. In addition to the firms' technical qualification, Bank guidelines note that the firms shortlisted should represent the member countries in a 'reasonably balanced way'.[29] The final selection is based on a comparative evaluation of the proposals taking into consideration a number of factors, particularly the substance of the technical proposal, the past international experience of the firm and the professional qualifications of the technical staff proposed. Financial negotiations are entered into only after a firm has been selected on technical grounds, and cost is therefore not a major consideration.[30]

While domestic consultants can in principle be recruited for or collaborate on Bank projects, in practice ADB consultancy policies are based on international competition and have taken little note of the principle of promoting domestic consultants. In contrast to the World Bank, which allows both international competition and a choice restricted to local firms, the ADB will only finance domestic consultants if they are selected through the competitive international submission of proposals, but not if the borrower decides in advance to use domestic consultants. Moreover, if domestic consultants are selected, the Bank will only finance the same costs as for foreign consultants, that is professional staff, international travel, the foreign exchange cost of computer services, and imported vehicles and equipment. Local costs such as non-professional staff, hire of vehicles, and office rentals will only be financed up to a ceiling of 10 per cent of the technical assistance grant, if specially approved by the Bank's board of directors.[31] These restrictions inhibit domestic consultants from using their principal asset, local resources, and encourage them to increase the import content of their proposals. In comparison the World Bank often finances the total cost of consultants.

The Bank's prequalification requirements for shortlisting and the criteria applied in the evaluation of proposals, which both emphasise a firm's previous international experience, have a tendency to work against consultants from DMCs and domestic consultants. Moreover, the fact that costs are not considered in comparing bids works to the disadvantage of local consultants, whose costs may be substantially lower than those of consultants from donor countries. Following considerable pressure from its borrowers, the Bank has taken one measure to favour local consultants and to encourage consultants from developed countries to collaborate with domestic consultants. Compared with the ADB's original guidelines on the use of consultants,[32] the revised guidelines circulated in 1979 contain an additional proviso on the evaluation of proposals stipulating that, all other factors being equal, preference will be given to firms proposing collaboration with domestic consultants, and to domestic consultants or consultants from other DMCs who submit their own proposals.[33] The borrowing countries, however, found the practical implications of this stipulation inadequate and have continued to push for a more substantial revision of the Bank's consultancy policy.[34]

As Table 6.3 shows, the distribution of consultancy contracts has been considerably more concentrated than procurement contracts in general, and has shown little tendency to decline. Of all consultants used on Bank projects by 1974, 93.8 per cent were from developed countries and 5.9 per cent from developing countries. In 1986 the corresponding figures were 82.1 and 10 per cent. In contrast to its relatively low share in procurements, the US is the largest source of consultants, followed by Japan, the UK, Canada, West Germany, Switzerland, Italy, France and Australia. Of the DMCs, only India, South Korea, Taiwan and the Philippines have been awarded significant consultancy contracts in other countries under international competitive procedures, while domestic consultants have been awarded only 3.3 per cent of all contracts, mainly in Indonesia, South Korea, Malaysia and the Philippines.

Although effective policy changes have not been undertaken, there is growing dissatisfaction not only in the borrowing countries, but also among Bank projects staff, with the present consultancy system, particularly in terms of finding appropriate technical solutions, making use of available expertise and ensuring local participation in rural development projects. The proceedings of a Bank seminar on rural development held in 1984, for example, summarise the problem as follows:

Current Bank procedures for project preparation consist of provision of funds for feasibility studies by consultants. These consultants are generally recruited from outside the executing agency and the region and have limited exposure to local conditions. As a result project proposals in feasibility studies not infrequently fail to identify specific constraints or relevant experience and development potentials of the project area and the willingness of the population to participate. An alternative way of project preparation could be to provide facilities to local level organizations and executing agencies to formulate the project at an early stage of project identification.[35]

## Local Cost Financing

The question of whether loan funds should be used to cover the foreign exchange cost of projects, mainly for imported capital goods, or whether funds should also be earmarked to cover local costs in the borrowing country, particularly labour and operational costs, has been the subject of extensive policy debate in the ADB and other aid agencies. Opposition to local cost financing has been justified mainly on the grounds that it undermines the borrowers' domestic mobilisation of resources for a project. On the other hand, the technological bias inherent in restrictive local cost financing policies, and the fact that particularly low-income countries with very limited resources have increasing difficulties in meeting local cost expenses on projects, have long been recognised as justification for increasing the financing of local costs. Both the Pearson Commission Report of 1969 and the Brandt Commission Report of 1979 recommend that a larger proportion of development finance be used to cover local costs.[36]

There is also a connection between local cost financing and the question of procurements, in that the former is a direct measure to allow the spending of loan money in the borrowing country rather than through international procurement. Particularly due to its potentially detrimental effect on their share of procurement contracts, many donors have been opposed to extensive local cost financing.

The question of whether or not local costs are financed has an impact on several aspects of project planning. First, restrictive local cost financing policies and procedures have an intrinsic bias towards imported, capital-intensive technology. Projects with an emphasis on employment creation through the use of labour-intensive techniques require a considerable proportion of funds for domestic inputs, particularly labour, locally produced tools and equipment, and operational costs which the borrowing country may be unable to include in its budget. If loan funds cannot be used for the labour-intensive components, planners will tend to seek capital-intensive solutions. Research has indicated the close relationship between the availability of loan funds for local costs and the viability of labour-intensive technologies as an option for project planners.[37]

Second, lack of local cost financing encourages the preparation of investment-oriented rather than operationally oriented projects. In road projects, for example, this takes the form of a bias in favour of construction rather than maintenance projects. As Tendler observes, in conventional highway and road projects, loan funds are usually used for construction costs while the borrower is required to finance the operational costs of maintenance. In Tendler's example, the project's requirements for counterpart funding had initially resulted in the borrower's budgetary resources being diverted from maintenance, and as sufficient loan funds were not set aside for local costs, maintenance programmes were unable to keep up with construction programmes.[38] Third, as Tendler points out, foreign exchange financing tends to promote large, centralised rather than small, decentralised projects.[39]

In the ADB numerous donors, particularly Japan and the US, have opposed local cost financing on the grounds that it reduces the borrowers' resource mobilisation. The DMCs, again, have continuously demanded greater lending for local costs. The members of the Canadian, Dutch and Nordic voting group have also favoured increasing the financing of local costs, as one policy statement put it, due to the direct bearing of the issue 'on the eradication of mass poverty and the meeting of basic human needs'.[40]

The ADB's local cost financing policy has been relatively restrictive. Initially the Bank financed only the foreign exchange costs of projects, but in 1974 a policy amendment was introduced under which up to 5 per cent of lending from ordinary resources and 10 per cent from special funds could be used for local costs, and later this was revised to 5 per cent of ordinary loans and 15 per cent of ADF lending.[41] Consequently, between 1974 and 1981 a total of $461 million, or 5.5 per cent of all lending, was earmarked for local costs, mainly for the agriculture and agro-industries sector.[42]

Compared with the demand for local cost financing by the borrowing countries, and with the requirements of different sectors to implement policy changes, financing of local costs has been very limited. The ceilings on local cost financing have resulted in different treatment being accorded to similar requests from different countries. Concerns with efficiency and speedy project preparation have also worked against the financing of local costs. Due to the internal procedures and staff time involved in justifying proposals for local cost financing, a Bank study notes that 'there is a tendency to avoid proposing [local cost financing] in projects in some countries'.[43] While the funding of local costs in agriculture and agro-industry, which in 1974–81 totalled $269.5 million, or some 10.5 per cent of lending for this sector, has provided marginal scope for changing project content, the transport sector's share, which amounted to only 4.3 per cent of new loan approvals in 1974–81 can be considered to have inhibited moving towards more labour-intensive road projects.

The Bank's study of operational priorities and plans for the 1980s recommended that the Bank significantly liberalise its local cost policies, by adopting standard percentages, in the case of the lowest income countries ranging from 70 to 90 per cent of total project costs, for which local cost finance would be provided. The report also recommended that even within these relatively high ranges, flexibility should be allowed for suitable project selection in areas such as rural roads and social infrastructure.[44] In 1983 the Bank's local cost financing policies were made more flexible,[45] although due to the political context of the issue considerably less so than required by the borrowers. While Japan has acknowledged the need to expand local cost financing, the Reagan administration has continued to be opposed, as exemplified by the statement of the US representative at a recent annual meeting that 'the primary activity of the ADB must continue to be financing the foreign exchange component of . . . development projects'.[46]

# 7 Irrigation and Rural Development Projects

Loan projects are the ADB's primary vehicle for implementing its rural development policy. Between 1968 and 1986 the Bank approved 265 agricultural and rural development loans worth a total of about $6174 million, accounting for 31.7 per cent of all ADB lending.[1] In addition road construction and improvement projects, which are classified by the Bank under infrastructure, play a significant role in shaping rural development. In 1968–86 the ADB approved 57 road construction loans worth a total of $1472 million, or 7.6 per cent of all Bank lending. Chapters 7 and 8 examine the Bank's rural sector projects, with particular emphasis on two questions. First, how far are policy changes reflected in project content, and what are the major constraints on change at the project level? Second, to what extent have rural sector projects had an impact on the three policy objectives of the Bank's rural development policy: increasing production, creating employment and promoting a more equitable distribution of incomes?

Following a general discussion of the subsectors of rural lending, the chapters focus on the three most important subsectors: irrigation and rural development; credit (including both agricultural credit and credit for fisheries development); and road construction and improvement. Between them these subsectors account for approximately $3600 million or 70 per cent of all ADB lending of relevance to the rural sector in 1968–83.[2] To narrow down the focus of this study, to enable us to examine changes in the content of specific projects and to discuss project impact, the chapters concentrate on five groups of projects: irrigation and rural development projects in Indonesia (eight loans worth a total of $266.9 million) and the Philippines (eight loans worth $199 million); agricultural credit projects in Nepal (four loans worth $26.4 million); fisheries credit projects in Sri Lanka (two loans worth $16.5 million); and road construction and improvement projects in the Philippines (seven loans worth $203.5 million). These represent a relatively broad spread of Bank projects and provide reasonable grounds for a degree of generalisation.

## Rural Lending by Subsector and Policy Objectives

The principal indicator of the priority given by the Bank to the rural sector is its share of total lending. Table 7.1 outlines the development of the Bank's annual allocation for the rural sector. Rural lending has increased steadily in both real and relative terms, and can broadly be divided into three periods. Between 1968 and 1973 the rural sector accounted for an average of 16.8 per cent of all lending. The initial priority accorded to the sector can be attributed to the foodgrain shortages of the early 1960s, the first *Asian Agricultural Survey* and the emphasis placed on agriculture by Japan. This was followed by a decline in 1972. During the second period, from 1974 to 1978, the rural sector accounted for an average of 28.6 per cent of lending. In 1974–5 rural lending rose sharply, largely in response to the foodgrain shortages of 1972–3, and as the foodgrain situation improved rural lending levelled out in 1976–8. From 1979 onwards the Bank has continuously allocated a third of its loans to the rural sector. At the Bank's annual meeting in 1979, President Yoshida announced that the rural sector would continue to receive priority attention, and that rural lending would increase by 20 per cent on average for the next four years.[3] This target was not met, but since 1979 rural lending has, with the exception of a decline in 1985, increased steadily, accounting for an average of 33 per cent of all lending. Moreover, in the light of difficulties encountered in expanding lending in other sectors in the 1980s there have been indications that the rural sector's share might expand further in the second half of the 1980s.[4]

Table 7.1 also examines the development of average loan size for the rural sector, which follows the general development of loan size (see Table 5.1). Average loan size increased from $2 million in 1968 to $39.1 million in 1986, but two periods of significant increase also indicate a relationship between loan size and fund-channelling. In connection with the rapid expansion of rural sector lending in 1973–5, loan size increased from $6.6 million in 1972 to $18.9 million in 1975, and, in connection with the priority given by President Fujioka to expanding lending in the 1980s, loan size reached a peak of $44.6 million in 1984.

The subsectoral distribution of loans serves as an indicator of the Bank's priorities within the rural sector, and of the Bank's rural strategy. The Bank classifies its rural projects into seven subsectors:

    a) *Irrigation and rural development* includes both straightforward projects for the construction and rehabilitation of irrigation works

*Table 7.1* Annual ADB lending for agriculture and rural development, 1968–86

| Year | Total lending for sector ($ million) | OCR $ million (per cent) | SFR $ million (per cent) | Number of loans | Per cent of total lending | Annual increase in rural lending (per cent) | Annual increase in total lending (per cent) | Average loan size for sector ($ million) |
|---|---|---|---|---|---|---|---|---|
| 1968 | 2.0 | 2.0 (100.0) | – | 1 | 4.8 | – | – | 2.0 |
| 1969 | 27.3 | 13.7 (50.2) | 13.6 (49.8) | 6 | 27.8 | 1265.0 | 135.8 | 4.6 |
| 1970 | 45.8 | 16.8 (36.8) | 29.0 (63.5) | 12 | 18.6 | 67.4 | 150.4 | 3.8 |
| 1971 | 49.3 | 22.0 (44.6) | 27.3 (55.4) | 9 | 19.4 | 7.9 | 3.4 | 7.0 |
| 1972 | 32.8 | 13.3 (40.5) | 19.5 (59.5) | 5 | 10.4 | –33.5 | 24.4 | 6.6 |
| 1973 | 74.3 | 36.0 (48.5) | 38.3 (51.5) | 8 | 17.6 | 126.5 | 33.3 | 9.3 |
| 1974 | 134.0 | 64.2 (47.9) | 69.8 (52.1) | 14 | 24.5 | 80.3 | 29.9 | 9.6 |
| 1975 | 245.9 | 138.6 (56.4) | 107.3 (43.6) | 13 | 37.2 | 83.5 | 20.6 | 18.9 |
| 1976 | 200.9 | 90.4 (45.0) | 110.5 (55.0) | 12 | 25.9 | –18.3 | 17.5 | 16.7 |
| 1977 | 262.0 | 105.5 (40.3) | 156.5 (59.7) | 17 | 29.6 | 30.4 | 14.3 | 15.4 |
| 1978 | 310.7 | 108.6 (35.0) | 202.1 (65.0) | 18 | 26.8 | 18.6 | 30.7 | 17.3 |
| 1979 | 411.6 | 158.6 (38.5) | 253.0 (61.5) | 23 | 32.9 | 32.5 | 8.0 | 17.9 |
| 1980 | 467.9 | 197.9 (42.3) | 270.0 (57.7) | 22 | 32.6 | 13.7 | 14.7 | 21.3 |
| 1981 | 541.6 | 276.6 (51.1) | 265.0 (48.9) | 20 | 32.3 | 15.8 | 16.8 | 27.1 |
| 1982 | 621.3 | 297.3 (47.9) | 324.0 (52.1) | 22 | 35.9 | 14.7 | 3.2 | 28.2 |
| 1983 | 648.4 | 341.9 (52.7) | 306.5 (47.3) | 24 | 34.2 | 4.4 | 9.4 | 27.0 |
| 1984 | 758.0 | 509.0 (67.2) | 249.0 (32.8) | 17 | 33.9 | 16.9 | 18.0 | 44.6 |
| 1985 | 559.5 | 216.0 (38.6) | 343.5 (61.4) | 18 | 29.3 | –26.2 | –14.6 | 31.1 |
| 1986 | 822.2 | 394.3 (48.0) | 427.9 (52.0) | 21 | 31.7 | 47.0 | 4.9 | 39.2 |
| Total | 6173.9 | 2975.9 (48.2) | 3198.0 (51.8) | 280 | 31.9 | – | – | 22.0 |

*Note:* Figures may not tally due to rounding and to minor changes over time in the Bank's sectoral classification of projects.

*Source:* Calculated from ADB, *Agriculture in Asia, Statistical Appendices*, A Bank Staff Working Paper (March 1985), and *Annual Report* (1986).

and integrated rural development projects, which usually include both irrigation construction and various supporting components.

b) *Industrial crops and agro-industries* covers loans to support the production of plantation crops, mainly tea, rubber and oil palm, and of other crops, particularly sugar, jute and cotton, as well as rice processing and milling.

c) *Fisheries* loans have mainly been for onlending as credit for the purchase or mechanisation of boats and the construction of shore-based support facilities for marine fisheries, but they have also recently been extended to include inland fisheries and aquaculture.

d) *Livestock* loans, which are limited in number, have supported livestock raising for both meat production and as draft animals and for transportation.

e) *Forestry* loans, which are all relatively recent and which are also limited in number, have been for either planting and reforestation, forestry extraction and processing, or a combination of the two.

f) *Agricultural support services* include a number of different types of projects, mainly loans to support national agricultural development banks providing rural credit, seed production projects, and projects for the construction of storage facilities. Over half of support services loans have been for credit projects.

g) *Fertiliser* loans have been given for the construction or expansion of fertiliser plants.[5]

The subsectoral distribution of rural lending is set out in Tables 7.2 and 7.3 and indicates the shift in the Bank's priorities. Until the mid-1970s irrigation, industrial crops and agro-industry, fisheries and fertiliser production were the most important subsectors, reflecting the Bank's straightforward concern with enhancing agricultural production. Since the mid-1970s, more emphasis has been placed on subsectors ostensibly designed to benefit relatively small-scale producers. Lending for irrigation has increased and at the same time the subsector has expanded to encompass integrated rural development projects. Lending for agricultural support services, particularly credit projects, has increased substantially, making this the second largest subsector, while lending for both agro-industries and fertiliser projects has declined. Between 1977 and 1986, irrigation and rural development and agricultural support services between them accounted for over 62 per cent of all rural loans. While the relative share of fisheries projects has declined, in terms of volume fisheries is the third most important rural subsector. Loans have also been given for livestock development and forestry. In the early 1980s

*Table 7.2* Distribution by subsector of ADB loan approvals for agriculture, rural development and road construction and improvement, 1968–86 ($ million)

| | Irrigation & rural development | Industrial crops & agro-industry | Fisheries | Livestock | Forestry | Agricultural support services | Fertiliser production | Programme loans | Special assistance for selected projects | Total sector | Road construction & improvement |
|---|---|---|---|---|---|---|---|---|---|---|---|
| 1968 | | 2.0 | – | – | – | – | – | – | – | 2.0 | 7.2 |
| 1969 | 12.1 | 5.2 | 10.0 | – | – | – | – | – | – | 27.3 | – |
| 1970 | 13.5 | 10.6 | 9.2 | – | – | – | 10.0 | – | – | 45.8 | 28.6 |
| 1971 | 38.2 | 7.4 | – | 0.3 | – | 2.4 | – | – | – | 49.3 | 27.0 |
| 1972 | 13.9 | – | 18.9 | – | – | 3.4 | – | – | – | 32.8 | 43.3 |
| 1973 | 15.9 | 20.3 | 11.1 | – | – | – | 27.0 | – | – | 74.3 | 27.8 |
| 1974 | 83.2 | 19.7 | 15.8 | – | – | 15.3 | – | – | – | 134.0 | 41.4 |
| 1975 | 56.1 | 37.1 | 33.2 | – | – | 9.4 | 110.0 | – | – | 245.9 | 67.2 |
| 1976 | 153.8 | – | 27.0 | 3.6 | – | 14.0 | 2.5 | – | – | 200.9 | 92.0 |
| 1977 | 193.4 | 5.3 | 21.6 | – | 30.0 | 11.7 | – | – | – | 262.0 | 116.5 |
| 1978 | 148.0 | 65.4 | 68.0 | 12.4 | 8.0 | – | – | 8.9 | – | 310.7 | 98.0 |
| 1979 | 204.6 | 37.1 | 42.9 | 53.3 | – | 19.9 | 28.0 | 25.8 | – | 411.6 | 27.0 |
| 1980 | 283.5 | 63.8 | 75.8 | – | 1.7 | 43.1 | – | – | – | 467.9 | 133.9 |
| 1981 | 291.8 | 35.0 | 34.1 | 24.7 | 11.0 | 46.0 | 72.0 | 27.0 | – | 541.6 | – |
| 1982 | 308.7 | 30.7 | 92.4 | 40.9 | 35.0 | 113.6 | – | – | – | 621.3 | 223.0 |
| 1983 | 264.9 | – | 39.1 | – | 50.7 | 140.8 | – | 93.0 | 60.0 | 648.4 | 65.5 |
| 1984 | 320.5 | 102.0 | 50.0 | 60.0 | 32.5 | 63.0 | – | 130.0 | – | 758.0 | 115.3 |
| 1985 | 330.5 | 14.0 | 65.0 | 53.0 | 38.0 | 20.0 | – | 39.0 | – | 559.5 | 230.0 |
| 1986 | 276.9 | 171.1 | 64.9 | 4.3 | – | 279.0 | 26.0 | – | – | 822.2 | 128.5 |
| *Total* | 3009.5 | 626.7 | 679.0 | 252.5 | 206.9 | 781.5 | 275.5 | 323.7 | 60.0 | 6215.4 | 1472.1 |
| Number of projects | 121 | 33 | 38 | 15 | 13 | 28 | 8 | 11 | (4) | 267 | 57 |

*Note:* Figures may not tally due to rounding. The discrepancy between total sector lending and the corresponding figure in Table 7.1 is due to changes in the Bank's sectoral classification of projects.

*Source:* Calculated from ADB, *Agriculture in Asia, Statistical Appendices*, A Bank Staff Working Paper (March 1985), and ADB, *Annual Report* (1968–86).

Table 7.3  Distribution by subsector of ADB loan approvals for agriculture and rural development, from 1968–70 to 1984–6 (per cent, based on three-year moving averages)

| | Irrigation & rural development | Industrial crops & agro-industry | Fisheries | Livestock | Forestry | Agricultural support services | Fertiliser production | Programme loans | Special assistance for selected projects | Total sector |
|---|---|---|---|---|---|---|---|---|---|---|
| 1968–70 | 34.0 | 23.6 | 25.6 | – | – | 3.2 | 13.2 | – | – | 100.0 |
| 1969–71 | 52.2 | 18.9 | 15.7 | 0.3 | – | 4.7 | 8.1 | – | – | 100.0 |
| 1970–72 | 51.3 | 14.1 | 22.0 | 0.2 | – | 4.4 | 7.7 | – | – | 100.0 |
| 1971–73 | 43.6 | 17.7 | 19.2 | 0.2 | – | 2.1 | 17.3 | – | – | 100.0 |
| 1972–74 | 49.9 | 16.5 | 19.0 | – | – | 6.3 | 11.2 | – | – | 100.0 |
| 1973–75 | 34.2 | 17.0 | 13.2 | – | – | 5.4 | 30.2 | – | – | 100.0 |
| 1974–76 | 50.5 | 9.8 | 13.1 | 0.6 | – | 6.7 | 19.4 | – | – | 100.0 |
| 1975–77 | 56.9 | 6.0 | 11.6 | 0.5 | – | 5.0 | 15.9 | – | – | 100.0 |
| 1976–78 | 64.0 | 9.2 | 15.1 | 2.1 | 4.2 | 3.3 | 0.3 | 1.2 | – | 100.0 |
| 1977–79 | 55.6 | 11.0 | 13.5 | 6.7 | 4.9 | 3.2 | 2.8 | 3.5 | – | 100.0 |
| 1978–80 | 53.4 | 14.0 | 15.7 | 5.5 | 3.9 | 5.3 | 2.3 | 2.9 | – | 100.0 |
| 1979–81 | 54.9 | 9.6 | 10.7 | 5.5 | 0.8 | 7.7 | 7.0 | 3.7 | – | 100.0 |
| 1980–82 | 54.2 | 7.9 | 12.4 | 4.0 | 0.9 | 12.4 | 4.4 | 1.7 | – | 100.0 |
| 1981–83 | 47.8 | 3.6 | 9.1 | 3.6 | 2.9 | 16.6 | 4.0 | 6.6 | 3.3 | 100.0 |
| 1982–84 | 44.1 | 6.5 | 9.0 | 5.0 | 5.3 | 15.7 | – | 11.0 | 3.0 | 100.0 |
| 1983–85 | 46.6 | 5.9 | 7.8 | 5.8 | 5.8 | 11.4 | – | 13.3 | 3.1 | 100.0 |
| 1984–86 | 43.4 | 13.4 | 8.4 | 5.5 | 3.3 | 16.9 | 1.2 | 7.9 | – | 100.0 |
| *Cumulative* (1968–86) | 48.4 | 10.1 | 10.9 | 4.1 | 3.3 | 12.6 | 4.4 | 5.2 | 1.0 | 100.0 |

*Note:*  Figures may not tally due to rounding.

*Source:*  Calculated from ADB, *Agriculture in Asia, Statistical Appendices*, A Bank Staff Working Paper (March 1985) and ADB, *Annual Report* (1968–86).

programme lending has increased, and in 1983 funds were also allocated to provide 'special assistance for selected projects'.

The change in development strategy is also evident from the emergence of several new project types. Alongside construction-oriented irrigation projects, integrated rural development projects have been designed with the explicit purposes of ensuring that low-income groups can benefit from improved irrigation. Projects in other subsectors, particularly agricultural credit and fisheries projects, have also started to mention small farmers and the rural poor as specific target groups, although there is little indication of change in the actual substance of these projects. In addition, ADB lending for road construction has gradually shifted from paved highways and primary roads to feeder roads in rural areas. However, the Bank has been relatively cautious in introducing new types of projects, and the number of innovative projects has remained low.

Examined in terms of the sector's policy objectives, ADB projects have continued to be production-oriented, with appraisal reports justifying projects on grounds of economic returns based on increased production or output. The changes that have taken place between 1968 and the early 1980s have been intended either to enhance projects' effectiveness in increasing production, or to direct projects towards increasing the output of specific target groups. In the case of irrigation projects, the creation of on-farm and off-farm employment has been included as a secondary consideration, although in other rural projects there is little evidence of concern for employment creation. As projects have become more target-group oriented, there are indications that the benefit has shifted somewhat to lower income groups and relatively small-scale farmers. However, as virtually all projects are centred around production, it is clear that those owning or controlling productive assets are the main beneficiaries. Some projects have benefited marginal farmers, but subsistence farmers and landless labourers are largely beyond the projects' reach, particularly as loans have not included or been tied to effective measures for land reform and have rarely been concerned with off-farm employment. Thus, ADB projects on the whole have not been directed to a reduction of rural income disparities.

Following a Bank-sponsored regional seminar on rural development in October 1984, two staff members undertook an analysis of the impact of Bank-financed projects on rural employment creation, which served as a resource paper at an ADB–ILO regional workshop on rural employment creation in November 1986. The study reviewed

83 agricultural sector projects financed by the Bank in 1973–85, representing nearly 70 per cent of all agricultural sector projects approved in that period. The review projected that the employment position of about 7.8 million people improved as a result of the projects and that the project construction works created 1.2 million man-years of employment.[6]

In his foreword to the proceedings of the workshop and the study, M. Zaki Azam, Director of the Bank's Agriculture Department (East) notes that 'rural employment creation was not the main objective of these projects, and, given the current dimension of this problem, the impact of Bank-financed projects on rural employment has been relatively limited'.[7] Both the study and the workshop proceedings make recommendations on how the Bank could increase the employment-orientation of its rural projects. These include the systematic gathering of data on projects' employment and welfare impact, to be used as benchmarks in assessing proposals and project performance, and the broadening of project selection criteria to include, among other things, the number of jobs generated in relation to project cost. These would require changes in the 'Project Benefits and Justification' section of consultants' feasibility studies and Bank appraisal reports, and the introduction of new performance indicators to be used together with the EIRR, and would also lead to a stronger emphasis on employment and income questions in the assessment of project performance in PCRs and PPARs. Other recommendations include increasing labour-substitution in the civil works components of Bank projects, giving priority to sectorally-linked projects, and paying greater attention to upland areas and small-farmer and community-oriented proposals.[8] While implementing the above recommendations would contribute significantly to redirecting Bank projects, it is important to remember that many of them are similar to those made in Bank reports and policy documents in the mid- and late 1970s, and that their implementation is likely to be subject to the same constraints as earlier recommendations.

The above-cited study on the employment impact of Bank projects also emphasises the constraining role of the policies and programmes of the borrowing countries on reorienting Bank lending. The borrowers' role can be seen from two angles. On the one hand, the DMCs have pushed for many of the changes in operational policies and practices discussed in Chapter 6, which are important in providing a framework for increasing the impact of Bank projects on unemployment and poverty. The South Asian countries have been particularly vocal in calling for the Bank to increase the focus of its lending on rural employment creation and poverty alleviation.

On the other hand, the policies pursued by the DMCs in the Bank, the degree to which their national development programmes have or have not effectively tackled unemployment and poverty, and the type of projects for which the DMCs are willing to borrow to a significant degree reflect national power structures and vested interests and have also constrained Bank lending. At the policy level, the exclusion of land reform from Bank programmes is perhaps the best example of the influence exerted by the borrowers. Not only is land reform not mentioned in official policy documents, but, with the exception of irrigation projects in the Philippines discussed below, projects have not been linked to or made conditional on the implementation of land reform by the borrowing government.

There are also shortcomings in other aspects of national development programmes. As Jha and Polman point out, while the DMCs' socio-economic policies and development plans and programmes emphasise the problem of unemployment, the concern is not substantially reflected in development budgets or the implementation of the programmes, which have in many cases continued to focus on increasing productivity.[9] In the Philippines, for example, the policy priority given to unemployment by the Marcos government was not always translated into budgetary allocations and actual programmes. In contrast there are indications that the Aquino government is more concerned with implementing employment-oriented programmes. Thus, while it was possible for aid agencies to direct their lending to employment creation within the policy framework of the Marcos years, but with practical constraints, under the Aquino government they are being requested to do so and, at least initially, government programmes are being directed accordingly. Finally, at the project level vested interests in the DMCs reflect not only on the selection of projects and project components for financing but, as this and the following chapter indicate, on the distribution of project benefits.

## Irrigation Projects and Rural Development Projects

In volume, irrigation and rural development is the most important subsector. Between 1968 and 1986 lending for this subsector totalled $3009.5 million, accounting for 48.4 per cent of ADB lending for agriculture and 15.4 per cent of all lending. The fact that from 1983 to 1986 one of the Bank's four projects departments dealt exclusively with irrigation and rural development projects also attests to the central role of this subsector. In the light of the experience gained from the green revolution, several alternatives for channelling capital assistance into irrigation can be discerned.[10] First, investment can concentrate on either large-scale construction, such as major dams and canals, or small-scale construction, specifically minor dams and secondary and tertiary canals. Foreign aid in the 1960s focused on large-scale construction, but in the 1970s it gradually shifted towards medium- and small-scale construction. The issue is of significance from the point of view of technology, employment, and project beneficiaries. Compared with large-scale construction, small-scale irrigation schemes require relatively less capital-intensive technology and thus have considerable potential for increasing off-farm employment at the construction stage of a project.[11] Small-scale systems are also more likely to ensure the distribution of water at the farm level.

Second, projects can either be 'conventional' irrigation projects or integrated rural development projects built around investment in irrigation. 'Conventional' irrigation projects are concerned mainly with the construction or improvement of physical structures, and were an integral part of investment programmes connected with the green revolution. Integrated rural development projects, again, incorporate a broad range of measures intended to enhance the socio-economic impact of irrigation investment, for specific target groups or in specific target areas, and are an outgrowth of the rural development debate of the 1970s.

The Bank classifies projects in this subsector as either irrigation projects or rural development projects. The former category covers projects concentrating on capital investment in the irrigation system, while a recent paper on rural development projects by Satish Jha, at the time a division manager in the Irrigation and Rural Development Department, defines the latter as 'rural based *multi-component* development projects which aim at improving living conditions with emphasis on agricultural infrastructure facilities in rural areas'.[12] However, as irrigation is a main component of most of the Bank's rural development projects, the paper goes on to note that strict distinction with irrigation projects is difficult. According to Jha the principal difference between the two types of projects lies in their objectives. Irrigation projects are concerned with agricultural development, and their focus is on raising productivity and farm incomes, while the focus of rural development projects is on 'poverty eradication and institutional reform to provide poor groups with access to basic production assets (particularly land and water) and supportive services, etc'.[13]

A second major difference between the two types of projects concerns their planning and implementation. There is considerable uniformity of design in the ADB's irrigation projects, which usually consist of the rehabilitation, improvement or construction of major canals, field networks and inspection and access roads along the canals, demonstration farms, and the provision of agricultural support services. As such their planning and administration is relatively straightforward for both Bank staff and borrowing governments. Rural development projects are more complex, aim at achieving both quantifiable production-oriented objectives and socio-economic objectives which are difficult to quantify, involve numerous components requiring different areas of technical specialisation, and require suitable sequencing of project inputs. Consequently they are more difficult to plan and implement. The dilemma posed by the importance of rural development projects for poverty alleviation, on the one hand, and the difficulties encountered in their preparation and implementation, on the other, is summed up by Jha as follows:

> The overall conclusion drawn is that rural development projects are complicated and difficult to manage and implement. Yet, these types of projects are too important in the Bank's DMCs to be left untouched. The real attack on rural poverty, which has been the growing development concern with most of the DMCs, is to be made only by such multi-sectoral projects. The challenge ahead lies in Bank's [sic] innovativeness to help design appropriate rural development projects which could be expeditiously implemented to be self-sustaining after the implementation phase of projects. This innovativeness would very much depend upon understanding of local resource potential and institutional constraints as well as people's participation in project design and implementation. Thus, comparatively much more time is required for proper preparation and planning and this might be appropriately reflected in Bank's [sic] country strategy, project planning and programming.[14]

The Bank's lending for irrigation and rural development is set out in Table 7.4.[15] Two trends are apparent. First, lending for the subsector has increased almost continuously from $15.9 million in 1973 to $264.9 million in 1983, and has relatively constantly accounted for slightly over half of the Bank's lending for the agricultural sector. The slight decline in 1983 can be explained by the fact that in 1983 $60 million went to provide 'special assistance for selected projects',

Table 7.4 ADB lending for irrigation projects and rural development projects, 1968–83

| | Total lending for subsector ($ million) | OCR ($ million) | SFR ($ million) | Irrigation projects ($ million) | Number of irrigation projects | Rural development projects ($ million) | No. of rural development projects | Rural development projects as % of total |
|---|---|---|---|---|---|---|---|---|
| 1968 | – | – | – | – | | – | – | – |
| 1969 | 12.08 | 0.89 | 11.20 | 12.08 | 3 | – | – | – |
| 1970 | 13.52 | 1.40 | 12.12 | 4.17 | 3 | 9.35 | 2 | 69.2 |
| 1971 | 38.20 | 22.00 | 16.20 | 38.20 | 4 | – | – | – |
| 1972 | 13.94 | – | 13.94 | 5.94 | 1 | 8.00 | 1 | 57.4 |
| 1973 | 15.90 | 7.80 | 8.10 | 6.30 | 2 | 9.60 | 1 | 60.4 |
| 1974 | 83.20 | 51.00 | 32.20 | 32.20 | 4 | 51.00 | 3 | 61.3 |
| 1975 | 56.10 | 56.10 | – | 43.90 | 3 | 12.20 | 4 | 21.7 |
| 1976 | 153.82 | 63.38 | 90.44 | 77.28 | 4 | 76.54 | 4 | 49.8 |
| 1977 | 193.40 | 105.50 | 87.90 | 101.40 | 5 | 92.00 | 4 | 47.6 |
| 1978 | 148.04 | 80.59 | 67.45 | 91.18 | 5 | 56.86 | 4 | 38.4 |
| 1979 | 204.60 | 107.10 | 97.50 | 135.10 | 6 | 69.50 | 2 | 34.0 |
| 1980 | 283.45 | 155.90 | 127.55 | 208.45 | 8 | 75.00 | 3 | 26.5 |
| 1981 | 291.80 | 178.30 | 113.50 | 231.30 | 5 | 60.50 | 2 | 20.7 |
| 1982 | 308.73 | 150.03 | 158.70 | 230.35 | 6 | 78.38 | 2 | 25.4 |
| 1983 | 264.85 | 209.35 | 55.50 | 249.85 | 7 | 15.00 | 1 | 5.7 |
| Total | 2081.63 | 1189.33 | 892.30 | 1467.70 | 66 | 613.93 | 32 | 29.5 |

Note:   Figures may not tally due to rounding.

Sources:   ADB, Agriculture in Asia, Statistical Appendices, A Bank Staff Working Paper (March 1985), Rural Development in Asia and the Pacific, Volume I, Papers and Proceedings of the ADB Regional Seminar on Rural Development (April 1985), and Annual Report (1983).

many of which were irrigation projects (see Table 7.2). Second, the relative share of conventional irrigation projects has continued to increase, while that of integrated rural development projects has declined. There was a marked increase in the share of rural development projects in 1974 and 1976–7, but between 1978 and 1982 the loan funds earmarked for rural development projects remained constant, and in 1983 they declined sharply. In relative terms, funds for integrated rural development projects have declined continuously, while increasing funds have been allocated for irrigation projects. In 1983–6 lending for this subsector has levelled out and decreased slightly (see Tables 7.2 and 7.3). This can be attributed to the growing difficulty of justifying investment in irrigation in terms of economic returns, as investment in irrigation structures has become more costly, while the price of principal crops such as rice has declined.

On the whole, the Bank's approach to irrigation development has changed little in the period covered by this study. A paper by a staff member of the Bank's Post-Evaluation Office notes that in general the ADB has supported capital-intensive, medium- to large-scale schemes, rather than small-scale irrigation.[16] Only relatively minor modifications have been introduced, such as increasing the information available on beneficiaries by introducing a system of 'project benefit monitoring and evaluation' (PBME) for selected rural sector projects,[17] and increasing the degree to which investment in physical facilities is supplemented with institutional support.[18]

The ADB's strong focus on irrigation projects based on capital investment in medium- and large-scale construction and limited involvement in integrated rural development projects can be explained in the light of both political and organisational factors. Construction-oriented projects are familiar to international consultants and contractors; they can readily be split up into components which are suitable for ICB and require substantial foreign exchange for earth-moving and construction machines and equipment and relatively little local cost financing. Rural development projects, on the other hand, place more emphasis on developing innovative approaches and making use of local resources, and involve such issues as local cost financing and the use of consultants from developing countries. The increase in lending for rural development projects in 1974–7 coincided with considerable political pressure from donor governments for international agencies to develop new project modalities for dealing with rural poverty, while the subsequent stagnation in the preparation of rural development projects has accompanied a period of growing emphasis by donors on their own economic and commercial interests.

The dominance of consulting companies from industrial countries in preparing the Bank's projects is significant in shaping the Bank's approach to irrigation and rural development at the project level. The proceedings of a Bank seminar on rural development in 1984 point out the limited exposure of many foreign consultants to local conditions and problems, their lack of awareness of relevant local experience and the resultant shortcomings in feasibility studies prepared by such consultants.[19] In his paper presented to the seminar, Jha also attributes inadequacies in the design of rural development projects to 'the lack of exposure of consulting firms [of the donor countries] to the development process occurring in the DMCs as well as their strong bias towards engineering and technical aspects'.[20]

A second explanation for the Bank's low and declining lending for rural development projects can be found at the organisational level. The preparation of rural development projects takes longer and their implementation has encountered more difficulties and delays than that of ADB projects on average.[21] The recent study on aid by Cassen and associates indicates that the performance of irrigation projects is more favourable than that of integrated rural development projects, a finding which is confirmed by a 1985 World Bank report on project performance.[22] The decline in pressure from many donors for poverty-oriented projects in the early 1980s, combined with the increased pressure within the Bank for compliance with annual lending targets, can be assumed to have contributed to a preference among division managers for administratively straightforward irrigation projects, with a relatively high likelihood of achieving their objectives, over more problematic rural development projects. In an article on the irrigation strategy being supported by the World Bank in India, Wade similarly suggests that ease of project formulation and loan implementation are significant in explaining why the World Bank has adopted a package approach based on capital investment in main system construction, rather than exploring alternative approaches.[23]

## Irrigation in Indonesia

In both Indonesia and the Philippines, the ADB's rural lending has, in a manner reminiscent of that of the World Bank, concentrated on irrigation. Between 1969 and 1983 Indonesia received 22 irrigation loans, worth a total of $588.42 million, while the Philippines received 18 loans worth $376.5 million. In Table 7.5, the substance of sixteen of these projects, eight from either country, is summarised to provide an overview of the development of the Bank's irrigation lending. In addition to information on loan size, local cost financing, and the irrigated area covered by the projects, the table compares the principal project components, and the economic and social justification for the projects, based on appraisal reports and PPARs.

The primary objective of the Bank's irrigation projects in Indonesia has been to increase rice production, particularly with a view to making Indonesia self-sufficient in foodgrain production, an objective which the country achieved in the early 1980s. In this context the main concern of irrigation projects has been with promoting improved cropping patterns – double cropping and in some cases triple cropping – thus raising farm output and incomes. Since the second agricultural survey in 1977 stressed the need for increased employment, appraisal reports for irrigation projects have also attempted broadly to quantify the increased agricultural employment resulting from production increases and off-farm employment during a project's construction period. Appraisal reports have also mentioned various other benefits, such as reduced flood damage, and improved water supply and health conditions, although these have not been quantified. In terms of project components, irrigation projects have concentrated predominantly on irrigation works – the construction of dams, weirs, pump stations, main canals, secondary and in some cases tertiary canals, and inspection and access roads. Since the late 1970s projects have included a number of other components, particularly rural water supply, soil conservation and erosion control, and have specified the agricultural support services to be provided by the government. Loan funds have also been earmarked for local costs.

Of the three policy objectives examined in this study, there are clear indications that irrigation projects have contributed to the achievement of two: increasing production and creating employment. Bank post-evaluations of irrigation loans indicate that these have resulted in significant production increases,[24] and this conclusion is confirmed by the available post-evaluations of Bank irrigation projects in Indonesia.[25] Both Booth, in her study of irrigation in Indonesia, and the evaluation of a USAID-funded irrigation project in Indonesia have reached similar conclusions regarding the impact of investment in irrigation on rice production.[26]

Table 7.5 The main elements of 16 selected ADB irrigation loans to Indonesia and the Philippines, 1969–83

| Year | Project | Loan amount ($ million) | Local cost financing ($ million & per cent) | Land irrigated (hectares) | Project components | | | | | | Economic & social justification | | | |
|---|---|---|---|---|---|---|---|---|---|---|---|---|---|---|
| | | | | | Irrigation works** | Rural water supply | Rural health services | Land development/ erosion control | Gov't: agric. support serv. | Gov't: land reform | Agric. prod. | Farm incomes | Employ-ment | Other benefits*** |
| | *Indonesia* | | | | | | | | | | | | | |
| 1969 | Tajum irrigation | 0.99 | – | 3 200 | × | – | – | – | – | – | × | × | – | – |
| 1970 | Gambarsari-Pesanggrahan irrigation | 2.70 | – | 20 000 | × | – | – | – | – | – | × | × | – | – |
| 1971 | Sempor dam and irrigation | 9.20 | – | 16 240 | × | – | – | – | – | – | × | × | – | – |
| 1978 | Bali irrigation | 18.00 | 8.20 (46) | 11 630 | × | × | – | × | × | – | × | × | × | × |
| 1979 | Tulungagung drainage | 39.00 | 12.00 (31) | 21 000 | × | – | – | – | × | – | × | × | × | × |
| 1980 | Cibaliung irrigation | 35.00 | 8.50 (24) | 13 100 | × | × | – | × | × | – | × | × | × | × |
| 1982 | Irrigation package loan | 77.00 | 10.00 (13) | 42 780 | × | – | – | – | – | – | × | × | – | – |
| 1983 | Second irrigation sector loan | 85.00 | 24.00 (28) | 45 000 | × | – | – | – | × | – | × | × | × | × |
| | *Philippines* | | | | | | | | | | | | | |
| 1969 | Cotabato irrigation | 2.50 | – | 7 430 | × | – | – | – | × | – | × | × | × | × |
| 1973 | Angat-Magat agric. dev.* | 9.60 | – | 66 800 | × | – | – | – | × | × | × | × | × | × |
| 1973 | Davao del Norte irrigation | 4.20 | – | 11 820 | × | – | – | – | – | × | × | × | – | – |
| 1978 | Second Agusan irrigation | 14.00 | – | 8 000 | × | × | × | × | × | × | × | × | × | × |
| 1979 | Bukidnon irrigation | 15.00 | 10.00 (24) | 11 400 | × | × | × | – | × | – | × | × | × | × |
| 1979 | Bicol irrigation* | 41.00 | 10.00 (24) | 14 260 | × | × | × | × | × | – | × | × | × | × |
| 1982 | Third Davao irrigation | 45.30 | 10.00 (22) | 9 000 | × | – | × | × | × | – | × | × | × | × |
| 1983 | Irrigation sector loan | 67.40 | 18.80 (28) | 37 600 | × | – | – | – | – | – | × | × | × | × |

\* Classified by ADB as rural development projects.

\*\* Construction of dams, weirs, main, secondary and tertiary canals, and inspection and access roads.

\*\*\* Includes benefits from improved flood control, sanitary water supply, health services etc.

*Source:* ADB *PPARs* and *Appraisal Reports*.

In assessing the projects' impact on employment, a distinction should be made between on-farm and off-farm employment. No detailed estimates of the amount of employment created are included in Bank PPARs, which can be attributed to the fact that employment creation was not a major policy objective at the time the Bank's early irrigation projects were planned. However, more recent irrigation project appraisal reports include calculations of fairly extensive employment creation in rice production, and through the utilisation of labour-intensive construction techniques. As Booth points out, rice cultivation in Indonesia is unusually labour-intensive, and the more intensive cropping patterns permitted by improved irrigation have created substantial additional employment for surplus agricultural labour.[27] It can reasonably be assumed that the increased production brought about by Bank projects has been accompanied by a corresponding increase in on-farm employment.

The impact of Bank irrigation projects on off-farm employment has only been examined in one evaluation report, of the Sempor dam and irrigation project, which was implemented between 1971 and 1979. In the project, the dam was built by a Japanese contractor in cooperation with a local contractor, and was highly capital-intensive, while canal construction was carried out by local contractors, making extensive use of unskilled labour and relatively labour-intensive construction techniques.[28] However, the local contracts were funded from government funds, while the loan was used to cover the foreign exchange costs of capital goods and paying the Japanese contractor. The data on the Sempor dam project presented in Table 7.6 also clearly illustrate the high employment-creating potential of funds

*Table* 7.6 Breakdown of machinery and unskilled labour costs for different construction activities in the Sempor dam and irrigation project

| *Type of works* | Breakdown of total costs (per cent) | | |
|---|---|---|---|
| | *Machinery* | *Unskilled labour* | *Materials and others* |
| Dam | 45 | 2 | 53 |
| Main canals | 24 | 42 | 34 |
| Main drainage | 25 | 45 | 30 |
| Secondary canals | 11 | 52 | 37 |
| Tertiary canals | 6 | 75 | 19 |

*Source*: ADB, *PPAR on the Sempor Dam and Irrigation Project in Indonesia*, (October 1982) p. A30.

allocated for the construction of small-scale canals, particularly tertiary canals, compared with the much lower employment-creating impact of the medium- to large-scale construction favoured by the Bank.

Assessing the distribution of the benefits among the rural populace is more problematic. Numerous studies have pointed out constraints on the equitable distribution of the benefits of improved irrigation.[29] Thus even the benefits of projects with physical structures designed for equitable water distribution are often unevenly distributed. Moreover, viewed within the context of the entire rural sector, irrigation projects – which involve investment in either irrigated land, in the case of rehabilitation projects, or potentially irrigable land, in the case of projects bringing new land under irrigation – are designed to benefit small and medium farmers who are being integrated into the market economy, while significantly poorer socio-economic groups, particularly subsistence farmers in rain-fed areas, and landless labourers, remain beyond the reach of irrigation projects. These observations are supported by the Bank's post-evaluation of the Tajum irrigation project, which concludes that the project's benefits were not distributed equally with regard to farm size and location, and that the landless, who accounted for 52 per cent of the population in the project area, benefited little from the project.[30]

The assumptions set out in ADB appraisal reports indicate that while irrigation projects will benefit relatively small holdings, the farm incomes of owner-operators are expected to increase much more in real terms than those of sharecroppers. Landless labourers are only expected to benefit through increased employment opportunities, and even this assumption may often be optimistic. The appraisal report for the $35 million Cibaliung irrigation project approved in 1980 demonstrates the inherent bias in favour of larger holdings:

> The main beneficiaries of the Project will be farmers in the Project area. As a result of the Project facilities, the farmers would be able to adopt more intensive and modern methods of farming. It is estimated that the average net earnings from a typical owner operated farm (1 ha) in the future in a 'with Project' condition would increase to about [$1027] a year from the present level of [$368] a year. In the case of the smaller 0.5 ha sharecropping farmer, the increase would be to about [$368] from [$131] a year.[31]

The appraisal report of the $77 million irrigation package loan approved in 1982 describes the project's beneficiaries as farm households and the landless poor. The report goes on to describe the

project's employment impact, which is apparently how the Bank sees
the project as benefiting the landless poor:

> A large proportion of the civil works construction will be carried out by
> labour-intensive techniques to reduce costs and to provide employment
> opportunities to the unemployed skilled and unskilled labour in the area.
> The project is expected to generate 51,000 man-years of employment
> during the construction phase and 11,700 man-years of employment on a
> continuous basis in agricultural operations on full development.[32]

Two factors should be pointed out which tend to detract from the
amount of additional employment created for landless labourers in
the project area. First, the PPAR of the Sempor dam project indicates
that while construction increased employment, the bulk of the labour
force was recruited by the local contractors from districts other than
that of the project.[33] Second, according to the post-evaluation of the
Tajum irrigation project, the additional agricultural employment
created by the project benefited mainly farmers and their families
and absorbed relatively less landless poor.[34]

## Irrigation and Rural Development in the Philippines

The ADBs irrigation lending to the Philippines differs from that to
Indonesia in that the projects have been more integrated, encompassing
broader socio-economic objectives and a larger number of project
components. Of the 18 irrigation and rural development loans made
by the Bank to the Philippines by 1983, three projects, the Angat-
Magat integrated agricultural development project (1979), the Bicol
River Basin irrigation development project (1981), and the Palawan
integrated area development project (1981), for which the ADB lent
a total of $97.6 million, are classified by the Bank as rural development
projects.[35] However, several other of the ADB's irrigation loans are
similar in scope and approach and could easily also be included in
this category (see Table 7.5).

As in Indonesia, in the Philippines ADB investment in irrigation
has aimed at supporting government efforts to achieve – and more
recently to maintain – self-sufficiency in rice production. Projects
have focused on allowing intensified cropping patterns and the
introduction of agricultural inputs, thus raising farm incomes and
creating jobs. Compared with most irrigation projects in Indonesia,
many projects in the Philippines have, in addition to irrigation and

flood control works, included the construction of tubewells to provide villages with water supply, the construction of village health stations and the establishment of schistosomiasis control programmes. Appraisal reports and loan agreements have also specified the agricultural support services to be provided by the government and made reference to the importance of the government's land reform programme for the achievement of project objectives (see Table 7.5).

The question of land reform in Philippine irrigation projects is of particular interest, as this is one of the very rare examples of land reform being included in ADB projects. In the mid- and late 1970s the appraisal reports and loan agreements for these projects included a relatively standard statement to the effect that the Philippine government had given its assurance that high priority would be accorded to its land reform programme in the project area, and giving a date by which the land reform would be completed.[36] As a Bank report observes, this implies that bringing about a more equitable distribution of incomes was also a project objective.[37] Critics of the Marcos government's land reform programme, however, maintained that even fully implemented the programme would do little to improve income distribution, pointing out, for example, that the landless did not benefit from the programme, and that the benefits to tenant farmers were severely constrained by the exclusion of a wide range of crops and the fact that landlords were allowed to retain a substantial share of their holdings.[38]

In practice the implementation of land reform, even in the ADB project areas, was not successful. Evaluations of Bank irrigation projects indicate that the Marcos government was reluctant to implement land reform and did not meet the deadlines specified in project appraisals. PPARs explicitly point out that while the government complied with other loan covenants, those concerning land reform were not satisfactorily met.[39] Apparently as a result of this non-compliance and due to the politically sensitive nature of the issue, land reform was no longer mentioned in irrigation project appraisals after 1980.[40]

Of the three major policy objectives, irrigation projects in the Philippines can be considered relatively successful in increasing rice production and creating on-farm employment. Evaluation reports indicate that projects have led both to an expansion in the irrigated area and to significantly higher yields per hectare.[41] As in Indonesia, appraisal reports stress the impact projects will have on both agricultural and off-farm employment. These observations are in line with the conclusions of an evaluation report on USAID investment in irrigation in the Philippines.[42] More important, however, is the question of whether the Bank's integrated approach to irrigation and rural development in the Philippines has been any more successful in reaching the poor than the Bank's other irrigation projects. The question is discussed below in the light of the limited evidence available.

An examination of the Angat-Magat and Bicol River Basin integrated rural development projects shows that the main difference between these and regular irrigation projects lies in their multi-sectoral nature. They are basically irrigation projects, but also include components such as road construction, rural water supply, health stations and schistosomiasis control, under Bank financing, and land reform and the provision of agricultural support services, under government inputs. The support services and rural roads are intended to enhance the projects' impact on agricultural output, and mainly benefit farmers. Land reform is intended to equalise the distribution of assets and incomes, but has not been effectively implemented. Consequently, improved water supply and health services are the only project components which stand to benefit non-farm, low-income groups in project areas.

The economic and social justification in the Bank's appraisal of the Bicol River Basin project – which is part of a broader project also receiving funds from USAID and the EC and includes rural roads and water supply, but no health component – demonstrates the close similarity between irrigation and rural development projects:

> The Project has been formulated as a multi-sectoral area development program, with primary emphasis on irrigation and flood control, aimed at increasing rice production, promoting employment, and improving income and living standards of the rural population. Situated in an area of small farms, the Project will benefit predominantly low income farm families. The Project will provide 3 basic economic and social needs of the area: (i) development of irrigation, flood control and rice culture; (ii) construction of farm-to-market roads; and (iii) installation of rural water supply systems. The project will assist in meeting the Government's objectives of increased food production and achieving and sustaining self-sufficiency in rice. Investment in the Project is justifiable in terms of its value to the national economy, as well as in terms of enhancement of rural incomes and other socio-economic benefits.[43]

The report goes on to list as the project's main benefits increased incomes for farmers and increased agricultural and off-farm employment. Similar benefits are described in the PPAR of the Angat-Magat project.[44] It thus seems that there is only relatively minor difference in the content of, and little substantial difference in the distribution of the benefits of, irrigation projects and irrigation-based, integrated rural development projects, although the latter are purportedly more poverty-oriented.

Two additional comments are required concerning irrigation projects' impact on income distribution. First, the irrigable ricelands on which Bank projects concentrate are by definition not the most depressed areas, nor are small and medium farmers at the bottom of the income scale in such areas. As Ayres points out in his discussion of who benefits from World Bank irrigation projects in the Philippines, while World Bank staff contend that the major beneficiaries are farmers owning less than three hectares, they also concede that the projects 'were not benefiting the poorest of the poor since potentially irrigable areas in which projects were undertaken were already better off than those rainfed areas where the really miserable were located'.[45]

Second, research has shown that farmers' ability to take advantage of improved irrigation depends on the degree to which their farming is commercialised, and on their access to credit and inputs. The World Bank has been criticised for including as an integral part of its irrigation development strategy a substantial increase in irrigation water fees. Such charges are justified as a means of covering the cost of investing in and operating irrigation systems, and some studies suggest a strong positive relationship between user charges and maintenance of facilities.[46] Critics, on the other hand, have pointed to the financial burden they constitute for marginal and subsistence farmers. ADB projects have incorporated a similar policy of encouraging borrowers to raise water charges significantly. For example, under the Davao del Norte project irrigation fees were raised from $3.7 and $5.2 per hectare for wet season and dry season paddy at the time of appraisal in 1973 to $20.7 and $31 respectively at project completion in 1981. According to the PPAR, 74 per cent of all farms in the project area were below three hectares, and most of these were only one or two hectares in size. With the increased farm incomes expected at full project development, the report concluded that farmers with two hectares and above would be able to meet increased irrigation fees, while tenants of one hectare holdings would 'not have sufficient income to meet living expenses, unless additional off-farm income is available to them'.[47]

# 8 Rural Credit and Road Projects

Following irrigation and rural development, rural credit and road construction and improvement are the two most important subsectors of ADB lending for the rural sector. This chapter examines the ADB's approach to both subsectors, the extent to which projects have changed over time, the role of political and organisational factors in shaping projects, and project impact. The rural development policy set out in the second Asian agricultural survey envisaged extensive investment in credit to small farmers, to enhance the impact of irrigation projects and other investment in agricultural production, and to promote a more equitable distribution of incomes. It also entailed complementing agricultural employment with extensive off-farm employment, mainly in labour-intensive public works. This chapter indicates that while lending for both subsectors has increased substantially since the mid-1970s, the change in project content has been very limited. Lending for rural credit has expanded, but has continued to be directed to local development finance institutions for onlending through existing channels, and the ADB has not effectively implemented small-farmer credit projects. In road construction the Bank has moved from financing highways to a combination of major roads and feeder roads, but has not incorporated labour-intensive technology in its projects.

## RURAL CREDIT

The provision of institutional credit for the purchase of irrigation equipment, inputs such as fertiliser, seeds and pesticides, and for farm mechanisation, is an integral part of both agricultural modernisation and rural development strategies. In modernisation strategies, irrigation and inputs play an important role in supporting the yield-raising potential of the HYVs. Consequently the green revolution's failure to meet expectations of increased productivity, and the unequal distribution of production increases, was largely blamed on the lack of inputs and credit for the purchase of inputs, and led to a heightened emphasis on the role of credit and support services in the

144

reorientation of rural development policies in the 1970s. This is reflected in the second agricultural survey, in various Bank policy papers prepared in the late 1970s and in the ADB's lending for credit and other support services, which has increased very substantially since 1979 (see Tables 7.2 and 7.3). At the same time, rural credit has itself come under strong criticism, particularly because of its limited accessibility to small farmers and its potential to lead farmers into a cycle of excessive indebtedness.[1]

The Bank's rural credit lending has encompassed two main types of projects: credit in support of crop production, and credit for fisheries and livestock development.[2] By 1984, the Bank had made 14 loans totalling $284.5 million which it classified as agricultural credit loans (see Table 8.1). However, most of the Bank's fisheries loans were also made to support credit facilities for the mechanisation of fishing boats, and many of the Bank's livestock and agro-industry loans have credit components. Consequently, by the end of 1983, loans or loan components to support institutions providing credit for different productive activities in the rural sector had been given for 47 projects, accounting for about $500 million or 12 per cent of all Bank lending for the rural sector.[3]

*Table* 8.1 ADB lending for agriculture credit, as of 1984

| Country | Years | No. of projects | Amount ($ million) | OCR | SFR |
|---|---|---|---|---|---|
| Bangladesh | 1975–83 | 3 | 77.53 | – | 77.53 |
| Indonesia | 1971–82 | 3 | 33.67 | 27.57 | 6.10 |
| Nepal | 1970–80 | 4 | 26.40 | – | 26.40 |
| Pakistan | 1982 | 1 | 50.00 | – | 50.00 |
| Philippines | 1982 | 1 | 36.00 | 36.00 | – |
| Sri Lanka | 1979 | 1 | 10.90 | – | 10.90 |
| Thailand | 1983 | 1 | 50.00 | 50.00 | – |
| Total | | 14 | 284.50 | 113.57 | 170.93 |

*Source*: ADB, *Annual Reports*.

Most credit projects consist of two components: medium- and long-term credit for onlending to farmers or fishermen for the acquisition of irrigation facilities, fishing vessels, marine engines and various types of farm equipment, and an institution-building component to strengthen the local development finance institution(s) through which funds are channelled. Credit projects can correspondingly be examined in terms of both their institutional impact and their impact on production, employment and incomes. A draft sector policy paper on agricultural credit prepared in 1984 by the Agricultural Support Services Division of the Agriculture Department indicates that due to the high risk and low debt recovery associated with rural credit, and strong government support, the financial viability of rural credit institutions is often low.[4] However, as the case of the Agricultural Development Bank of Nepal (ADBN) below demonstrates, the problem of the lack of institutional viability may also stem from the ready or excessive access credit institutions have had to ADB loans. This, in turn, is a direct consequence of the emphasis placed by the Bank on fund-channelling.

In terms of policy objectives, credit projects are designed to support increases in foodgrain production and other types of output, and evaluations conducted by the Bank have confirmed the positive impact of Bank-funded credit projects on output. Due to various constraints both in the Bank's operational policies for project preparation and in the socio-economic structure of the borrowing countries, the distribution of the benefits of credit projects has been strongly biased in favour of relatively large-scale producers. The Bank's draft policy paper sums up the distributional impact of credit projects as follows:

> Post-evaluation reports indicate that a larger share of the benefits was cornered by the relatively more affluent. The fact that many Bank projects provided for only those types of farm equipment which individual small farmers could not afford to own accounted for one of the reasons for missing the small group. That the project benefits were open equally for the big and small, and that the onlending agencies perceived greater degree of creditworthiness with the big were other reasons. Bank-aided credit projects addressed only the farmers, whereas the great bulk of the rural poor were the landless or the marginal farmers.[5]

The skewed distribution of benefits can be attributed to a combination of factors, including the strong focus in preparation and appraisal on the projects' EIRR based on increased output, the greater perceived creditworthiness of larger producers mentioned above, and the paucity of viable institutions for providing small-farm credit in many borrowing countries. Project content has also been constrained by the Bank's procurement and local cost financing policies. It is interesting to note that credit projects are built almost entirely around the procurement of imported equipment, mainly irrigation pumps, tractors, power tillers and marine diesel engines, and that these have been procured in accordance with Bank procurement policies with disregard for, and at times in conflict with, the preferences of farmers in borrowing countries.[6]

Particularly since the second survey, the Bank has stressed the role of small-farmer credit as an integral part of its rural development policy. However, as the examples of the small farmers' groups in Nepal and fisheries cooperative societies in Sri Lanka below indicate, there is a lack of adequate small-farmer organisations at the local level. The projects examined did not incorporate institution-building components to strengthen such organisations, but preferred to rely on existing credit arrangements. This can to a large degree be attributed to the many complex issues involved in projects channelling credit to small farmers, compared with the simplicity of direct lending to local development finance institutions for onlending. The 1984 draft policy paper recognises many of the problems in the Bank's credit projects and suggests a number of remedial measures, including directing more credit to smaller producers and strengthening projects' institution-building function, but has been the subject of prolonged discussion and scrutiny in the Bank. It was expected to be finalised and submitted to the board during the third quarter of 1987.

## Agricultural Credit in Nepal

The ADBN was established in 1968 as the principal source of institutional credit for Nepal's agricultural development, and has served as one of the main channels of ADB assistance to Nepal's rural sector. Since the outset of its operations, the ADBN has received regular and substantial support from the ADB in the form of technical assistance totalling $765 000, a $1.1 million UNDP technical assistance grant executed by the Bank, and four loans between 1971 and 1980 worth a total of $26.4 million, constituting 14.4 per cent of ADB lending to the country's rural sector. The ADBN has also served as the executing agency for the credit components of numerous other ADB projects in Nepal. In principle, the ADBN lends to individual farmers directly, as well as through cooperatives, village committees and groups of small farmers, but in practice the bulk of its lending has been directly to individual farmers, due mainly to the weakness of cooperatives and farmers' groups in Nepal.

The ADB's four loans to the ADBN were given to cover the foreign exchange cost of importing agricultural machines, farm and irrigation equipment and a variety of inputs, which farmers purchased with credits extended by the ADBN. The major components of these loans are listed in Table 8.2, and to a certain extent reflect the shift in the Bank's policy objectives. The first two projects were aimed at modernising and mechanising agricultural production. Eighty-five per cent of the first loan was used for the purchase of tractors, 10 per cent to import irrigation pumpsets, and the balance for vehicles and office equipment for the ADBN. Of the second loan, 58 per cent was used for the construction of cooperative warehouses and cold storage facilities, and 42 per cent for the purchase of tractors and power tillers.

*Table* 8.2  Breakdown of ADB agricultural credit projects in Nepal by major components, 1971–86

|  | Credit project | | | |
| --- | --- | --- | --- | --- |
|  | *I* | *II* | *III* | *IV* |
| *Loan amount ($ million)* | $2.4 | $3.0 | $6.0 | $15.0 |
| *Years of implementation* | 1971–76 | 1974–80 | 1977–81 | 1980–86 |
| *Major components* | | | | |
| Tractors | 380 | 150 | – | – |
| Power tillers | – | 300 | – | 700 |
| Pumpsets | 1160 | – | 4000 | 1300 |
| Tubewells | – | – | 2800 | 1200 |
| Dugwells | – | – | 400 | – |
| Cold storage facilities | – | 3 | – | – |
| Warehouses | – | 78 | – | – |
| Fertiliser | – | – | incl. | – |
| Water turbines | – | – | – | 160 |
| Imported livestock | – | – | – | 2290 |
| Biogas plants | – | – | – | 2000 |
| Office equipment | incl. | – | incl. | incl. |

*Source*:  ADB *Appraisal Reports* and *PPARs*.

The two more recent loans focused on irrigation, the provision of inputs, and farm mechanisation. The third loan proposed to direct most of the loan proceeds to small farmers, and included income distribution as an explicit objective,[7] while the fourth loan was aimed at increasing production and employment, and was also intended to contribute to alleviating energy and environmental problems.[8] The third loan was used for the purchase of fertiliser and irrigation equipment, and the fourth for pumpsets, tubewells and power tillers, as well as three new components: water turbines, biogas plants and livestock.

ADB lending for agricultural credit in Nepal is an example of the result in terms of rapidly increasing project size and relatively standardised project content of the pressure within the Bank for fund-channelling. On the one hand, the ADB has provided a constant flow of concessional finance to the ADBN, with loan size increasing from $2.4 million in 1971 to $15 million in 1980. A fifth agricultural credit loan of $24 million was approved in 1987.[9] On the other hand, the loans' low disbursement rate and serious implementation problems cast doubt on the capacity of the ADBN and Nepalese farmers to absorb such rapidly expanding credit. The expansion of ADB lending to the ADBN should be seen at least partly as arising from organisational pressures for increased lending, and seems to have taken place with considerable disregard for institutional, economic and financial considerations at the country level.

The post-evaluation reports of the first two loans were critical of the financial status of the ADBN, and drew particular attention to its deteriorating profitibility and poor debt management.[10] By the end of the third loan, however, the ADB's post-evaluation mission noted a 'substantial improvement' in the bank's financial situation and expressed general satisfaction with its performance. The mission's report did, however, point out the low repayment rate of ADBN loans by farmers, which it blamed on the ADBN's spending relatively more effort on meeting lending targets associated with aid programmes than on monitoring loan repayment.[11]

An external consultant who participated in the preparation of another ADB rural project connected with the ADBN in 1984 is considerably more critical of the outcome of ADB lending to the ADBN. According to an independent account published by the consultant, the continuous flow of Bank loans and other forms of foreign assistance, which were provided to the ADBN in abundance at concessional terms, combined with lax supervision of loan conditions, have completely undermined the bank's viability as a financial institution. The ADBN's situation in 1984 is described by the consultant as follows:

> [In Nepal] the fifth credit line for the 'Agricultural Development Bank, Nepal' . . . is being prepared, although neither have the agreed conditions under the first credits been complied with nor has the objective of promoting production been achieved. The Nepalese bank, a money distributing institution, does not bother about the reconciliation of accounts

with its clients, makes investments amounting to millions of monetary units without contracts, rarely bothers about the continuously increasing debtors' accounts, does not make any provisions for bad and doubtful debts and has been showing losses for many years.[12]

The account goes on to discuss the substantial improvement in the ADBN's financial position reported by the ADB at the completion of the third credit project:

But in 1982/3, a clumsily manipulated profit was shown which should have been recognised by any trainee in his second year of banking training, which was, however, reported back to Manila by the 'experts' of the Asian Development Bank as a 'turning point' and 'poised to take off'. The Agricultural Development Bank maintains its liquidity only by borrowing again and again from external sources, and since one does not want to see the word 'write-off' at the Asian Development Bank, only positive social achievements are being included in the filtered reports. If one wanted seriously to rehabilitate the Agricultural Development Bank of Nepal, many years would be required for the reconciliation of accounts and revision of loan agreements, in order to determine, first of all, the true losses. But, financing, distribution, and misuse continue.[13]

The consultant blames the above situation on the ready availability of assistance on such concessional terms that neither ADB staff nor Nepalese officials are very concerned about adherence to the principles of 'sound' financing. The account ends with a critical comment on development aid and the role of international consultants:

The socio-economic conditions of the rural population, the catastrophical institutional situation of the Agricultural Development Bank, the cooperatives and so-called 'small farmers groups' will continue to deteriorate, if the money continues to flow and no radical changes are undertaken. I know that I will not make friends in the 'development aid business' with this article, where people with eloquent ambivalence prefer not to address the genuine problems. However, I know as a banker that hypocrisy, dishonesty and window-dressing do not help our profession and the institutions entrusted to us; this also applies to advisory services.[14]

Recent disclosures within the ADB about the financial situation of the ADBN confirm the above account and in 1986 led to a board inquiry into and delay in the approval of an ADB aquaculture loan which included a $6.5 million credit component channelled through the ADBN.[15]

In terms of policy objectives the projects have had only limited impact on agricultural production and employment, and no positive impact on income distribution. In the Bank's own assessment the projects have been partially successful in raising productivity. Post-evaluation reports indicate that the farm mechanisation and irrigation facilities funded with project credits contributed to increasing yields, but that the increases were considerably less than estimated in project appraisals.[16]

The projects' impact on employment has been mixed. On the one hand, farm mechanisation tended to displace labour, while on the other, increased production also entailed increased labour utilisation. In the first and second projects, on the farms which purchased tractors, labour demand in the preparation of the seed-bed declined, but was to a certain degree offset by increased demand for labour in other operations.[17] In the first project, on the farms which purchased pumpsets, demand for labour in both seed-bed preparation and other activities increased.[18]

In the light of Nepal's high level of unemployment and abundant low-cost labour, however, serious questions can be raised about any project giving priority to labour-displacing farm mechanisation, and it is fair to conclude that the first two projects' impact on employment was marginal. The two more recent projects have had more impact on employment. The third project led to increased use of hired labour on the farms where pumpsets and tubewells were installed.[19] The fourth project includes employment creation as an objective, but while it can be assumed that the pumpset and tubewell components led to increased employment, the farm mechanisation component can be expected to have little employment impact.

Finally, the available evidence indicates that the projects have not contributed to economic equity, and have probably reinforced Nepal's skewed distribution of incomes. First, the projects have concentrated on the Terai region along Nepal's border with India, which is the most prosperous of Nepal's three regions, and have neglected the hill region, in which about 60 per cent of the population live, mostly in considerable economic hardship.[20] This can largely be justified by the fact that the production of Nepal's agricultural surplus is concentrated in the Terai. The fourth credit project has to some degree attempted to balance this disparity by expanding its coverage to some districts in the hill and mountain regions.[21]

More important is the question of the direct beneficiaries of ADBN credits supported by the ADB projects. A significant limitation is posed by the fact that the ADBN only extends production credits and will not provide loans for the purchase of land. Landless tenants and small farmers seeking loans to buy land are consequently reliant on traditional, non-institutional credit arrangements. As the above-cited consultant describes the situation, nearly 90 per cent of all loans to buy land in Nepal are financed by private money-lenders or landlords, involving very disadvantageous terms for the peasants and small farmers.[22] ADBN loans, again, are extended mainly to relatively large farmers in a position to expand their operations.

The Bank's own PPARs confirm that the principal benefit from the four loans is in many cases going to the largest farm households and in virtually all cases to households with above average holdings. On the first credit project, while the average farm size in the project area was 1.54 hectares and that of the Terai region was placed at 2.41 hectares, the average size of the farms which purchased pumpsets with project credits varied from 6.7 to 10.5 hectares, while the farms purchasing tractors ranged from 12.9 to 21.5 hectares.[23]. In the light of the data presented by Feldman and Fournier on land distribution in the Terai, this places the pumpset beneficiaries in the 15 per cent of the households with the largest holdings, and the tractor beneficiaries in the top 5 per cent.[24] In the second project, the tractor component benefited farmers with holdings of at least 7 hectares, while power tillers were purchased by farmers with between 2 and 6 hectares.[25]

The third loan shows little change in the distribution of project benefits. Although the appraisal report proposed to distribute two thirds of the irrigation equipment to farmers with holdings below 2.68 hectares, in fact only 5 per cent of the ADBN loans went to small farmers' groups through agricultural cooperatives, while the rest of the loans went to individual farmers.[26] According to the PPAR, the ADBN was reluctant to lend to small farmers' groups and cooperatives due to weaknesses in their organisation and management.[27] Consequently the average size of the farms receiving loans under the project was 6.15 hectares. The PPAR concludes that the project did not contribute to social equity, and points out some questionable practices under the loan:

> Even though small farmers with land holdings of 0.67 ha could now obtain tubewell loans from ADBN, large farmers maintain a more advantageous position because they can obtain as many pumpsets and tubewells as they need as long as they are able to meet the ADBN's lending conditions in terms of collateral and farm size requirement. No restriction on the number of tubewells or pumpsets is imposed by ADBN for its loans to individual

farmers. The large farmers clearly took advantage of the subsidised farm credits available to them. The [post-evaluation mission] was informed that some large farmers acquired four to five pumpsets and 10 to 12 tubewells under the Project.[28]

While data was not available on the impact of the fourth credit project, the experience of the first three gives an indication of how loans for power tillers, pumpsets and tubewells are distributed, while the appraisal report notes that the biogas plants 'would be affordable mainly by relatively well-off farmers'.[29]

## Fisheries Mechanisation in Sri Lanka

The mechanisation of marine fisheries in Sri Lanka is a typical example of a fisheries development programme supported by the ADB, and of an equipment-oriented lending programme designed to increase rural production, but with no apparent impact on either employment or income distribution.[30] In the period being examined, Sri Lanka's fisheries received a total of $17.215 million in Bank assistance, consisting of $615 000 in technical assistance grants and two concessional loans, one of $3.1 million in 1972 and a second of $13.5 million in 1981. The two loans were channelled through two state-owned banks, to provide funds for onlending for the procurement of fishing vessels, engines and equipment under the government's programme for the mechanisation of fishery. Originally the funds were intended to be onlent to fisheries cooperative societies, but due to the cooperatives' organisational and financial weakness, virtually all loans under the government programme, and all those funded by ADB loans, have been made to private fishermen. A major point on which both the Bank and the government have been criticised was consequently the lack of institutional and technical support to the cooperative societies.[31]

Sri Lanka's fisheries modernisation programme was set in motion by the government in 1958, and was based on the mechanisation of traditional craft and the introduction of a four-man, 3.5-ton mechanised craft to replace the sailing boats traditionally used for deep-sea fishing. Since the introduction of the programme, changes have been made in both the size of motors used and in some of the equipment, but essentially the programme has continued to be built around expanding the commercial use of the 3.5-ton mechanised boats.[32] The programme has received substantial foreign assistance, particu-

larly from the FAO, the World Bank and the ADB. The first
ADB loan was used to buy 200 3.5-ton vessels, 30 11-ton vessels,
maintenance equipment, and some transportation and refrigeration
equipment to facilitate marketing.[33] Based on the first project's
negative experience with the larger vessels, the second loan placed
more emphasis on the 3.5-ton boats, and provided credit for the
purchase of 400 complete vessels, 200 replacement engines, sails and
other equipment. It also introduced 50 boats of a new 12-ton class.

The principal impact of fisheries mechanisation has been an increase
in fish production. On the other hand, the programme has had little
impact on either unemployment or poverty. According to Alexander
the employment opportunities created by the programme have been
negligible compared with the expanding work force in fishing villages.
Alexander also concludes that mechanisation has resulted in an
expansion and restructuring of the élite owning and operating fishing
vessels, but has not been of any significant benefit to peasants in
fishing villages. This he attributes mainly to the fact that, due to
the greatly increased expenditures and credit requirements which
mechanisation entails and the terms and collateral requirement of
government and private credit, only the relatively prosperous can
afford to invest in mechanisation.[34]

The above conclusions are confirmed by the information available
on the two ADB projects. Marine fish production has increased
substantially during the same period as the fishing fleet was mechanised, and has enabled the country to maintain its level of consumption
while reducing its dependence on fish imports, although some doubts
have been raised about the extent to which this can be directly
attributed to mechanisation. The catch of the vessels funded under
the first ADB project, for example, was much lower than appraisal
estimates, and there is evidence that extensive fleet mechanisation in
the late 1970s was not accompanied by a corresponding increase in
production.[35] Alexander attributes problems in raising production to
the fact that the mechanisation programme assumed that both
fishermen's values and attitudes and the available supportive facilities
would be similar to those in an urban community, although in practice
this was usually not the case.[36] ADB reports, again, have drawn
attention to the fact that the utilisation of the boats was less intensive
than planned, which is related to factors such as fishermen's reluctance
to undertake the multi-day fishing trips that mechanised vessels make
possible.[37]

The programme's impact on employment has been very limited.

Each boat employs four men, in addition to which it has been estimated that for every five active fishermen one person is employed in related occupations, including boat repair and marketing.[38] In the light of these figures, the entire programme, which distributed an average of 240 vessels a year between 1977 and 1982, has created about 1150 jobs annually. The 3.5-ton vessel component of the first ADB loan created about 960 jobs, while the corresponding component in the second project can be estimated to have created about 1920. According to Alexander even if the programme were considerably larger, it would 'do little to alleviate the very high rates of unemployment in the fishing villages'.[39] Alexander also points out a tendency for the relatively highly paid jobs on mechanised boats to be concentrated within the boat-owning families.[40]

Finally, data gathered by the ADB indicate that the fisheries mechanisation projects have expanded and strengthened local economic élites. According to an impact evaluation study by the Bank, the main beneficiaries of the projects are the skippers and owners of the new vessels, the three crew members, and their families.[41] Subloans for the purchase of boats were not made to cooperative societies as planned, but directly to either skipper/owners or shore-bound owners who hired skippers to operate the boats, and consequently the owners and skippers were the principal beneficiaries of raised incomes. As the evaluation report puts it, the estimated annual income of $1220–2440 from a boat 'would put new shore-bound owners in the upper middle class nationally' while skipper/owners earned considerably more.[42] The average earnings of the crew members, again, were estimated at between $537 and $732 per annum, which puts them significantly above Sri Lanka's per capita income.

## ROAD CONSTRUCTION AND IMPROVEMENT

As the development policies of the donor governments in the early 1970s began to place more emphasis on combating poverty and promoting income distribution and employment, civil construction and rural works programmes received increasing attention as a means of achieving these objectives.[43] Labour-intensive public works schemes have played an important role in the rural development strategies of the World Bank, the ILO and various bilateral programmes, including those of the Swedish International Development Authority (SIDA), USAID and the Netherlands, and have to a varying degree been incorporated in the projects of these agencies. Similarly both the second agricultural survey and the Bank's policy paper outlining priority areas for the rural sector in the 1980s stress the significance of labour-intensive public works as a means of providing off-farm employment and additional income for the rural poor, and as an integral part of the Bank's rural development policy.

The literature on the role of roads in development programmes suggests that two issues are of particular importance: the selection criteria used in deciding which roads to invest in, and the type of construction technology used.[44] The criteria used in deciding whether to invest in expressways, primary or secondary roads, or rural roads, and the people served by these roads, obviously reflect the development objectives of a road investment programme. These objectives are also reflected in the specific factors included in the economic analysis carried out during project preparation and appraisal. Howe has classified the evolution of quantitative selection criteria for road investment into four broad phases: the use of a purely engineering assessment of road needs, simple cost-benefit analysis, the introduction of generalised socio-economic indicators as preselection criteria prior to the actual cost-benefit analysis, and the introduction into the decision-making framework of income distribution as an explicit social consideration.[45]

Within this classification, the second stage, simple cost-benefit analysis, has been widely applied since the 1960s, in the form of various methods of calculating the economic savings to road users resulting from the construction or improvement of a road. The third stage entails recognising that different roads serve different socio-economic purposes, and considering the number, socio-economic position and economic activity of the people using a road prior to the application of purely economic criteria. As an example, Howe cites the fact that in expanding its lending to include rural roads and feeder roads the World Bank included agricultural production as a separate economic criterion, and took indirect note of various other factors, including employment generation. Finally, as an example of the relatively advanced institutionalisation of income distribution as a selection criterion, Howe refers to the IDB, which in 1979 introduced a requirement that a low-income level be identified for each borrowing country, and that, in addition to the economic, financial and technical criteria usually applied to projects, the IDB must ensure that 50 per cent of its resources benefit such low-income individuals.[46]

The type of construction technology used on road projects is closely related to the selection criteria, and to the projects' impact on employment and incomes. In broad terms road construction technology can be either capital-intensive, using mainly machines and equipment, or labour-intensive, using mainly unskilled and semi-skilled labour, hand tools, relatively simple equipment and draft animals, and only using machines for selected operations. Extensive research by the World Bank and the ILO has demonstrated that labour-intensive methods are technically feasible for the construction of gravel-surfaced feeder roads, and are, when properly implemented, economically competitive within the wage levels of low-income and many middle-income developing countries. Of the ADB countries, these include not only group A countries but group B countries such as Indonesia, the Philippines and Thailand.[47] While producing roads of a technically acceptable standard, the principal advantages of labour-intensive methods are that they generate significant employment for unskilled labour, channel public expenditure directly to raising the incomes of low-income groups, save foreign exchange otherwise spent on importing machines and fuel, and at low wage levels result in financial savings.[48] However, due to the strong influence of construction technology developed for high-wage industrial economies, particularly the Southeast Asian countries have adopted capital-intensive methods even where labour-intensive methods would be feasible.

Approximately three quarters of the roads built or improved by the ADB are funded through road construction and improvement loans planned and administered by the Infrastructure Department's Airports and Highways Division, while about one quarter are incorporated in irrigation or integrated rural development loans. In the following, only the road projects of the Airports and Highways Division are examined. Between 1968 and 1983 such projects accounted for $998.35 million or 7.4 per cent of all Bank lending. The main features of these projects, are outlined in Table 8.3.

As can be seen from the table, the first constraint on the impact of the Bank's road construction loans relates to the fact that over 88 per cent of road lending has been from the Bank's OCR, which are earmarked for the higher income DMCs. Consequently road construction loans have concentrated markedly on the middle-income borrowing countries in East and Southeast Asia, with Indonesia, the Philippines, South Korea and Thailand between them accounting for 74.1 per cent of all ADB lending for roads. In contrast, lending for

Table 8.3 ADB lending for road construction and improvement, 1968–83

| Country | Year(s) of approval | No. of loans | Total amount ($ million) | OCR ($ million) | SFR ($ million) | Per cent | Total kilometres built or improved | Type of roads (kilometres) | | |
|---|---|---|---|---|---|---|---|---|---|---|
| | | | | | | | | Expressways | Primary (national) & secondary (provincial) roads | Feeder roads |
| Afghanistan | 1973 | 1 | 14.90 | – | 14.90 | 1.5 | 266 | – | 266 | – |
| Bangladesh | 1977 | 1 | 15.00 | – | 15.00 | 1.5 | 22 | – | 22 | – |
| Burma | 1983 | 1 | 27.00 | – | 27.00 | 2.7 | 220 | – | 220 | – |
| Indonesia | 1976–82 | 6 | 217.21 | 217.21 | – | 21.8 | 3268 | – | 1829 | 1439 |
| Laos | 1983 | 1 | 8.00 | – | 8.00 | 0.8 | 143 | – | 53 | 90 |
| Malaysia | 1971–82 | 7 | 80.64 | 80.64 | – | 8.1 | 458 | – | 394 | 64 |
| Nepal | 1972–83 | 3 | 32.40 | – | 32.40 | 3.2 | 330 | – | 80 | 250 |
| PNG | 1972–83 | 3 | 37.80 | 28.00 | 9.80 | 3.8 | 406 | – | 406 | – |
| Philippines | 1970–82 | 8 | 203.95 | 203.95 | – | 20.4 | 3178 | – | 1988 | 1190 |
| Singapore | 1972 | 1 | 1.10 | 1.10 | – | 0.1 | – | – | – | – |
| South Korea | 1968–82 | 6 | 181.75 | 181.75 | – | 18.2 | 1415 | 88 | 1327 | – |
| Sri Lanka | 1980 | 1 | 10.00 | – | 10.00 | 1.0 | 158 | – | 158 | – |
| Taiwan | 1968–71 | 1 | 32.00 | 32.00 | – | 3.2 | 43 | 43 | – | – |
| Thailand | 1974–80 | 4 | 136.60 | 136.60 | – | 13.7 | 1486 | 134 | 1352 | – |
| Total | | 46 | 998.35 | 881.25 | 117.10 | 100.0 | 11393 | 265 | 8095 | 3033 |

Source: Compiled from ADB Appraisal Reports, PPARs and Annual Reports.

road construction in the relatively low-income South Asian countries, and Burma and Laos, accounts for only 10.7 per cent of road loans, and has ranged from no projects in Pakistan and one each in Afghanistan, Bangladesh, Burma, Laos and Sri Lanka to three in Nepal. Thus, while the group B and C borrowing countries, with a total of approximately 359 million inhabitants, have benefited from loans for the construction or improvement of 10 254 kilometres of roads, the low-income group A countries, with a total of 355 million inhabitants, have received loans for only 1139 kilometres of roads.

In most countries ADB lending has concentrated on primary and secondary roads, and loans for the extensive construction of feeder roads have only been given to Indonesia, the Philippines and Nepal. In terms of general selection criteria, lending has gradually shifted from expressways and primary roads to a combination of primary and secondary roads as well as rural feeder roads. The shift to roads serving rural areas is reflected in the breakdown of loan approvals by road type, in Table 8.4.[49] From 1968 to 1974 the Bank supported major highways projects and the rehabilitation and improvement of primary roads, such as the North–South freeway and Taipei–Yangmei freeway in Taiwan, the Seoul–Inchon expressway in South Korea, the Hetauda–Narayangarh road in Nepal, and the Bang Na–Pattaya highway in Thailand. Selection was based on heavy traffic volume and the role of the roads in stimulating economic growth in capital cities and major industrial areas.

In 1973–5 the Bank started to supplement the construction of highways and national roads with provincial and feeder roads, and also started to lend for so-called road improvement projects aimed at upgrading existing roads and stimulating economic activity in provincial areas. The first project to include feeder roads was the Tarlac–Santa Rosa road project in the Philippines, which was approved in 1973, and the first road improvement loan, to South Korea, was approved in 1974. The third phase, in which over half of the roads built with Bank loans have been rural roads, can be said to have started in 1982, with the approval of two road projects with substantial feeder road components, in Indonesia and the Philippines, followed in 1983 by feeder road projects in Nepal and Laos.

Until the mid-1970s the Bank's economic analysis of road projects centred around a single economic benefit: savings in vehicle operating costs. In a few instances this was supplemented with calculations of savings in road maintenance costs. Since the late 1970s, as Bank lending expanded to include feeder roads, the calculation of the

Table 8.4 ADB road lending by type of road, 1968–83

| Type of road built/improved | 1968–69 | 1970–71 | 1972–73 | 1974–75 | 1976–77 | 1978–79 | 1980–81 | 1982–83 | Total |
|---|---|---|---|---|---|---|---|---|---|
| Expressways (km) | 30 | 43 | – | 138 | – | 54 | – | – | 265 |
| Primary and secondary roads (km) | – | 232 | 988 | 542 | 1359 | 1239 | 1950 | 1785 | 8095 |
| Feeder roads (km) | – | – | 40 | 64 | 190 | 450 | – | 2289 | 3033 |
| Total kilometres built/improved | 30 | 275 | 1028 | 744 | 1549 | 1743 | 1950 | 4074 | 11393 |
| Total road lending ($ million) | 7.20 | 55.00 | 71.05 | 108.55 | 208.51 | 125.00 | 133.94 | 288.50 | 998.35 |

Source: ADB Appraisal Reports and PPARs.

economic benefits of rural roads has often included incremental agricultural production. Within the four phases of development of selection criteria distinguished by Howe, the ADB has clearly moved from the second to the third stage, from simple cost-benefit analysis to the introduction of rural development as a generalised preselection criterion. Correspondingly it can be assumed that recent road lending is of more direct benefit to people in rural areas. However, compared with the World Bank and USAID, which both lent extensively for rural roads in the 1970s, the ADB has been slow to include feeder roads in its loans. Moreover, as the discussion of road projects in the Philippines demonstrates, there is little indication that the Bank is effectively institutionalising either income distribution or employment as explicit selection criteria.

In terms of technology, ADB road projects have been predominantly capital-intensive, and much less attention has been paid to exploring labour-intensive alternatives than by the World Bank, USAID and other bilateral agencies. This can be attributed to a combination of political and organisational factors. At the political level, it is important to remember that the Bank's two major donors are also the two most important manufacturers of heavy construction equipment and have been instrumental in shaping the Bank's procurement policies and practices. Within the context of the Bank's general selection criteria, the restrictions inherent in the Bank's consultancy, procurement and local cost financing policies have significantly shaped Bank road projects. Initial Bank lending for highways and major national and provincial roads precluded the use of labour-intensive techniques. While the inclusion of feeder roads in Bank projects in principle provided scope for the use of labour-intensive techniques, in practice loan funds have been earmarked almost entirely for the foreign exchange costs of projects, and have been used mainly to import equipment and machines, even in the case of contracts being awarded to domestic contractors.

At the organisational level, the apparent reluctance of the Airports and Highways Division to consider labour-intensive alternatives can be explained by a number of factors, including the complexity of planning and administering labour-intensive projects and their anticipated low disbursement rate, both of which conflict with management's emphasis on annual lending targets, and a general preference by the Bank for projects which accommodate rather than attempt to change prevailing policies of the borrowing governments. While two projects in Bangladesh incorporated labour-intensive techniques, no effort has been made to introduce such methods in the more equipment-oriented Southeast Asian countries. In contrast, both the World Bank and USAID have seen it as their role to advise recipient governments of different alternatives and have developed detailed guides and manuals to assist staff and government officials in planning labour-intensive projects.[50] Appropriate technology was an area of some priority in the ADB between 1977 and 1980, when the Bank published a report on incorporating appropriate technology into its activities and organised several regional seminars on appropriate technology, including one co-sponsored by the ILO on road construction and maintenance. However, these activities had little visible impact on loan planning, and since 1980 the Bank has shown much less interest in the question of technological choice.

## Road Construction in the Philippines

The alternatives for investment in road construction in the Philippines include all of the options outlined in the preceding section. Roads in the Philippines are classified into four groups: national roads, provincial or secondary roads, city and municipal roads, and *barangay* or feeder roads, which serve mainly as farm-to-market roads.[51] In addition, there are numerous lower standard tracks and trails connecting more remote villages and hamlets to the road network. Particularly since the 1970s feeder roads have received increasing priority in government road construction and rural development programmes. This is exemplified by the fact that of the roads built in 1973–7, 18 per cent were concrete, 10 per cent were asphalt, and 72 per cent were gravel.[52]

A number of studies and pilot projects have also demonstrated that the construction of gravel-surfaced feeder roads in the Philippines is both technically and economically feasible using labour-intensive methods. Since this was initially demonstrated in a study and pilot project conducted by the ILO in 1973,[53] the rise in fuel prices has significantly increased the foreign exchange savings potential and cost competitiveness of labour-intensive methods. Government policies have also been open to labour-intensive alternatives. The four-year development plan for fiscal years 1974–7 stressed the generation of employment opportunities in all sectors of the economy, and included a USAID-financed study on the combinations of labour and equipment which would result in maximum labour utilisation without sacrificing quality and efficiency, particularly in public works construction.[54] The following five-year plan, for 1978–82, emphasised that labour-intensive road construction methods should be used 'whenever technically and economically justifiable not only to generate jobs but also to develop local skills and indigenous resources, promote self-reliance, and minimise the depletion of foreign exchange for capital equipment', thus leaving considerable scope for aid agencies to implement labour-intensive projects.[55]

Between 1970 and 1982 the ADB gave the Philippines seven major loans totalling $203.45 million, one technical assistance loan of $0.5 million, and seven technical assistance grants totalling $1.77 million for road construction and improvement. The technical assistance was mainly used to finance feasibility studies for the seven loans, while the loans covered a large share of construction and improvement costs. During this period the ADB shifted its priority from primary roads to a combination of primary and secondary paved roads and feeder roads. The first two road loans were for the construction of two primary roads in Mindanao, the Cotabato–General Santos road and the Iligan–Cagayan de Oro–Butuan road. Four of the five road loans approved between 1973 and 1982 have consisted of combinations of paved roads and feeder roads, while one loan in 1980 was only for primary roads. In 1986 the Bank approved a further loan of $82 million for the fourth road improvement project, to 'rehabilitate and improve national roads and provide detailed engineering for rural roads in several areas of the country'.[56] The basic details of the first seven loans are set out in Table 8.5.

The type of roads selected and the socio-economic groups to benefit from projects are largely determined by the project objectives and the benefits considered in calculating the projects' EIRR. In terms of objectives, the initial road loans were concerned with increasing the country's transport capacity, while more recent projects have also included the objective of increasing agricultural production. The economic analysis of the initial projects was based on savings in vehicle operating costs and, to a lesser degree, on savings in road maintenance costs. In the Mindanao secondary and feeder roads project and the third road improvement project, which include 450 and 510 kilometres of feeder roads respectively, the net value added of the incremental agricultural production was introduced as a separate criterion for those rural roads expected to enhance agricultural production significantly. No projects included either income distribution or employment as specific selection criteria, although the

*Table 8.5* ADB road construction loans to the Philippines, 1970–82.

| Year | Project* | Loan amount ($ million) | Local cost financing ($ million) | Economic analysis | | | | Type of roads (kms) | | | | Nationality of consultants (& associates) |
| --- | --- | --- | --- | --- | --- | --- | --- | --- | --- | --- | --- | --- |
| | | | | Vehicle operating costs | Road maintenance savings | Increased agricultural production | Employment or income distribution mentioned in appraisal | Total kms built or improved | Primary | Secondary | Feeder | |
| 1970 | Cotabato–General Santos road project | 10.60 | – | × | – | – | – | 209 | 209 | – | – | US (US) |
| 1972 | Iligan–Cagayan de Oro–Butuan road project | 22.25 | – | × | × | – | – | 310 | 310 | – | – | Italy (Phil) |
| 1973 | Tarlac–Santa Rosa & feeder roads project | 3.60 | – | × | – | – | – | 81 | 41 | – | 40 | US (Phil) |
| 1977 | Road improvement project | 45.00 | 4.00 | × | × | × | – | 517 | 327 | – | 190 | US, France (US, Denmark, Phil) |
| 1978 | Mindanao secondary & feeder roads project | 24.00 | 4.00 | – | – | – | – | 558 | – | 108 | 450 | Japan (US, Phil) |
| 1980 | Second road improvement project | 30.00 | 5.00 | × | – | – | – | 540 | 540 | – | – | US, Denmark, Phil |
| 1982 | Third road improvement project | 68.00 | 12.00 | × | × | × | × | 963 | 453 | – | 510 | US, Denmark, Phil |
| *Total* | | 203.45 | 25.00 | 7 | 4 | 2 | 3 | 3178 | 1880 | 108 | 1190 | |

* A technical assistance loan of $0.5 million in 1975 for the feasibility study for the Mindanao secondary and feeder roads project is not included.

*Source:* Compiled from ADB *Appraisal Reports*, *PCRs* and *PPARs*.

appraisal reports of both the above projects contained brief discussions of the projects' envisaged impact on employment (see Table 8.5).

The projects were all implemented using capital-intensive technology, which can be attributed to a combination of factors, including the Bank's general selection criteria, the project consultants and contractors and the relatively low level of local cost financing. The consultants hired to prepare the feasibility studies play a key role in determining both the roads selected and the type of technology used, within the framework of Bank and government priorities. It is significant that in the Philippines, the feasibility studies for ADB road projects were prepared by foreign consultants, mainly from the US. The fact that the initial loans were entirely for foreign exchange costs, while only about 17 per cent of more recent loans have been earmarked for local costs, has also limited the extent to which labour-intensive methods could, even in theory, have been considered. In the projects for which details of the contractors are available, it is also interesting to note that construction was virtually entirely carried out by contractors from South Korea and the US.[57]

In terms of impact, the information available indicates that the Bank's road projects have been relatively successful in increasing transport capacity, reducing transport costs and facilitating economic growth, to the benefit of industries, agricultural producers and vehicle operators. On the other hand, the projects' impact on employment has been limited and their impact on income distribution negligible. The PPARs of the first two projects suggest that the main socio-economic impact of the project roads was to stimulate industrial and agricultural production.[58] The impact of the Tarlac–Santa Rosa project, again, was mainly agricultural. According to the PPAR, the project facilitated the transportation of agricultural produce to market, and of agricultural inputs to farms, thus stimulating rice and vegetable production; the project also stimulated other economic activities, and, as a secondary benefit, provided rural inhabitants with better access to public services.[59]

As with irrigation projects, road projects' potential impact on employment is twofold. Indirectly, roads create employment by enabling agricultural and industrial production to expand, and directly, roads can be used to create jobs through labour-intensive construction. The fact that no data is available about road projects' impact on employment is in itself indicative of the low priority accorded by the Bank to the issue. In general it can be assumed that projects have indirectly increased employment, but that due to their capital-intensive technology, their direct job-creating impact has been low. The question of indirect employment creation through agricultural production is only discussed in two more recent appraisal reports, and although the reports also mention the creation of off-farm employment, no consideration is given to labour-intensive technology.[60]

Due to the paucity of data it is also difficult to assess precisely the projects' impact on incomes. However, it is clear that the main beneficiaries of new and improved roads are vehicle operators and road users, mainly industrial and agricultural producers, while marginal and subsistence farmers and landless labourers will derive little benefit from roads. Bank PPARs suggest that while primary roads linking areas of agricultural and industrial production with cities and ports tend to benefit large-scale producers, feeder road projects benefit both large- and small-scale rural producers. The PPAR of the Cotabato–General Santos project emphasises the road's role mainly from the point of view of extractive production:

> The Project area is predominantly agricultural. It has vast areas of rich soil with great potential for agricultural development. The area traversed by the Project road produces bananas for export and a huge pineapple plantation has been developed by Dole Philippines, Inc. Timber, rice and coconuts are also produced in the area. An improved transportation facility was therefore vital for the continued growth of agriculture and the Project provided a link with the two seaports. Agricultural products for both domestic consumption and export can now be transported with ease.[61]

The Iligan–Cagayan de Oro–Butuan road, again, benefited both agricultural producers and industries in the road area.[62] The appraisal of a primary road project approved in 1980 indicates that the Bank expects vehicle operators, producers and middlemen to benefit from the roads, but that the benefit to small-scale farmers will depend on the degree to which they become integrated in the market economy:

> Vehicle operators will be the most immediate beneficiaries of reduced operating costs on the Project roads. Since the road transport industry consists of a large number of owner-operators and companies which operate on a small scale, the benefits to the industry will be widely distributed. It can be reasonably assumed, that improvements of operating conditions will benefit users in the form of more frequent and more reliable transport services. Small-scale farmers are also expected to benefit if they can be induced to participate in the market economy through sale of agricultural surplus. It is the tradition of rural areas of the Philippines to

rely on the services of middlemen to purchase surplus produce and arrange for transport. It is likely that surplus production will be encouraged if purchasing agents will penetrate further into the countryside because of easier and cheaper transport for at least part of the way between farms and marketing centers.[63]

While feeder roads more directly benefit rural areas, legitimate doubts can be raised about their impact on income distribution. An evaluation of USAID-funded rural road projects in the Philippines indicates that the distribution of benefits ranged from relatively equal to strongly biased in favour of large producers.[64] The question of income distribution was discussed in the appraisal of only one ADB road loan to the Philippines, the 1978 Mindanao secondary and feeder roads project. However, a closer examination of the appraisal report seriously calls into question its optimistic assessment of the project's impact on income distribution:

Although not quantifiable because of lack of reliable income distribution data in the Project area, it can be reasonably expected that the Project will have some favourable income distribution effect. A major part of quantified economic benefits in the form of net value added on incremental agricultural production is expected to go directly to farm producers thus raising their standards of living, which on the average are lower than in urban areas. In terms of numbers, a significant portion of farm producers would be small and average farmers. Farm households having average or below average holdings (5 ha. or less) constitute about 75–80 per cent of total farm households in South Cotabato and in Misamis Oriental provinces, although their share in the cultivated area was only about 40–45 per cent. Large and medium farmers will also benefit though it is expected that these farmers will provide greatly increased employment opportunties to farm labor, who belong to the poorest section of the rural community. Farm labor will also additionally benefit, especially in Northern Mindanao, as improved roads will provide them with better and easier (and probably less costly) access to off-farm employment during the off-season months in nearby towns. Furthermore, the Project is expected to provide job opportunities to about 2,000 people during the Project implementation period.[65]

The above quotation is correct in noting that the project will favour rural households over urban, but it is difficult to agree with the rest of its logic. In fact, the above figures suggest a substantial bias in favour of large holdings. Assuming that all farmers are able to increase production equally, which is in itself a generous assumption, it can be reasoned that of the project's principal quantified benefit, the net value added on incremental production, the 20–25 per cent of farmers with above average holdings will account for 55–60 per cent while the 75–80 per cent of farmers with average or below average holdings will account for only 40–45 per cent. Landless labourers will benefit only through increased job opportunities on large farms, and from improved access to employment in towns, although it should be pointed out that the latter is a benefit which does not accrue exclusively to landless labourers. To assume from this that the project roads will have a favourable impact on income distribution is, to say the least, tenuous.

In comparing ADB road lending with the different alternatives for road investment in the Philippines, it is the contention of this study that while the ADB's strong focus on national and provincial roads, using capital-intensive technology, is probably justified in terms of generating a high EIRR, it would have been possible to identify feeder roads serving low-income rural areas, and to consider labour-intensive alternatives, which would have significantly increased the projects' impact on rural incomes and employment. The Bank's lending pattern seems largely to be a reflection of the low priority given by the Bank's Airports and Highways Division to rural roads and labour-intensive techniques. This, in turn, is connected with the Bank's practice of using consultants and contractors mainly from developed countries, the limited funds for local cost financing, and the strong push by management for departments to meet high lending targets. While conclusions of this nature, comparing actual programmes with counter-factual alternatives, must remain speculative, it is significant that the proportion of cement and asphalt roads built in the Philippines with ADB loans is considerably higher than that of overall government spending on roads. A brief comparison with recent USAID and World Bank road projects in the Philippines also serves to demonstrate how other aid agencies have directed a larger proportion of their capital assistance to feeder roads and labour-intensive technology.

USAID lending to the Philippines for road construction and improvement, particularly since the 1970s, has focused on feeder roads, lower standard penetration roads, and rural tracks and trails, with the specific objective of benefiting rural low-income groups. In 1974 and 1978 USAID gave the Philippines two loans totalling $39 million to support the government's rural road programme. The loans were used in their entirety for the construction and improvement of 794 kilometres of feeder and penetration roads and related bridges, with the selection criterion that each road should form 'all or part of a continuous system linking a farm area with a nearby farm or market'.[66] An evaluation of the two projects indicated that the beneficiaries were not limited to the rural poor, and criticised the projects' capital-intensive construction techniques.[67] However, compared with the ADB projects, the USAID-funded roads were aimed more directly at low-income beneficiaries in rural areas. In the 1980s, the USAID programme in the Philippines has taken significant steps to introduce labour-intensive construction technology, first with a pilot project in 1982 and then by using labour-intensive methods in a project to build and upgrade rural tracks and trails.[68]

In a similar manner the World Bank's lending for roads in the Philippines since the mid-1970s has concentrated on feeder roads and has, albeit on a limited scale, introduced labour-intensive methods. The IDA-financed Philippine rural infrastructure project I, which was approved in 1978, included both irrigation and road components, of which the latter consisted of the construction and improvement of 1160 kilometres of feeder roads. Of these, 57 kilometres were built using labour-intensive techniques. This has been followed by the incorporation of labour-intensive construction on a much broader scale in World Bank road projects in the mid-1980s. Thus, in terms of both selection criteria and technology, the World Bank and USAID have taken steps to introduce income distribution and employment criteria into their road projects in the Philippines which have not been matched by the ADB. The similarity of the political parameters of the three programmes suggested that the explanation for the difference is predominantly organisational.

# 9  Conclusion

## The ADB and Rural Development

Betweeen 1967 and the mid-1980s the ADB's development policy for the rural sector, as reflected in the two Asian agricultural surveys prepared by the Bank and the resulting policy papers, underwent fundamental changes. The Bank's initial policy of modernising agricultural production, mainly through investment in irrigation, agricultural inputs and seed varieties, was thoroughly revised in the mid-1970s, leading to the emergence of a rural development policy emphasising that increasing production should be accompanied by substantial measures to create employment and promote a more equal distribution of rural incomes, and drawing some attention to the question of land reform. Within the broad classification of rural development strategies suggested by Griffin, and to the extent that such a classification for national policies can be applied to an international agency, the ADB moved from a technocratic strategy to one with considerable elements of reformism.[1] The policy change can largely be explained in the light of the 1972–4 food crisis and changes in the rural development policies of the World Bank and the international donor community, and received particularly strong endorsement from the Bank's smaller donors and the Carter administration in the US.

At the same time, there is evidence of considerable Japanese influence on the Bank's rural development policy, derived from Japan's concern with its food security and emphasising the need to increase foodgrain production in Southeast Asia, mainly through investment in irrigation. Concrete indicators of this influence include the central role played by Japan in initiating the first *Asian Agricultural Survey*, in setting up the ASF and, later, the ADF, and in promoting its proposal for large-scale investment in Asian irrigation through various channels, including the Trilateral Commission and the ADB. The irrigation-based Japanese model for agricultural development shaped the approach to Asian agriculture set out in the first survey in 1968, and there is evidence that it has continued to influence thinking in the Bank into the 1980s. Particularly in that the main objective of the Japanese approach is increasing agricultural production, it has detracted from the degree of emphasis placed by the Bank on a more directly poverty-oriented approach.

170

At the level of operational policies and practices, the changes which it can be argued are required for the effective implementation of the Bank's policy change are less evident and have been relatively cautious and slow, whether measured against recommendations made in the Bank's own policy reports, particularly the second agricultural survey, the sector paper on agriculture and rural development, and the more recent study on the Bank's operational priorities for the 1980s,[2] or the steps taken by the World Bank and a number of other aid agencies toward the implementation of their rural development policies. The Bank has been slow to expand the proportion of loans available for financing local costs, has been reluctant to implement preferential margins for procurements from developing countries to the same extent as other international development agencies, and has not taken effective policy steps to promote consultants from the borrowing countries or incorporate local-level expertise into projects. The ADB's allocation of lending by country is more or less in line with that of the other multilateral banks. Country allocation of OCR loans has concentrated on the middle-income borrowing countries, to a certain degree reflecting the political preferences of Japan and the US, while ADF lending for low-income countries has been relatively low, due to funding constraints.

The share of Bank lending for agriculture and rural development has increased steadily, but the Bank has been very cautious in changing its project modalities. Since the mid-1970s, project identification criteria have placed greater emphasis on the rural sector, but projects have continued to focus on increasing agricultural production and have taken few steps to incorporate poverty alleviation, employment creation or income distribution. In the three subsectors in which projects were examined, lending increased substantially in both real and relative terms. Projects also underwent a certain amount of adjustment. In irrigation projects in Indonesia and the Philippines, the Bank has increased the number of supporting components, mainly with a view to enhancing project efficiency. In its agricultural credit loans to Nepal and fisheries loans to Sri Lanka, the ADB indicated a concern with channelling more credit to small producers, but did not incorporate appropriate institutional measures to accomplish this in its projects. In road construction, the Bank has moved from funding highways and primary roads to a combination of main roads and rural feeder roads.

On the other hand, there is relatively little indication of broader project innovation or a significant shift to new types of projects corresponding to the objectives of the Bank's rural development policy. Chapters 7 and 8 touched on three such project types: irrigation-based, integrated rural development projects as opposed to large-scale, construction-based irrigation projects; small-farmer credit projects as opposed to agricultural credit loans to national development finance institutions for direct onlending; and labour-intensive as opposed to capital-intensive rural road projects. Since the mid-1970s the Bank has prepared and implemented integrated rural development projects on a limited scale, but there is no evidence of any significant degree of ADB involvement in either of the other two innovative project types.

Project impact was examined in the light of three objectives: agricultural production, employment and income distribution – although it should be noted that the latter two were only adopted as rural sector policy objectives by the Bank in the 1970s. The general conclusion to which the groups of projects examined point is that ADB projects have in many instances succeeded in promoting agricultural production, but have had only limited impact on employment and no significant impact on income distribution. In fact, by improving the productive capacity of relatively high income groups, available data indicate that many projects had a tendency to enhance rather than reduce rural income disparities. Recent adjustments in project content have somewhat broadened the range of project beneficiaries, but projects have continued to be built around the objective of increasing production and have only in a few isolated instances included specific measures to increase off-farm employment or income distribution. Consequently, while the benefit to some small farmers has increased, projects have had very little impact on the most depressed segments of the rural population, which remain outside mainstream production, namely farmers in rain-fed areas, marginal and subsistence farmers, and landless labourers.

Explanations for this gap between the Bank's policy and its operational practice were discussed at two levels, the political and the organisational, based on the premise that a distinction can be made between the respective roles of these two groups of factors in determining Bank lending for rural development. Chapters 3, 4 and 6 clearly indicated the dominant role played by donor policies and interests in shaping the Bank's development policy and operational policies. Chapers 5, 7 and 8, again, demonstrated the extent to which various organisational factors – particularly the concern of the Bank's management with fund-channelling and the resulting quantitative

definition of organisational output in terms of annual lending targets –
have influenced subsectoral lending policies and project formulation
and content.

The allocation of lending by country, and the Bank's apparent
reluctance to modify its procurement, consultancy and local cost
financing policies are largely a reflection of the political and economic
concerns of the Bank's donors, but to a certain extent also reflect
administrative considerations. While projects are formulated within
the framework of operational policies, there is also a close relationship
between project content and organisational factors. Management's
concern with annual lending targets, disbursement targets and administrative efficiency has contributed to streamlining project planning
and implementation, but in the three subsectors examined there
were also indications that it has enhanced tendencies in projects
departments towards the preparation of large projects, easily manageable projects, relatively rapidly disbursing projects, projects with a
short cycle, 'repeater' projects and projects with a relatively uniform
design. There are clear areas of conflict between these tendencies
and the changes in the Bank's rural development policy, and to
this extent they have worked against innovation and change. This
conclusion can also be examined in the context of the discussion on
the relationship between the quantity and the quality of aid.[3] Broadly,
this study suggests that the ADB's concern with the quantity of
lending, defined in terms of fund-channelling, has detracted from the
quality of lending, defined in terms of developmental effectiveness,
or in terms of the ability of project formulation and implementation
to serve as an effective vehicle for changing development policies.

Constraints on the Bank's rural development projects are also
evident in the policies of the borrowing governments and in socio-
economic conditions at the field level, although these are largely
beyond the Bank's direct control. The virtual exclusion of land reform
from official Bank policy documents and from lending programmes
can be attributed mainly to the policies of the borrowing governments,
as exemplified by the lack of success in the implementation of land
reform on Bank-financed irrigation projects in the Philippines. The
fact that the rural development policies of the DMCs have not always
been translated into budget allocations and effective development
programmes has also presented an obstacle to the redirecting of Bank
lending. In Nepal, for example, the use of ADB loan funds was
constrained by the lending policies of the ADBN, which favour large
farmers and do not include lending for the purchase of land. At the

field level, the impact of most projects has been constrained by the bias inherent in production-oriented projects in favour of relatively large landowners and producers, and by the inability of the lowest income groups to take advantage of project benefits.

On the other hand, compared with the leading role assumed by the World Bank in rural development and its active role in shaping and changing its borrowers' rural sector policies, the ADB has not taken strong measures to encourage its borrowers to adopt poverty-oriented policies. This can partly be attributed to the cautious approach of the Bank's first three presidents to sensitive policy issues, but the Bank's active support in the 1980s for private-sector oriented policy changes clearly indicates that the question of the type of policies the Bank encourages its borrowers to adopt is also political.

In the context of the literature on aid agencies and development banks, the conclusions of this study on the content and impact of ADB lending support some of the conclusions of more vehement critics such as Payer about the political orientation of aid.[4] At the same time, the study supports many of the specific conclusions of more moderately critical studies and evaluations regarding the role of organisational factors.[5] The general conclusion is that development policy and operational policies are formulated within a political framework, but that projects are formulated in an organisational context, and that many of the constraints on project change are organisational. While the change in the Bank's rural development policy reflects a fundamental shift in the international aid community's perception of the problems of the rural sector, the limited degree of innovation and change in ADB projects has significantly impaired the Bank's ability to implement the policy change, and has confined the Bank to a very conventional approach at the project level. This lends credence to the case made by Rondinelli for a much more flexible and innovative approach to project planning.[6]

## The Prospects for Change

The practical implications of this study can also be discussed at both the political and organisational levels. To increase the developmental effectiveness of the ADB's rural lending, this study has pointed to the need for substantial revisions in various operational policies, including increasing the emphasis on operational issues related to poverty alleviation, increasing the flow of funds to the poorest countries, increasing lending for local costs, and revising procurement and consultancy policies. None of these issues are new to the discussion on the role of the multilateral banks,[7] and they have all been raised in various ADB reports, including the second agricultural survey and the study on the Bank's operational priorities for the 1980s.[8] However, they are also to a large extent determined by donor interests, and initially lead us to a discussion of the Bank's political power structure, in particular questions of decision-making, voting power and the financial influence of the member governments.

On many political questions and most of the above operational issues, the broad conflict in the Bank is between donors and borrowers, although in some areas a distinction can also be made between the policies and interests of Japan, the US and the smaller donors. The more limited approach to questions of decision-making and voting power – and the one that has tended to dominate any discussion within the Bank on the redistribution of power – examines the distribution of votes among donors in relation to their financial contributions. In contrast to formal voting power based on OCR subscriptions, the leading role played by Japan and the smaller donors in funding the ADF, and in particular the drop in the US share in the cost-sharing formula, have at different times led the smaller donors to raise the question of increasing their voting power and representation on the board of directors. While minor adjustments in capital subscriptions and voting power have been made, the issue is constrained by the 40 per cent ceiling set on non-regional votes by the Bank's charter.

The question of political influence in development banks has also been discussed from the broader viewpoint of the distribution of influence between donors and borrowers, mainly in response to the developing countries' demands for more control over the banks.[9] In 1979 the Brandt Commission recommended a number of measures to stabilise and depoliticise the flow of multilateral finance to the developing countries, including the proposal that donors abstain from imposing political conditions on the operations of the multilateral banks, and that the borrowing countries be given a greater role in the banks' decision-making and management. The Brandt Commission also put forward for consideration the establishment by the international community of a new 'World Development Fund', based on universal membership and 'in which decision-making is more evenly shared between lenders and borrowers to supplement existing institutions and diversify lending policies and practices'.[10] Subsequent shifts in donor policies, however, have tended to increase rather than reduce the linkage between funding and policy control, as exemplified in 1987 by the efforts of the US to increase its voting power in the IDB and Japan's push for more votes in the ADB, and highlight the difficulty of approaching operational reform through a reform of political power structures.

Measures to increase the developmental effectiveness of ADB lending can be discussed more fruitfully at the organisational level. This study has indicated the substantial gap between the ADB's rural development policy and the ability of projects effectively to implement this policy. With a view to enhancing the effectiveness of the Bank's rural lending, it has been argued that Bank projects should focus on a broader range of policy objectives than just agricultural production, and that to achieve these objectives steps should be taken to develop and implement appropriate technical, administrative and operational solutions, with greater emphasis on change and innovation at the project level. Two organisational issues are of particular importance: the definition of organisational output and the project formulation process.

The definition of organisational output adopted by successive ADB presidents has concentrated on quantitative targets related to different aspects of the Bank's fund-channelling cycle, initially to the Bank's international standing and credit rating, and more recently to loan approvals and disbursements. Obviously an appropriate balance needs to be struck between management objectives connected with the Bank's ability to lend money, which is its principal means of action, and the developmental content of loan projects. However, this study indicates that the ADB has tended to emphasise the former, to the detriment of the latter, and that there is considerable scope for the Bank to increase the priority given to the developmental aspects of its outputs. As the recent report commissioned by the Development Committee Task Force on Concessional Flows notes, the problem can be tackled either by 'weakening the effect of quantity incentives or strengthening the quality incentives'.[11]

Ideally management targets and incentives related to the organisational output of projects departments and staff should be tied to the achievement of the objectives of the Bank's development policies. Objective achievement, however, is documented at the end of the project cycle, mainly in connection with the PCR and PPAR. Due to the length of the project cycle and, among other things, staff turnover, relating regular managerial assessment of organisational output directly to development objective achievement is therefore not practicable. However, there is significant scope for linking definitions of the Bank's output – whether quantitative or qualitative – to an assessment of the identification, preparation and appraisal stages of a project's anticipated development impact, in terms not only of the production increases reflected in the EIRR, but, for example, employment, the distribution of project benefits, and specific target groups. Correspondingly, the possibilities for expanding the Bank's project identification criteria and economic analysis methodology could, once again, be reconsidered.

The emphasis placed by McNamara in the 1970s on the quantification in World Bank appraisals of the small farmers and rural poor expected to benefit from a project was criticised on a number of counts, including the difficulty of precisely defining or verifying such figures. It was nevertheless significant in providing departments and staff with an incentive to define their output in terms of development objectives rather than fund-channelling. Much the same can be said of the IDB's requirement that projects should be planned so that at least a set proportion of the beneficiaries fall below a precisely defined income level. The IDB's programme for financing small projects is also an interesting initiative to overcome the shortcomings of large-scale lending and provide funds directly to target groups without ready access to credit.

A study on the future role of the World Bank in rural development, supported jointly by the Inter-American Foundation and the World Bank, draws conclusions which might also be relevant to the ADB. Broadly, the study suggests that the World Bank should move from 'poverty lending' to lending for 'grassroots development', by creating linkages between its large-scale rural development projects and small-scale programmes in borrowing countries. Specific measures recommended by the study include that the World Bank develop new ways to work directly with grassroots level non-governmental organisations, establish a small projects fund, and develop a broader range of innovative projects. At the same time the study acknowledges that this approach will require more staff time for project planning and may entail a slower implementation pace for projects.[12]

In contrast to present pressure for ADB staff to meet quantitative lending targets, there is considerable scope for the Bank's management to devise means of assessing the performance of projects divisions in terms of the achievement of the development objectives set out in Bank policy, and for introducing organisational measures to encourage innovation. The current stagnation in demand for ADB loans could be viewed as an opportunity for paying closer attention to questions of project quality, rather than a reason for redoubling efforts to expand annual lending, possibly at the cost of project quality.

Finally, a broader look could be taken at the role of the project formulation process in shaping project content. Significantly more emphasis could be placed on the first three stages of the project cycle (identification, preparation and appraisal) as a means of identifying and giving consideration to a range of investment possibilities and alternative approaches, as opposed to the cycle's more limited function at present of processing projects for board approval. This might be achieved by stressing the importance of the identification stage, and coordination between programme and projects staff in project identification, in contrast to the present division of labour in which identification is primarily the responsibility of country programme staff, with the technical projects departments becoming involved at the preparation stage. In this context it is particularly interesting to note that the 1987 reorganisation of the World Bank combined at the level of country groups the operational management functions which were previously divided between programmes and projects departments.[13] Consideration could also be given to the potential role of decentralisation as a means of increasing the Bank's involvement in and responsiveness to the planning process in the borrowing countries. Ultimately, however, the extent to which project formulation and content can be revised depends on the willingness of the Bank's management to move from its present definition of organisational output in terms of fund-channelling to a notion more directly related to achieving the objectives of development.

# Notes and References

## 1 Introduction

1. The multilateral development banks are generally defined as consisting of the World Bank Group (the IBRD, IDA and IFC), and the three regional development banks, the Inter-American Development Bank (IDB), the African Development Bank (AFDB) and the Asian Development Bank (ADB).
2. World Bank, *The McNamara Years at the World Bank, Major Policy Addresses of Robert S. NcNamara 1968–1981* (Baltimore: The Johns Hopkins University Press, 1981), pp. 231–63.
3. ADB, *Asian Agricultural Survey* (University of Tokyo Press, 1968).
4. ADB, *Rural Asia: Challenge and Opportunity* (New York: Praeger, 1977).
5. ADB, *Agriculture in Asia, Its Performance and Prospects, the Role of ADB in its Development*, A Bank Staff Working Paper, (Revised March 1985), p. 5.
6. Mason E. S., and Asher R. E., *The World Bank Since Bretton Woods* (Washington, D.C.: The Brookings Institution, 1973).
7. Dell S., *The Inter-American Development Bank, A Study in Development Financing* (New York: Praeger, 1972).
8. Amegavie Y. C., *La Banque Africaine de Développement*, (Paris: Editions A. Pedone, 1975), and Fordwor K. D., *The African Development Bank, Problems of International Cooperation*, (Oxford: Pergamon Press, 1981).
9. White J., *Regional Development Banks* (London: Overseas Development Institute, 1970).
10. Krasner S. D., 'Power Structures and Regional Development Banks', *International Organization*, Vol. 35 (Spring 1981) pp. 303–28.
11. Syz J., *International Development Banks* (New York: Oceana Publications, 1974).
12. Reid E., *The Future of the World Bank* (Washington, D.C.: International Bank for Reconstruction and Development, September 1965).
13. Reid E., *Strengthening the World Bank* (Chicago: The Adlai Stevenson Institute, 1973).
14. Tendler J., *Inside Foreign Aid* (Baltimore and London: The Johns Hopkins University Press, 1975).
15. van de Laar A., *The World Bank and the Poor* (The Hague: Martinus Nijhoff Publishing, 1979).
16. Ayres R. L., *Banking on the Poor, The World Bank and World Poverty* (Cambridge and London: The MIT Press, 1984).
17. Hayter T., *Aid as Imperialism* (Harmondsworth: Penguin, 1971), and van de Laar, op. cit. p. 6.
18. For example, Feder E., 'Capitalism's Last-ditch Effort to Save Underdeveloped Agriculture: International Agri-business, the World Bank

179

and the Rural Poor', *Journal of Contemporary Asia*, Vol. 7 (1977) pp. 56–78; Payer C., 'The World Bank and the Small Farmers', *Journal of Peace Research*, Vol. XVI (1979) pp. 243–312; and Lappé F. M., Collins J. and Kinley D., *Aid as Obstacle, Twenty Questions about Our Foreign Aid and the Hungry* (San Francisco: Institute for Food and Development Policy, 1981).

19. Bello W., Kinley D. and Elinson E., *Development Debacle: The World Bank in the Philippines* (San Francisco: Institute for Food and Development Policy, 1982).
20. Payer C., *The World Bank, A Critical Analysis* (New York and London: Monthly Review Press, 1982).
21. Krishnamurti R., *ADB – The Seeding Days* (Manila: ADB Printing Section, 1977).
22. Huang P.-W. Jr., *The Asian Development Bank, Diplomacy and Development in Asia* (New York: Vantage Press, 1975).
23. Watanabe T., *Towards a New Asia, Memoirs of the First President of the Asian Development Bank* (Singapore, 1977).
24. White, op. cit.
25. Tsao J. H., 'The Asian Development Bank as a Political System' (University of Oklahoma: Ph.D. dissertation, 1974).
26. Krasner, op. cit.
27. Yasutomo D. T., *Japan and the Asian Development Bank* (New York: Praeger, 1983).
28. For example Krasner, op. cit., White, op. cit., and Ayres R., 'Breaking the Bank', *Foreign Policy*, No. 43 (Summer 1981), pp. 104–20.
29. Tendler, op. cit.
30. For example Cassen R., 'The Effectiveness of Aid', *Finance and Development* (March 1986) p. 13.
31. Rondinelli D. A., 'International Assistance Policy and Development Project Administration: The Impact of Imperious Rationality', *International Organization*, Vol. 30 (Autumn 1976) pp. 573–605, and *Development Projects as Policy Experiments* (London and New York: Methuen, 1983) particularly pp. 1–22.
32. Ascher W., 'New Development Approaches and the Adaptability of International Agencies: The Case of the World Bank', *International Organization* Vol. 37 (Summer 1983) pp. 415–39.
33. Ayres (1983) op. cit. pp. 51–75.
34. This section has drawn considerably from Heiskanen I. and Martikainen T., 'On Comparative Policy Analysis: Methodological Problems, Theoretical Considerations, and Empirical Applications', *Scandinavian Political Studies*, Vol. 9 (1974) pp. 9–22, and International Labour Office, Bureau of Programming and Management, *Procedures for the Design and Evaluation of ILO Projects*, Volume II, Technical Co-operation (Geneva, June 1979) particularly pp. 2–9.
35. Hirschman A., *Development Projects Observed* (Washington, D.C.: The Brookings Institution, 1967).
36. van de Laar, op. cit. p. 3.
37. Payer (1982) op. cit. and Ayres (1983) op. cit.

38. Llorente R., 'Managing the Implementation of Projects: The ADB Approach', *ADB Quarterly Review* (October 1985) pp. 10–14.
39. ADB, *Notes on Post-Evaluation Activities* (no date given). Until the late 1970s PPARs were called post-evaluation reports.
40. Ibid. p. 2.
41. Payer C., 'Researching the World Bank', in Torrie J. (ed.), *Banking on Poverty, The Global Impact of the IMF and the World Bank* (Toronto: Between the Lines, 1983) pp. 80–8.
42. Road construction is classified by the Bank under transport and communications, but is included in this study because of its significance in rural areas.

## 2 The Asian Development Bank

1. The World Bank, which is formally both a UN specialised agency and a multilateral bank, the International Labour Organisation, with a tripartite decision-making structure including government, employer and worker representatives, and the International Fund for Agricultural Development, with three categories of members (developed countries, oil-exporting developing countries, and other developing countries), are the exceptions.
2. In 1974 ECAFE was renamed the UN Economic and Social Commission for Asia and the Pacific (ESCAP).
3. ADB, *Technical Assistance Activities* (1985) p. 12.
4. Krishnamurti R., *ADB – The Seeding Days* (Manila: ADB Printing Section, 1977) pp. 75–8.
5. Ibid.
6. Ibid. pp. 51–4.
7. Yasutomo D. T., *Japan and the Asian Development Bank* (New York: Praeger, 1983) p. 59.
8. Krishnamurti, op. cit. p. 80.
9. For a discussion of mutual interests and differences in the interests of donors and recipients, see Cassen R., Jolly R., Sewell J. and Wood R. (eds.), *Rich Country Interests and Third World Development* (London and Canberra: Croom Helm, 1984) pp. 7–36.
10. Bowring P., 'A Quiet Revolution', *Far Eastern Economic Review* (19 May 1983) pp. 54–6.
11. Rowley A., 'We'll Do It Our Way', *Far Eastern Economic Review* (14 May 1987) pp. 68–70.
12. ADB, *Agreement Establishing the Asian Development Bank* (4 December 1965–31 January 1966) Article 28.
13. Ibid. Article 31.
14. Ibid. Article 30.
15. Krishnamurti, op. cit. p. 72.
16. Yasutomo, op. cit. pp. 111–13.
17. Krasner S. D., 'Power Structures and Regional Development Banks', *International Organization*, Vol. 35 (Spring 1981) p. 312.

## 3  Donor Policies and Interests

1. For example White J., *Japanese Aid* (London: Overseas Development Institute, 1964) and Dore R., 'Japan and the Third World: Coincidence or Divergence of Interests', in Cassen et al. (eds.) op. cit. pp. 128–55. For a somewhat contrasting view, see Loutfi M. F., *The Net Cost of Japanese Foreign Aid* (New York: Praeger, 1973) pp. 47–67.
2. Statement by the Japanese Governor, ADB, *Summary of Proceedings, Second Annual Meeting of the Board of Governors* (Sydney, 10–12 April 1969) pp. 41–2.
3. Japan External Trade Organization, *Economic Cooperation of Japan* (Tokyo, various issues).
4. Ibid. (Tokyo, 1979) p. 23.
5. Japan External Trade Organization, *White Paper on International Trade* (Tokyo, 1976).
6. Sato E., 'Japan's Role in Asia', *Contemporary Japan*, Vol. XXVIII, (May 1967) pp. 691–8, and Aichi K., 'Japan's Legacy and Destiny of Change', *Foreign Affairs*, Vol. 48 (October 1969) pp. 32–3.
7. Yasutomo D. T., *Japan and the Asian Development Bank* (New York: Praeger, 1983) pp. 30–40, and Huang P.-W., Jr., *The Asian Development Bank, Diplomacy and Development in Asia* (New York: Vantage Press, 1975) pp. 19–23.
8. Rix A., *Japan's Economic Aid, Policy-making and Politics* (London: Croom Helm, 1980) pp. 125–9.
9. White J., *Regional Development Banks* (London: Overseas Development Institute, 1970) p. 80.
10. Statement by the Japanese Alternate Governor, ADB, *Summary of Proceedings, Fifth Annual Meeting of the Board of Governors* (Vienna, 20–22 April 1972) p. 59.
11. Statement by the Japanese Alternate Governor, ADB, *Summary of Proceedings, Eighth Annual Meeting of the Board of Governors* (Manila, 24–26 April 1975) pp. 83–4.
12. Ocampo S., 'An Ice Age for Aid', *Far Eastern Economic Review* (23 April 1982) pp. 74–5, and Bowring P., 'A Borrower Be', *Far Eastern Economic Review* (7 May 1982) pp. 63–4.
13. White, op. cit. p. 80.
14. Ibid.
15. Yasutomo, op. cit. pp. 120–1.
16. Statements by the Japanese Governor, ADB, *Summary of Proceedings, Fifteenth Annual Meeting of the Board of Governors* (Manila, 28–30 April 1982) and *Summary of Proceedings, Sixteenth Annual Meeting of the Board of Governors* (Manila, 4–6 May 1983).
17. Rowley A., 'The Tokyo Initiative', *Far Eastern Economic Review* (7 May 1987) pp. 139–40, and 'We'll Do It Our Way', *Far Eastern Economic Review* (14 May 1987) pp. 68–70.
18. Sanderson F. H., *Japan's Food Prospects and Policies* (Washington, D.C.: The Brookings Institution, 1978) p. 13.
19. Ibid.
20. Kojima K., 'Japan's Role in Asian Agricultural Development', *Japan*

*Quarterly*, Vol. XIV (April–June 1967) pp. 158–64, and Okita S., 'The Proper Approach to Food Policy', *Japan Echo*, Vol. V (1978) pp. 49–57.

21. The notion of 'development import' is discussed in Rix A., 'The Mitsugoro Project: Japanese Aid Policy and Indonesia', *Pacific Affairs*, Vol. 52 (Spring 1979) pp. 42–63.
22. Okita, op. cit. p. 56.
23. Yasutomo, op. cit. p. 106.
24. Sato, op. cit. pp. 694–5.
25. Takita K., 'ADB-ing Agriculture', *Far Eastern Economic Review* (22 December 1966) pp. 593.
26. Watanabe T., 'The Asian Development Bank Starts Functioning', *Contemporary Japan*, Vol. XXVIII (May 1967) p. 701.
27. Takita, op. cit. p. 594.
28. ADB, *Asian Agricultural Survey* (University of Tokyo Press, 1968) p. v.
29. Statement by the Japanese Alternate Governor, ADB, *Summary of Proceedings, First Annual Meeting of the Board of Governors* (Manila, 4–6 April 1968) p. 45.
30. The text of the letter is quoted in Tsao J. H., 'The Asian Development Bank as a Political System' (University of Oklahoma: Ph.D. dissertation, 1974).
31. Yasutomo, op. cit. p. 108.
32. Statement by the Japanese Alternate Governor, ADB, *Summary of Proceedings, Third Annual Meeting of the Board of Governors* (Seoul, 9–11 April 1970) p. 51.
33. Statement by the Japanese Governor, ADB, *Summary of Proceedings, Tenth Annual Meeting of the Board of Governors* (Manila, 21–23 April 1977).
34. Compare United States, Department of the Treasury, *United States Participation in the Multilateral Development Banks in the 1980s* (Washington, D.C., February 1982) pp. 47–57, with Sanford J. E., *U.S. Foreign Policy and Multilateral Development Banks* (Boulder: Westview Press, 1982) pp. 19–40.
35. Ibid. pp. 3 and 48.
36. Ibid. p. 3.
37. Rowley A., 'Ideology Before Need', *Far Eastern Economic Review* (14 February 1985) p. 72.
38. See President Johnson's speech at Johns Hopkins University, *The New York Times* (8 April 1965). The background to US participation in the Bank is discussed by Geyelin P., *Lyndon B. Johnson and the World* (New York: Praeger, 1966) pp. 276–83.
39. Sanford, op. cit. pp. 158–9.
40. United States, Senate, *Hearing Before the Committee on Foreign Relations, Ninety-second Congress, First Session on S. 749 to Authorize United States Contributions to the Special Funds of the Asian Development Bank* (2 April 1971) is representative of the issues raised by Congress regarding ADB appropriations.
41. Statement by the US Governor *ad interim*, ADB, *Summary of Proceedings, Tenth Annual Meeting of the Board of Governors* (Manila, 21–23 April 1977) pp. 177–84.

42. This policy shift was set out in Reagan's speech at the World Bank–IMF meeting in September 1981, *The New York Times* (30 September 1981). Also see Lubar R., 'Reaganizing the Third World', *Fortune* (16 November 1981) pp. 80–90.

43. Statement by the US Governor *ad interim*, ADB, *Summary of Proceedings, Fourteenth Annual Meeting of the Board of Governors* (Honolulu, 30 April–2 May 1981) p. 160.

44. United States, Department of the Treasury, op. cit.

45. Schoultz L., 'Politics, Economics and US Participation in Multilateral Development Banks', *International Organization*, Vol. 36 (Summer 1982) pp. 566–71, and Sanford J. E., 'Restrictions on United States Contributions to Multilateral Development Banks', *Journal of International Law and Economics*, Vol. 15 (1981) pp. 560–73.

46. Clark W., 'Robert McNamara at the World Bank', *Foreign Affairs*, Vol. 60 (Fall 1981) p. 181.

47. Sanford J. and Goodman M., 'Congressional Oversight and the Multilateral Development Banks', *International Organization*, Vol. 29 (Autumn 1975) p. 1058.

48. Schoultz (1982), op. cit. pp. 549–50, and *Human Rights and United States Policy toward Latin America* (Princeton: Princeton University Press, 1981) pp. 296–8.

49. Schoultz (1982), op. cit. p. 559.

50. Ibid. pp. 551–5.

51. *Far Eastern Economic Review* (7 May 1976) p. 86.

52. Schoultz (1982), op. cit. p. 559.

53. United States, Agency for International Development, *U.S. Economic Aid to Thailand: Three Decades of Cooperation* (1983).

54. Statement by the US Governor, ADB, *Summary of Proceedings, Eighth Annual Meeting of the Board of Governors* (Manila, 24–26 April 1975) p. 137.

55. Statement by the US Governor, ADB, *Summary of Proceedings, Ninth Annual Meeting of the Board of Governors* (Jakarta, 22–24 April 1976), p. 153.

56. Statement by the US Governor *ad interim*, ADB, *Summary of Proceedings, Tenth Annual Meeting of the Board of Governors* (Manila, 21–23 April, 1977) pp. 180–1.

57. Ibid.

58. Statement by the US Alternate Governor, ADB, *Summary of Proceedings, Eleventh Annual Meeting of the Board of Governors* (Vienna, 24–26 April, 1978) p. 175.

59. Statement by the US Governor, ADB, *Summary of Proceedings, Twelfth Annual Meeting of the Board of Governors* (Manila, 2–4 May 1979) p. 158

60. United States, Department of the Treasury, op. cit.

61. Farnsworth C., 'Conable's Cautious Approach', *New York Times* (30 September 1986).

62. Harris S., 'Australia's Interests in Third World Development: The Perspective of a Resource Exporter', in Cassen et al. (eds.), op. cit. pp. 157–67.

63. Hoadley J. S., 'Small States as Aid Donors', *International Organization*, Vol. 34 (Winter 1980) pp. 121–37.
64. Ibid.
65. Statement by the Governor for Canada, ADB, *Summary of Proceedings, First Annual Meeting of the Board of Governors* (Manila, 4–6 April 1968) p. 30.
66. Ibid. pp. 30–1. This paragraph is also quoted by White, op. cit. pp. 80–1.
67. For example statement by the Temporary Alternate Governor for the United Kingdom, ADB, *Summary of Proceedings, Third Annual Meeting of the Board of Governors* (Seoul, 9–11 April 1970) p. 70.
68. Statement by the Governor for Finland, ADB, *Summary of Proceedings, Sixth Annual Meeting of the Board of Governors* (Manila, 26–28 April 1973) p. 70.
69. Statements by various Governors, ADB, *Summary of Proceeedings, Eleventh Annual Meeting of the Board of Governors* (Vienna, 24–26 April 1978).
70. Statements by various Governors, ADB, *Summary of Proceedings, Sixth Annual Meeting of the Board of Governors* (Manila, 26–28 April 1973).
71. Statement by the Temporary Alternate Governor for Sweden, ADB, *Summary of Proceedings, Eighth Annual Meeting of the Board of Governors* (Manila, 24–26 April 1975) p. 122.
72. Statement by the Temporary Alternate Governor for Canada, ADB, *Summary of Proceedings, Sixth Annual Meeting of the Board of Governors* (Manila, 26–28 April 1973) pp. 36–7.
73. Statement by the Alternate Governor for Sweden, ibid. p. 82.
74. Statement by the Australian Governor *ad interim*, ADB, *Summary of Proceedings, Seventh Annual Meeting of the Board of Governors* (Kuala Lumpur, 25–27 April 1974) p. 34.
75. Statement by the Temporary Alternate Governor for the Netherlands, ADB, *Summary of Proceedings, Eighth Annual Meeting of the Board of Governors* (Manila, 24–26 April 1975) p. 96.
76. Bowring P., 'A Quiet Revolution', *Far Eastern Economic Review* (19 May 1983) p. 55.

## 4 The Bank's Rural Development Policy

1. ADB, *Asian Agricultural Survey* (University of Tokyo Press, 1968).
2. ADB, *Paths to Progress, Selected Addresses by Takeshi Watanabe* (Manila, 1972) pp. 22–3.
3. ADB, *Asian Agricultural Survey*, op. cit. p. 31.
4. Ibid. p. 30.
5. Yamada N. and Lusanandana B., 'Rice Production in the ADB Region', in ibid. pp. 188–96.
6. Ibid. pp. 32–3.
7. Ibid. p. 89.
8. Ishikawa S., *Agricultural Development Strategies in Asia, Case Studies of the Philippines and Thailand* (ADB, 1970).

9. ADB, *Asian Agricultural Survey*, op. cit. p. 93.
10. Ibid. p. 105.
11. ADB, Board of Directors Meeting, *ADB's Role in Strengthening Agricultural Research in the Region* (22 July 1968).
12. ADB, Board of Directors Meeting, *ADB Operational Policies in the Field of Agriculture – Follow-up to Asian Agricultural Survey* (27 August 1968).
13. ADB, *Regional Seminar on Agriculture, Papers and Proceedings* (Hong Kong, 1969).
14. Schultz T. W., *Transforming Traditional Agriculture* (New Haven and London: Yale University Press, 1964).
15. For example Ohkawa K. and Johnston B. F., 'The Transferability of the Japanese Pattern of Modernizing Traditional Agriculture', in Thorbecke E., (ed.) *The Role of Agriculture in Economic Development* (New York and London, 1969) pp. 277–310.
16. ADB, *Asian Agricultural Survey*, op. cit. pp. 50–1.
17. Takase K. and Kano T., 'Development Strategy of Irrigation and Drainage', in ibid. pp. 518–20.
18. Hsieh S. C., and Ruttan V. W.' 'Environmental, Technological and Institutional Factors in the Growth of Rice Production: Philippines, Thailand and Taiwan', *Food Research Institute Studies*, Vol. VII (Stanford University Press, 1967) pp. 307–431.
19. Takase and Kano, op. cit. pp. 521 and 545.
20. Huntington S. P., *Political Order in Changing Societies* (New Haven and London: Yale University Press, 1968) pp. 380–96.
21. *Far Eastern Economic Review* (1 May 1969) p. 301.
22. Awanohara S., 'A Reprieve for Hungry Asia', *Far Eastern Economic Review* (29 April 1974) pp. 51–6.
23. World Bank, *The McNamara Years at the World Bank, Major Policy Addresses of Robert S. McNamara 1968–1981* (Baltimore: The Johns Hopkins University Press, 1981) pp. 136–67.
24. Ibid. pp. 171–89 and 208–29.
25. World Bank, *World Bank Operations, Sectoral Programs and Policies* (Baltimore and London: The Johns Hopkins University Press, 1972) pp. 3–18.
26. Ayres R. L., *Banking on the Poor, The World Bank and World Poverty* (Cambridge and London: The MIT Press, 1984) p. 76, and Hürni B. S., *The Lending Policy of the World Bank in the 1970s: Analysis and Evaluation* (Boulder: Westview Press, 1980) p. 45.
27. World Bank, *The McNamara Years at the World Bank*, op. cit. pp. 238–39.
28. Ibid. pp. 246–56.
29. Chenery H., Ahluwalia M. S., Bell C. L. G., Duloy J. H. and Jolly R., *Redistribution with Growth* (London: Oxford University Press, 1974) and Ayres, op. cit. p. 76.
30. World Bank, *Rural Development*, Sector Policy Paper (February 1975), *Agricultural Credit*, Sector Policy Paper (May 1975) and *Land Reform*, Sector Policy Paper (May 1975).
31. World Bank, *Annual Report* (1972–5).

32. ul Haq M., 'Changing Emphasis of the Bank's Lending Policies', *Finance and Development* (June 1978) p. 14.
33. Address by the President of the Bank, ADB, *Summary of Proceedings, Fifth Annual Meeting of the Board of Governors* (Vienna, 20–22 April 1972) p. 20.
34. Address by the President of the Bank, ADB, *Summary of Proceedings, Seventh Annual Meeting of the Board of Governors* (Manila, 26–28 April 1973) p. 21.
35. ADB, Board of Directors, *Land Reform and a Possible Approach in ADB's Operations* (5 November 1973).
36. Ibid. p. 4.
37. Ibid. pp. 13–18.
38. Address by the President of the Bank, ADB, *Summary of Proceedings, Seventh Annual Meeting of the Board of Governors* (Kuala Lumpur, 25–27 April 1974) pp. 23–4.
39. The survey was first printed by the Bank in 1977 under the title *Asian Agricultural Survey 1976* for distribution to member governments, and was later published in a somewhat revised version as ADB, *Rural Asia: Challenge and Opportunity* (New York: Praeger, 1978).
40. The team preparing the second survey also drew substantially from the 'rural-led, employment oriented strategy of growth' in Mellor J. W., *The New Economics of Growth, A Strategy for India and the Developing World* (Ithaca and London: Cornell University Press, 1976).
41. ADB, *Rural Asia: Challenge and Opportunity*, op. cit. foreword.
42. Ho K. P., 'Asian Agriculture's Decade in the Wrong Direction', *Far Eastern Economic Review* (15 September 1978) pp. 47–50.
43. The strategy is described in detail in ADB, *Rural Asia: Challenge and Opportunity*, op. cit. pp. 207–92.
44. Ibid. pp. 231–41.
45. Ibid. p. 242.
46. Ibid. pp. 244–45.
47. Ibid. pp. 256–61.
48. Ibid. pp. 269–92.
49. Ibid. pp. 295–317.
50. Address by the President of the Bank, ADB, *Summary of Proceedings, Tenth Annual Meeting of the Board of Governors* (Manila, 21–23 April 1977) pp. 29–34, and *Summary of Proceedings, Eleventh Annual Meeting of the Board of Governors* (Vienna, 24–26 April 1978) pp. 31–5.
51. ADB, *Economic and Financial Appraisal of Bank-assisted Projects*, Occasional Papers, No. 11 (January 1978), *Appropriate Technology and Its Application in the Activities of the Asian Development Bank*, Occasional Papers, No. 7 (April 1977) and *Promoting Small Scale Industries: The Role of the Asian Development Bank*, Occasional Papers, No. 9 (June 1977).
52. ADB, *Sector Paper on Agriculture and Rural Development* (Manila, 1979) and ADB, Board of Directors Meeting, *Bank's Role in Agriculture and Rural Development* (26 April 1979).
53. ADB, Board of Directors Meeting (26 April 1979), op. cit. p. 2.
54. Ibid. pp. 4–5.

55. Okita S., 'The Proper Approach to Food Policy.' *Japan Echo*, Vol. V (1978) p. 56.
56. Colombo U., Johnson D. G., and Shishido T. (assisted by Hayami Y., Hemmi K. and Takase K.), *Expanding Food Production in Developing Countries: Rice Production in South and Southeast Asia*, Report of the Trilateral Food Task Force, discussion draft (1977). For a discussion of the political background of the Trilateral Commission, see Ullman, R. H., 'Trilateralism: "Partnership" for What?' *Foreign Affairs*, Vol. 55 (October 1976) pp. 1–19.
57. Colombo et al., op. cit. p. 14.
58. Ibid. pp. 62–3.
59. For a brief discussion of the strategy's political implications, see Ball N., *World Hunger, A Guide to the Economic and Political Dimensions* (Santa Barbara and Oxford, 1981) pp. 131–2.
60. Colombo et al., op. cit., pp. 62–3.
61. Okita, op. cit. pp. 56–7.
62. Ibid.
63. Trilateral Commission, 'Comments on Food Task Force Discussion Draft' (unpublished, 20 February 1978).
64. Trilateral Commission, 'Expanding Food Production in Developing Countries: Rice Production in South and South East Asia', Follow up Meeting (unpublished, Paris, 25 February 1978).
65. Takase K., 'Food Production and Irrigation Development in Asia', *ADB Quarterly Review* (July 1982) pp. 6–8, and 'Irrigation Development and Cereal Production in Asia', *Asian Development Review*, Vol. 2 (1984) pp. 80–91.
66. Address by the President of the Bank, ADB, *Summary of Proceedings, Fourteenth Annual Meeting of the Board of Governors* (Honolulu, 30 April–2 May 1981) p. 27, and *Summary of Proceedings, Fifteenth Annual Meeting of the Board of Governors* (Manila, 28–30 April 1982) pp. 23–4.
67. ADB, *Review of Asian Agriculture: Its Past Performance and Future Development Needs*, Staff Working Paper (May 1983). An abbreviated version is presented in the form of an article by the then Deputy Director of the Bank's Agriculture and Rural Development Department, Tacke E. F., 'Performance and Development Needs of Asian Agriculture', *Asian Development Review*, Vol. 1 (1983) pp. 63–85.
68. ADB, *Agriculture in Asia, Its Performance and Prospects, the Role of ADB in Its Development*, A Bank Staff Working Paper (Revised March 1985).
69. Ibid. p. 109.
70. ADB, *Rural Development in Asia and the Pacific*, Volume I, Papers and Proceedings of the ADB Regional Seminar on Rural Development (April 1985), and ADB and ILO, *Rural Employment Creation in Asia and the Pacific*, Papers and Proceedings of the ADB's and the ILO's Regional Workshop on Rural Employment Creation (March 1987).

## 5 Organisational Constraints

1. Tendler J., *Inside Foreign Aid* (Baltimore and London: The Johns Hopkins University Press, 1975) particularly pp. 54–72.
2. Payer C., *The World Bank, A Critical Analysis* (New York and London: Monthly Review Press, 1982) p. 245.
3. The President's Acceptance Speech at the Inaugural Meeting of the Board of Governors, November 24–26, 1966, in ADB, *Paths to Progress, Selected Addresses by Takeshi Watanabe* (Manila, 1972) p. 5.
4. Watanabe T., 'The Asian Development Bank Starts Functioning', *Contemporary Japan*, Vol. XXVIII (May 1967) p. 700.
5. Watanabe T., *Towards a New Asia, Memoirs of the First President of the Asian Development Bank* (Singapore, 1977) particularly pp. 46–99.
6. Address by Inoue Shiro, ADB, *Summary of Proceedings, Sixth Annual Meeting of the Board of Governors* (Manila, 26–28 April 1973) pp. 19–20.
7. Address by Inoue Shiro, ADB, *Summary of Proceedings, Seventh Annual Meeting of the Board of Governors* (Kuala Lumpur, 25–27 April 1974) p. 21.
8. Address by Yoshida Taroichi, ADB, *Summary of Proceedings, Eleventh Annual Meeting of the Board of Governors* (Vienna, 24–26 April 1978) p. 21.
9. Address by Yoshida Taroichi, ADB, *Summary of Proceedings, Tenth Annual Meeting of the Board of Governors* (Manila, 21–23 April 1977) p. 39.
10. ADB, *Annual Report* (1982) gives new approvals as $1730.6 million, but annual reports since 1984 give the figure as $1683.6, due to cancellations. Thus, effective lending in 1982 increased by only 0.4 per cent.
11. ADB, *Address to the Board of Governors by Masao Fujioka*, Sixteenth Annual Meeting (Manila, 4–6 May 1983) pp. 4–5.
12. ADB, *Address to the Board of Governors by Masao Fujioka*, Seventeenth Annual Meeting (Amsterdam, 25–27 April 1984) p. 7.
13. Tasker R., 'Lender of First Resort,' *Far Eastern Economic Review* (17 May 1983) p. 69.
14. Clad J., 'Unhappy Returns', *Far Eastern Economic Review* (27 November 1986) p. 60.
15. Ibid. p. 61.
16. Ibid. pp. 60–3, Clad J., 'Unpalatable Loan to Burmese Cooperatives', ibid. pp. 64–6, Balfour F., 'Turning a Blind Eye', ibid. pp. 66–9, and Balfour F. and Clad J., 'Where There is a Will, There is a Way', ibid. pp. 63–5.
17. ADB, *Asian Agricultural Survey* (University of Tokyo Press, 1968) p. 67.
18. Bowring P., 'ADB: Searching for a Role,' *Far Eastern Economic Review* (22 April 1977) p. 46.
19. ADB, *Annual Report* (1985) pp. 39–59.
20. Jha S. C., 'ADB Experience with Rural Development Projects – A Critical Review', ADB, *Rural Development in Asia and the Pacific*, Volume I, Papers and Proceedings of the ADB Regional Seminar on Rural Development (April 1985) p. 73.

21. Clad, op. cit. pp. 64–6, and Balfour, op. cit. pp. 66–9.
22. United States, Department of the Treasury, *United States Participation in the Multilateral Development Banks in the 1980s* (Washington, D.C., February 1982) pp. 171–3, and Cassen R. and Associates, *Does Aid Work? Report to an Intergovernmental Task Force* (Oxford: Clarendon Press, 1986) pp. 309–11.
23. Deflating the annual approval and average loan size figures presented in Table 5.1 from current to constant values was considered but rejected for several reasons. First, it is statistically complex. Project costing takes into consideration price escalation during project implementation, which can last up to six years or more. Annual approval figures would therefore have to be purged of the inflation factor used to calculate price escalation in the first place, before they could be deflated. Owing to differences in the length and disbursement schedule of individual projects, approval figures would have to be purged project by project, which was not possible with the data available to the author. Moreover, an effort to deflate unpurged approval figures (which take price escalation into consideration) with the manufacturing unit value index (which increased in 1968–81, declined in 1982–4, increased slightly in 1985 and substantially in 1986) led to very ambiguous results. Lastly, the thinking and performance targets of the Bank's management have consistently been expressed in current rather than constant values.
24. Inter-American Development Bank, *Annual Report* (1986) p. 13.
25. Ibid.
26. Compare Llorente R., 'Managing the Implemenation of Projects: The ADB Approach', *ADB Quarterly Review* (October 1985) pp. 10–14, with Baum W. C., 'The World Bank Project Cycle', *Finance and Development* (December 1978) pp. 10–17. An updated discussion of the World Bank cycle can be found in Baum W. C. and Tolbert S. M., *Investing in Development, Lessons of World Bank Experience* (Oxford University Press, 1985) pp. 329–88.
27. ADB, *Economic Appraisal (Evaluation) of Agricultural and Rural Development Projects – Theoretical, Methodological and Operational Issues* (December 1983) pp. 1–3.
28. Ibid. p. 32.
29. Payer, op. cit. pp. 75–81, and Ayres R. L., *Banking on the Poor, The World Bank and World Poverty* (Cambridge and London: The MIT Press, 1984) pp. 62–4.
30. ADB, *Economic Appraisal (Evaluation) of Agricultural and Rural Development Projects*, op. cit. p. 32.
31. Ibid. pp. 8–9.
32. Clad, op. cit. pp. 60–3 and 64–6.
33. ADB, *Economic Appraisal (Evaluation) of Agricultural and Rural Development Projects*, op. cit. p. 38.
34. Ayres, op. cit. p. 63.
35. For example Schwartz H. and Berney R. (eds.), *Social and Economic Dimensions of Project Evaluation* (Washington, D.C.: Inter-American Development Bank, 1977).

36. Howe J. and Richards P. (eds.), *Rural Roads and Poverty Alleviation* (London: Intermediate Technology Publications, 1984) p. 41.
37. ADB, *Economic and Financial Appraisal of Bank-assisted Projects*, Occasional Papers, No. 11 (January 1978) pp. 31–8.
38. ADB, *Guidelines for Economic Analysis of Projects* (no date given) p. 1.
39. Ibid.
40. Ibid.
41. Rowley A., 'Clausen and a More Worldly World Bank', *Far Eastern Economic Review* (26 March 1982) p. 134.
42. Ayres, op. cit. pp. 64–7.
43. Ibid. p. 108.
44. Ascher W., 'New Development Approaches and the Adaptability of International Agencies: The Case of the World Bank', *International Organization*, Vol. 37 (Summer 1983) pp. 428–35.

## 6 Operational Policies and Practices

1. Please S., *The Hobbled Giant, Essays on the World Bank* (Boulder and London: Westview Press, 1984) pp. 85–90.
2. Ayres R. L., 'Breaking the Bank', *Foreign Policy*, No. 43 (Summer 1981) pp. 113–17, Wall R., 'Development, Instability and the World Bank', *Instant Research on Peace and Violence*, No. 2 (1977) and Krasner S. D., 'Power Structures and Regional Development Banks', *International Organization*, Vol. 35 (Spring 1981) pp. 314–19. The political concentration of World Bank lending is also discussed by Cohn T. H., 'Politics in the World Bank Group: The Question of Loans to the Asian Giants', *International Organization*, Vol. 28 (Summer 1974) pp. 561–71.
3. ADB, *Agreement Establishing the Asian Development Bank* (Manila, 4 December 1965–31 January 1966) Article 36.
4. ADB, *Questions and Answers* (October 1985) p. 27.
5. This table is modelled on the table in ADB, *Study of Operational Priorities and Plans for the Asian Development Bank for the 1980s* (Manila, 1983) p. 72.
6. Huang P.-W., Jr., *The Asian Development Bank, Diplomacy and Development in Asia* (New York: Vantage Press, 1975) pp. 67–8.
7. ADB, 'Increasing Business Opportunities Under ADB Operations', ADB Advertisement Supplement by W. D. Kluber, *Far Eastern Economic Review* (4 May 1979) p. 47.
8. King J. A., 'Procurement under World Bank Projects', *Finance and Development* (June 1975) pp. 6–7.
9. Sassoon D. M., 'Monitoring the Procurement Process', *Finance and Development* (June 1975) pp. 11–12, and World Bank, *Guidelines, Procurement under IBRD Loans and IDA Credits* (May 1985) pp. 36–8.
10. ADB, *Guidelines for Procurement under Asian Development Bank Loans* (Revised May 1981) p. 16.
11. Details of the special fund agreements can be found in ADB, *Special Funds, Rules and Regulations, Set Aside Actions, Contribution Agreements* (31 March 1972).

12. ADB, *Rural Asia: Challenge and Opportunity* (New York: Praeger, 1977) p. 314.
13. Statement by the Governor of Sri Lanka, ADB, *Summary of Proceedings, Twelfth Annual Meeting of the Board of Governors* (Manila, 2–4 May 1979) p. 132.
14. ADB, *Study of Operational Priorities*, op. cit. p. 133.
15. Clad J., 'The Foreseen Issues', *Far Eastern Economic Review* (30 April 1987) pp. 55–7.
16. Sassoon, op. cit. p. 12.
17. Clad, op. cit. p. 57.
18. ADB, *Study of Operational Priorities*, op. cit. p. 133.
19. It has also been suggested that this category includes a substantial element of 'hidden' Japanese procurements. See Clad J., 'Unhappy Returns', *Far Eastern Economic Review* (27 November 1986) p. 62.
20. Bowring P., 'ADB: Searching for a Role'. *Far Eastern Economic Review* (22 April 1977) p. 51.
21. Wideman B., 'Lending to the Poor', *The Times* (15 April 1977).
22. De Witt R. P., Jr., *The Inter-American Development Bank and Political Influence, with Special Reference to Costa Rica* (New York: Praeger 1977) pp. 39–43.
23. De Witt's calculations cover the World Bank, the IDB and the ADB and include US subscriptions to the banks, the banks' bond sales in the US and the banks' investments in the US, on the one hand, and US procurements, the banks' interest to US shareholders, the banks' long-term investments in the US, and the banks' administrative expenses in the US, on the other. The data for calculations of this extent for all ADB member countries were not available.
24. Statement by the US Temporary Alternate Governor, ADB, *Summary of Proceedings, Fifth Annual Meeting of the Board of Governors* (Vienna, 20–22 April 1972) pp. 91–2.
25. Statement by the US Temporary Alternate Governor, ADB, *Summary of Proceedings, Sixth Annual Meeting of the Board of Governors* (Manila, 26–28 April 1973) p. 94.
26. Clad J., 'Last Resort Lender', *Far Eastern Economic Review* (15 May 1986) p. 65.
27. Lee D., 'Contract Award by Asian Bank Prompts Questions', *The Washington Post* (28 April 1984) and Tan A., 'Burma Affair Puts ADB in Bad Light', *Bangkok Post* (29 June 1984).
28. Statement by the Indian Alternate Governor, ADB, *Summary of Proceedings, Twelfth Annual Meeting of the Board of Governors*, op. cit. p. 82.
29. ADB, *Guidelines on the Use of Consultants by Asian Development Bank and Its Borrowers* (April 1979) p. 1.
30. Ibid. pp. 8–13.
31. ADB, *Study of Operational Priorities*, op. cit. pp. 128–9.
32. ADB, *Use of Consultants by Asian Development Bank and Its Borrowers* (Revised Edition, May 1973).
33. ADB, *Guidelines on the Use of Consultants*, op. cit. p. 4.
34. Compare with World Bank, *Guidelines, Use of Consultants by World*

*Bank Borrowers and by the World Bank as Executing Agency* (August 1981) pp. 5–6.

35. ADB, *Rural Development in Asia and the Pacific*, Volume I, Papers and Proceedings of the ADB Regional Seminar on Rural Development (April 1985) p. 16.
36. Commission on International Development, *Partners in Development* (New York: Praeger, 1969) pp. 176–7, and Independent Commission on International Development Issues, *North–South: A Programme for Survival* (London: Pan Books, 1980) p. 232.
37. For example Tendler J., *Inside Foreign Aid* (Baltimore and London: The Johns Hopkins University Press, 1975) pp. 73–84.
38. Tendler, op. cit. p. 44.
39. Ibid. pp. 78 and 85–101.
40. Statements by various Governors, ADB, *Summary of Proceedings, Eleventh Annual Meeting of the Board of Governors* (Vienna, 24–26 April 1978).
41. ADB, *Appropriate Technology and its Application in the Activities of the Asian Development Bank*, Occasional Papers, No. 7 (April 1977) pp. 36–7.
42. ADB, *Study of Operational Priorities*, op. cit. p. 17.
43. Ibid. p. 101.
44. Ibid. pp. 101–2.
45. ADB, *Questions and Answers* (October 1985) pp. 17–18.
46. Statement by the US Governor, ADB, *Summary of Proceedings, Sixteenth Annual Meeting of the Board of Governors* (Manila, 4–6 May 1983).

## 7  Irrigation and Rural Development Projects

1. Owing to changes over time in the Bank's sectoral classification of projects, there are slight discrepancies between these figures, which are based on the Bank's 1986 *Annual Report*, and the figures in Tables 7.1 and 7.2.
2. Because of difficulties in obtaining source material, the analysis of projects concentrates on 1968–83.
3. Address by the President of the Bank, ADB, *Summary of Proceedings, Twelfth Annual Meeting of the Board of Governors* (Manila, 2–4 May, 1979) p. 26.
4. Clad J., 'Last-resort Lender', *Far Eastern Economic Review* (15 May 1986) pp. 64–5.
5. For a detailed discussion of these subsectors, see ADB, *Review of Asian Agriculture: Its Past Performance and Future Development Needs*, Staff Working Paper (May 1983) pp. 70–104.
6. Jha S. C. and Polman F. J., 'Analysis of the Impact of Bank-financed Projects on Rural Employment Creation', in ADB and ILO, *Rural Employment Creation in Asia and the Pacific*, Papers and Proceedings of the ADB's and the ILO's Regional Workshop on Rural Employment Creation (March 1987), pp. 52–3.
7. ADB and ILO, op. cit. p. iii.

8. Ibid. pp. 67–8 and 79–80.
9. Jha and Polman, op. cit. p. 51.
10. Berry L., Ford R. and Hosier R., *The Impact of Irrigation on Development: Issues for a Comprehensive Evaluation Study*, Program Evaluation Discussion Paper No. 9 (USAID, October 1980).
11. Thormann P. H., 'Labour-intensive Irrigation Works and Dam Construction: A Review of Some Research', *International Labour Review* (August–September 1972) pp. 151–66.
12. ADB, Irrigation and Rural Development Department, *Bank's Experience on Rural Development Projects*, Regional Seminar on Rural Development (15–23 October 1984) p. 1. This definition suggests that the term is interchangeable with what are usually called integrated rural development projects.
13. Ibid. p. 2.
14. Ibid. summary. The sensitivity of these issues in the Bank is reflected in the fact that the published proceedings of the seminar at which Jha presented this paper substantially tone down this statement. See Jha S. C., 'ADB Experience with Rural Development Projects – A Critical Review', ADB, *Rural Development in Asia and the Pacific*, Volume I, Papers and Proceedings of the ADB Regional Seminar on Rural Development (April 1985) p. 76.
15. The classification is based on a Bank paper covering lending from 1968 to 1983. As the distinction between the two types of projects is not always clear, it was not possible for the author to classify more recent projects consistently.
16. Bellekens Y. S., 'Evaluating Irrigation Development and System Performance: Some Lessons Learned from Experience', paper presented at the International Workshop on Methodologies for Evaluating the Performance of Irrigation Systems, Dhaka, Bangladesh (21–27 June 1985) p. 2.
17. ADB, *Guidelines on Project Benefit Monitoring and Evaluation for Agriculture, Irrigation and Rural Development Projects* (April 1984).
18. Takase K., 'Food Production and Irrigation Development in Asia', *ADB Quarterly Review* (July 1982) p. 8.
19. ADB, *Rural Development in Asia and the Pacific*, Volume I, op. cit. p. 16.
20. ADB, Irrigation and Rural Development Department, op. cit. p. 6.
21. Ibid. p. 14–15.
22. Cassen R. and Associates, *Does Aid Work? Report to an Intergovernmental Task Force* (Oxford: Clarendon Press, 1986) pp. 122–8, and World Bank, *Annual Review of Project Performance Results* (February 1986) p. 32–8.
23. Wade R., 'The World Bank and India's Irrigation Reform', *The Journal of Development Studies*, Vol. 18 (January 1982) pp. 171–84.
24. Bellekens, op. cit. p. 5.
25. For example, ADB, *PPAR on the Sempor Dam and Irrigation Project in Indonesia* (October 1982) pp. 1–7.
26. Booth A., 'Irrigation in Indonesia, Part II', *Bulletin of Indonesian Economic Studies*, Vol. XIII (July 1977) pp. 61–7, and Holloran S.,

Corey G. L. and Mahoney T., *Sederhana: Indonesia Small-scale Irrigation*, Project Impact Evaluation No. 29 (USAID, February 1982) pp. 5–6.

27. Ibid. p. 68.
28. ADB, *PPAR on the Sempor Dam and Irrigation Project in Indonesia*, op. cit. pp. A20–A30.
29. For example Wade R., 'Administration and the Distribution of Irrigation Benefits', *Economic and Political Weekly* (1 November 1975) pp. 1743–7, Bromley D. W., Taylor D. C. and Parker D. E., 'Water Reform and Economic Development: Institutional Aspects of Water Management in Developing Countries', *Economic Development and Cultural Change*, Vol. 28 (January 1980) pp. 370–3.
30. ADB, *Post-Evaluation of the Tajum Irrigation Project in the Republic of Indonesia* (September 1974) pp. 54–67.
31. ADB, *Appraisal of the Cibaliung Irrigation Project in the Republic of Indonesia* (October 1980) p. 35. Farmers' net earnings were given in Indonesian rupiahs and have been recalculated at the US dollar exchange rate prevailing at the time of the appraisal.
32. ADB, *Appraisal of the Irrigation Package Project and Tulungagung II and Bari Raya Irrigation Study in Indonesia* (August 1982) summary.
33. ADB, *PPAR on the Sempor Dam and Irrigation Project in Indonesia*, op. cit. p. 12.
34. ADB, *Post-Evaluation of the Tajum Irrigation Project in the Republic of Indonesia*, op. cit. pp. 62–5. A similar observation is made by Booth, op. cit. p. 72.
35. ADB, Irrigation and Rural Development Department, op. cit. p. 16.
36. For example ADB, *Appraisal of the Second Agusan Irrigation Project in the Republic of the Philippines* (September 1978) p. 8.
37. ADB, *PPAR on the Angat-Magat Agricultural Development Project in Philippines* (September 1981) p. 8.
38. Bello W., Kinley D. and Elinson E., *Development Debacle: The World Bank in the Philippines* (San Francisco: Institute for Food and Development Policy, 1982) pp. 73–7.
39. ADB, *PPAR on the Angat-Magat Agricultural Development Project in the Philippines*, op. cit. pp. A18 and A56, and *PPAR on the Davao del Norte Irrigation Project in the Republic of the Philippines* (April 1983) pp. A26 and A31.
40. For example ADB, *Appraisal of the Irrigation Sector Project and Fourth Mindanao Irrigation Study (MIS IV) in the Republic of the Philippines* (November 1983).
41. ADB, *PPAR on the Davao del Norte Irrigation Project*, op. cit. pp. 2–4.
42. Steinberg D. I., Caton D., Holloran S. and Hobgood T., *Philippines Small Scale Irrigation*, Project Impact Evaluation No. 4 (USAID, May 1980) pp. 6–7.
43. ADB, *Appraisal of the Bicol River Basin Irrigation Development Project in the Republic of the Philippines* (September 1979) p. 38.
44. ADB, *PPAR on the Angat-Magat Agricultural Development Project*, op. cit. pp. A42–A48.

45. Ayres R. L., *Banking on the Poor, The World Bank and World Poverty* (Cambridge and London: The MIT Press, 1983), p. 135.
46. Cassen R. and Associates, op. cit. p. 57.
47. ADB, *PPAR on the Davao del Norte Irrigation Project*, op. cit. p. 5. Irrigation fees were given in Philippine pesos and have been recalculated at the US dollar exchange rate prevailing at the time of appraisal and project completion.

## 8 Rural Credit and Road Projects

1. For a discussion of World Bank credit projects, see Payer C., *The World Bank, A Critical Analysis* (New York: Monthly Review Press, 1982) pp. 241–5, and Bello W., Kinley D. and Elinson E., *Development Debacle: The World Bank in the Philippines* (San Francisco: Institute for Food and Development Policy, 1982) pp. 77–80.
2. ADB, *Review of Asian Agriculture: Its Past Performance and Future Development Needs*, Staff Working Paper (May 1983) p. 100.
3. ADB, Agriculture Department, Agricultural Support Services Division, *Agricultural Credit Sector Policy Paper*, draft (February 1984) p. 1.
4. Ibid. p. 52.
5. Ibid. p. 56.
6. Ibid. pp. 62–6.
7. ADB, *PPAR on the Third Agricultural Credit Project in the Kingdom of Nepal* (May 1984) p. 5.
8. ADB, *Appraisal of the Fourth Agricultural Credit Project in Nepal* (October 1980).
9. The project was under preparation for several years, and following criticism of Bank support for the ADBN by the board of directors in 1986, it was scaled down from $30 to $24 million in early 1987. Compare ADB, *Operational Information on Proposed Projects* (July 1986) p. 12 and (May 1987) p. 11.
10. ADB, *Post-Evaluation of the Agricultural Credit Project in Nepal* (October 1977) pp. 20–1, and *PPAR on the Second Agricultural Credit Project in the Kingdom of Nepal* (October 1981) pp. A21–A31.
11. ADB, *PPAR on the Third Agricultural Credit Project*, op. cit. pp. 15–18.
12. Bechtel H., 'Banking – Art or Science?', *Zeitschrift für das Gesamte Kreditwesen*, 19 Heft (1984) p. 6, translated from German.
13. Ibid.
14. Ibid.
15. Balfour F., 'Turning a Blind Eye', *Far Eastern Economic Review* (27 November 1986) pp. 66–9.
16. ADB, *Post-Evaluation of the Agricultural Credit Project in Nepal*, op. cit. pp. 10–12, and *PPAR on the Third Agricultural Credit Project*, op. cit. pp. 32–5.
17. ADB, *Post-Evaluation of the Agricultural Credit Project in Nepal*, op. cit. p. 37, and *PPAR of the Second Agricultural Credit Project*, op. cit. p. A19.

18. Ibid.
19. ADB, *PPAR on the Third Agricultural Credit Project*, op. cit. p. 13.
20. Feldman D. and Fournier A., 'Social Relations and Agricultural Production in Nepal's Terai', *The Journal of Peasant Studies*, Vol. 4 (July 1976) pp. 447–52.
21. ADB, *Appraisal of the Fourth Agricultural Credit Project*, op. cit. p. 26.
22. Bechtel, op. cit. p. 6.
23. ADB, *Post-Evaluation of the Agricultural Credit Project in Nepal*, op. cit. pp. 12–13.
24. Feldman and Fournier, op. cit. pp. 462–3.
25. ADB, *PPAR of the Second Agricultural Credit Project*, op. cit. pp. 53 and A18–A19.
26. ADB, *PPAR of the Third Agricultural Credit Project*, op. cit. pp. 12–13.
27. Ibid. p. 34.
28. Ibid. p. 13.
29. ADB, *Appraisal of the Fourth Agricultural Credit Project*, op. cit. p. 30.
30. For a discussion of ADB lending for fisheries, see Azam M. Z., 'A Practical Approach to Fisheries Development', *ADB Quarterly Review* (October–November 1976) pp. 4–7.
31. ADB, *An Impact Evaluation Study on Bank Assistance to the Fisheries Sector in Sri Lanka* (May 1984) pp. 31–3.
32. The programme is discussed by Alexander P., 'Innovation in a Cultural Vacuum: The Mechanization of Sri Lankan Fisheries', *Human Organization*, Vol. 34 (Winter 1975) pp. 333–4.
33. ADB, *PPAR on the Fisheries Development Project in Sri Lanka* (March 1982) pp. 12–14.
34. Alexander, op. cit. pp. 342–3.
35. ADB, *An Impact Evaluation Study on Bank Assistance*, op. cit. pp. 18–21.
36. Alexander, op. cit. pp. 338–41.
37. ADB, *An Impact Evaluation Study on Bank Assistance*, op. cit. pp. 42–3.
38. Ibid. p. 20.
39. Alexander, op. cit. p. 342.
40. Ibid.
41. ADB, *An Impact Evaluation Study on Bank Assistance*, op. cit. pp. 21–5.
42. Ibid. p. 23.
43. Lewis J. A., 'The Public Works Approach to Low-end Poverty Problems: the New Potentialities of an Old Answer', *Journal of Development Planning*, No. 5 (1973) pp. 85–113, and Costa E., 'Maximising Employment in Labour-intensive Development Programmes', *International Labour Review* (1973) pp. 371–94.
44. Howe, J. and Richards P. (eds.), *Rural Roads and Poverty Alleviation* (London: Intermediate Technology Publications, 1984).
45. Ibid. p. 19.
46. Ibid. pp. 18–47.
47. Lal D., *Men or Machines, A Study of Labor-capital Substitution in Road*

*Construction in the Philippines* (Geneva: International Labour Office, 1978) and McCleary W. A. in collaboration with Allal M. and Nilsson B., *Equipment Versus Employment: A Social Cost-benefit Analysis of Alternative Techniques of Feeder Road Construction in Thailand* (Geneva: International Labour Office, 1976).

48. Coukis B. P. and Grimes O. F., Jr., 'Labour-based Civil Construction', *Finance and Development* (March 1980) pp. 32–5.
49. It is important to bear in mind that the table gives project output in terms of road kilometres, but does not distinguish between the significant cost differences of different road types, nor between those of road construction and road improvement. Thus, while emphasis has shifted to feeder roads in terms of kilometre output, in resource allocation there is still considerable emphasis on primary and secondary roads.
50. For example Thomas J. W. and Hook R. M., *Creating Rural Employment: A Manual for Organizing Rural Works Programs* (Harvard University, for the Agency for International Development, July 1977) and World Bank, Transportation Staff and Consultants, *Labor-based Construction Programs, A Practical Guide for Planning and Management* (Oxford University Press, 1983).
51. Llorente R., 'The ADB and Road Development in the Philippines', *ADB Quarterly Review* (October 1983) p. 13.
52. Republic of the Philippines, *Five-year Philippine Development Plan, 1978–1982* (Manila, September 1977) p. 250.
53. Lal, op. cit.
54. Republic of the Philippines, National Economic and Development Authority, *Four-year Development Plan FY 1974–77, Condensed Report* (April 1973) pp. 112–13.
55. Republic of the Philippines, *Five-year Philippine Development Plan*, op. cit. p. 253. There is also a provision that labour-intensive methods should be used unless they are over 10 per cent more costly and the construction time required is more than 50 per cent longer than for capital-intensive techniques.
56. ADB, *Annual Report* (1986) p. 51.
57. ADB, *PPAR on the Cotabato–General Santos Road Project in the Republic of the Philippines* (May 1980) pp. A9–A10, *PPAR, Iligan–Cagayan de Oro–Butuan Road Project in the Republic of the Philippines* (June 1984) pp. A10–A14 and *PPAR of the Tarlac–Santa Rosa and Feeder Roads Project in the Republic of the Philippines* (July 1982) pp. A13–A16.
58. ADB, *PPAR on the Cotabato–General Santos Road Project*, op. cit. pp. 26–7, and *PPAR, Iligan–Cagayan de Oro–Butuan Road Project*, op. cit. pp. 17–18.
59. ADB, *PPAR of the Tarlac–Santa Rosa Road and Feeder Roads Project*, op. cit. pp. 2–5.
60. ADB, *Appraisal of the Mindanao Secondary and Feeder Roads Project in the Republic of the Philippines* (November 1978) pp. 32–3, and *Appraisal of the Third Road Improvement Project in the Republic of the Philippines* (October 1982), pp. 43–5.

61. ADB, *PPAR on the Cotabato–General Santos Road Project*, op. cit. p. 28.
62. ADB, *PPAR, Iligan–Cagayan de Oro–Butuan Road Project*, op. cit. pp. 14–18.
63. ADB, *Appraisal of the Second Road Improvement Project in the Republic of the Philippines* (October 1980) p. 35.
64. Levy I., Zuvekas C., Jr., and Stevens C., *Philippines: Rural Roads I and II*, Project Impact Evaluation No. 18 (USAID, March 1981), pp. 8–10.
65. ADB, *Appraisal of the Mindanao Secondary and Feeder Roads Project*, op. cit. pp. 32–3.
66. Levy et al., op. cit. pp. 2–3.
67. Ibid. pp. 8–17.
68. Nilsson B., 'Labour-based/Equipment-supported Road Construction and Maintenance in the Philippines', A Position Paper (unpublished, March 1984).

# 9 Conclusion

1. Griffin K., *The Political Economy of Agrarian Change* (London and Tonbridge: The Macmillan Press, 1974) pp. 198–204.
2. ADB, *Rural Asia: Challenge and Opportunity* (New York: Praeger, 1977), *Sector Paper on Agriculture and Rural Development* (Manila, 1979), and *Study on Operational Priorities and Plans of the Asian Development Bank for the 1980s* (Manila, June 1983).
3. See Cassen R. and Associates, *Does Aid Work? Report to an Intergovernmental Task Force* (Oxford: Clarendon Press, 1986) pp. 309–11.
4. Payer C., *The World Bank, A Critical Analysis* (New York and London: Monthly Review Press, 1982).
5. For example Cassen R. and Associates, op. cit., Ayres R. L., *Banking on the Poor, the World Bank and World Poverty* (Cambridge and London: The MIT Press, 1984) and Tendler J., *Inside Foreign Aid* (Baltimore and London: The Johns Hopkins University Press, 1975).
6. Rondinelli D. A., *Development Projects as Policy Experiments* (London and New York: Methuen, 1983).
7. For example Reid E., *Strengthening the World Bank* (Chicago: The Adlai Stevenson Institute, 1973).
8. ADB, *Rural Asia: Challenge and Opportunity*, op. cit., and *Study on Operational Priorities and Plans*, op. cit.
9. For example Nsekela A. J., 'The World Bank and the New International Economic Order', *Development Dialogue*, No. 1 (1977) pp. 75–84.
10. Independent Commission on International Development Issues, *North–South: A Programme for Survival* (London: Pan Books, 1980) p. 255.
11. Cassen R. and Associates, op. cit. p. 310.
12. Annis S., 'The Next World Bank? Financing Development from the Bottom Up', *Grassroots Development*, Vol. 11 (1987) pp. 24–9.
13. World Bank, *A Guide to Institutional Changes, The World Bank Reorganization 1987* (May 1987) pp. 7 and 19–26.

# Bibliography

ADB, *Address to the Board of Governors by Masao Fujioka*, Sixteenth Annual Meeting (Manila, 4–6 May 1983).

ADB, *Address to the Board of Governors by Masao Fujioka*, Seventeenth Annual Meeting (Amsterdam, 25–27 April 1984).

ADB, *Agreement Establishing the Asian Development Bank* (Manila, 4 December 1965–31 January 1966).

ADB, *Agriculture in Asia, Its Performance and Prospects, The Role of ADB in its Development*, A Bank Staff Working Paper, (Revised March 1985).

ADB, *Agriculture in Asia, Statistical Appendices*, A Bank Staff Working Paper (March 1985).

ADB, *An Impact Evaluation Study on Bank Assistance to the Fisheries Sector in Sri Lanka* (May 1984).

ADB, *Annual Report* (1967–86).

ADB, *Appraisal of the Bali Irrigation Project in the Republic of Indonesia* (August 1978).

ADB, *Appraisal of the Bicol River Basin Irrigation Development Project in the Republic of the Philippines* (September 1979).

ADB, *Appraisal of the Bukidnon Irrigation Project and Third Mindanao Irrigation Study in the Republic of the Philippines* (July 1979).

ADB, *Appraisal of the Cibaliung Irrigation Project in the Republic of Indonesia* (October 1980).

ADB, *Appraisal of the Fourth Agricultural Credit Project in Nepal* (October 1980).

ADB, *Appraisal of the Irrigation Package Project and Tulungagung II and Baro Raya Irrigation Study in Indonesia* (August 1982).

ADB, *Appraisal of the Irrigation Sector Project and Fourth Mindanao Irrigation Study (MIS IV) in the Republic of the Philippines* (November 1983).

ADB, *Appraisal of the Mindanao Secondary and Feeder Roads Project in the Republic of the Philippines* (November 1978).

ADB, *Appraisal of the Second Agusan Irrigation Project in the Republic of the Philippines* (September 1978).

ADB, *Appraisal of the Second Irrigation Sector Project and West Nusa Tenggara Irrigation Study in Indonesia* (August 1983).

ADB, *Appraisal of the Second Road Development Project in the Republic of the Philippines* (October 1980).

ADB, *Appraisal of the Third Davao del Norte Irrigation Project in the Republic of the Philippines* (July 1982).

ADB, *Appraisal of the Third Road Improvement Project in the Republic of the Philippines* (October 1982).

ADB, *Appraisal of the Tulungagung Drainage Project in the Republic of Indonesia* (November 1979).

ADB, *Appropriate Technology and its Application in the Activities of the Asian Development Bank*, Occasional Papers, No. 7 (April 1977).

ADB, *Asian Agricultural Survey* (University of Tokyo Press, 1968).

ADB, *Economic and Financial Appraisal of Bank-assisted Projects*, Occasional Papers, No. 11 (January 1978).

ADB, *Economic Appraisal (Evaluation) of Agricultural and Rural Development Projects – Theoretical, Methodological and Operational Issues* (December 1983).

ADB, *Guidelines for Economic Analysis of Projects* (no date given).

ADB, *Guidelines for Procurement under Asian Development Bank Loans* (Revised May 1981).

ADB, *Guidelines on Project Benefit Monitoring and Evaluation for Agriculture, Irrigation and Rural Development Projects* (Revised April 1984).

ADB, *Guidelines on the Use of Consultants by Asian Development Bank and its Borrowers* (April 1979).

ADB, 'Increasing Business Opportunities under ADB Operations', Advertisement Supplement by Kluber W. D., *Far Eastern Economic Review* (4 May 1979) p. 47.

ADB, *Key Indicators of Developing Member Countries of ADB* (July 1986).

ADB, *Loan, Technical Assistance and Equity Approvals* (August 1984).

ADB, *Notes on Post-Evaluation Activities* (no date given).

ADB, *Operational Information on Proposed Projects* (various issues).

ADB, *Organizational Listing* (31 May 1983).

ADB, *Paths to Progress, Selected Addresses by Takeshi Watanabe* (Manila, 1972).

ADB, *Post-Evaluation of the Agricultural Credit Project in Nepal* (October 1977).

ADB, *Post-Evaluation of the Tajum Irrigation Project in the Republic of Indonesia* (September 1974).

ADB, *PPAR on the Angat-Magat Agricultural Development Project in the Philippines* (September 1981).

ADB, *PPAR on the Cotabato–General Santos Road Project in the Republic of the Philippines* (May 1980).

ADB, *PPAR on the Davao del Norte Irrigation Project in the Republic of the Philippines* (April 1983).

ADB, *PPAR on the Fisheries Development Project in Sri Lanka* (March 1982).

ADB, *PPAR, Iligan–Cagayan de Oro–Butuan Road Project in the Republic of the Philippines* (June 1984).

ADB, *PPAR on the Second Agricultural Credit Project in the Kingdom of Nepal* (October 1981).

ADB, *PPAR on the Sempor Dam and Irrigation Project in Indonesia* (October 1982).

ADB, *PPAR of the Tarlac–Santa Rosa and Feeder Roads Project in the Republic of the Philippines* (July 1982).

ADB, *PPAR on the Third Agricultural Credit Project in the Kingdom of Nepal* (May 1984).

ADB, *Project Completion Report of the Road Improvement Project in the Republic of the Philippines* (December 1985).

ADB, *Promoting Small Scale Industries: The Role of the Asian Development Bank*, Occasional Papers, No. 9 (June 1977).

ADB, *Quarterly Procurement Statistics* (various issues).

ADB, *Questions and Answers* (April 1984, and October 1985).

ADB, *Regional Seminar on Agriculture, Papers and Proceedings* (Hong Kong, 1969).

ADB, *Review of Asian Agriculture: Its Past Performance and Future Development Needs*, Staff Working Paper (May 1983).

ADB, *Rural Asia: Challenge and Opportunity* (New York: Praeger, 1977).

ADB, *Rural Development in Asia and the Pacific*, Volume I, Papers and Proceedings of the ADB Regional Seminar on Rural Development (April 1985).

ADB, *Rural Development in Asia and the Pacific*, Volume II, Country Papers Presented at the ADB Regional Seminar on Rural Development (April 1985).

ADB, *Sector Paper on Agriculture and Rural Development* (Manila, 1979).

ADB, *Special Funds, Rules and Regulations, Set Aside Actions, Contribution Agreements* (31 March 1972).

ADB, *Study of Operational Priorities and Plans of the Asian Development Bank for the 1980s* (Manila, June 1983).

ADB, *Summary of Proceedings, First–Seventeenth Annual Meeting of the Board of Governors* (Manila, 1967–1984).

ADB, *Use of Consultants by Asian Development Bank and Its Borrowers* (Revised Edition, May 1973).

ADB, *Technical Assistance Activities* (1985).

ADB, Agriculture Department, Agricultural Support Services Division, *Agricultural Credit Sector Policy Paper*, draft (February 1984).

ADB, Board of Directors Meeting, *ADB Operational Policies in the Field of Agriculture – Follow-up to Asian Agricultural Survey* (27 August 1968).

ADB, Board of Directors Meeting, *ADB's Role in Strengthening Agricultural Research in the Region* (22 July 1968).

ADB, Board of Directors Meeting, *Bank's Role in Agriculture and Rural Development* (26 April 1979).

ADB, Board of Directors, *Land Reform and a Possible Approach in ADB's Operations* (5 November 1973).

ADB, Board of Directors, *The Role of the Asian Development Bank in Agricultural Water Resources Development* (2 June 1970).

ADB, Irrigation and Rural Development Department, *Bank's Experience on Rural Development Projects*, Regional Seminar on Rural Development (15–23 October 1984).

ADB, and International Labour Organisation, *Rural Employment Creation in Asia and the Pacific*, Papers and Proceedings of the ADB's and the ILO's Regional Workshop on Rural Employment Creation (March 1987).

AICHI K., 'Japan's Legacy and Destiny of Change', *Foreign Affairs*, Vol. 48 (October 1969) pp. 21–38.

ALEXANDER, P., 'Innovation in a Cultural Vacuum: The Mechanization of Sri Lankan Fisheries', *Human Organization*, Vol. 34 (Winter 1975), pp. 333–44.

AMEGAVIE, Y. C., *La Banque Africaine de Développement* (Paris: Editions A. Pedone, 1975).

ANNIS, S., 'The Next World Bank? Financing Development from the Bottom Up', *Grassroots Development*, Vol. 11 (1987), pp. 24–29.

ASCHER, W., 'New Development Approaches and the Adaptability of International Agencies: The Case of the World Bank', *International Organization*, Vol. 37 (Summer 1983), pp. 415–39.

AYRES, R. L., *Banking on the Poor, The World Bank and World Poverty* (Cambridge and London: The MIT Press) 1984.

AYRES, R. L., 'Breaking the Bank', *Foreign Policy*, No. 43 (Summer 1981), pp. 104–20.

AZAM, M. Z., 'A Practical Approach to Fisheries Development', *ADB Quarterly Review* (October–November 1976) pp. 4–7.

BALL, N., *World Hunger, A Guide to the Economic and Political Dimensions* (Santa Barbara and Oxford, 1981).

BAUM, W. C., 'The World Bank Project Cycle', *Finance and Development*, Vol. 15 (December 1978) pp. 10–17.

BAUM, W. C., and TOLBERT, S. M., *Investing in Development, Lessons of World Bank Experience* (Oxford University Press, 1985).

BELLEKENS, Y. S., 'Evaluating Irrigation Project Development and System Performance: Some Lessons Learned from Experience', paper presented at the International Workshop on Methodologies for Evaluating the Performance of Irrigation Systems, Dhaka, Bangladesh (21–27 June 1985).

BELLO, W., KINLEY, D., and ELINSON, E., *Development Debacle: The World Bank in the Philippines* (San Francisco: Institute for Food and Development Policy, 1982).

BERRY, L., FORD, R., and HOSIER, R., *The Impact of Irrigation on Development: Issues for a Comprehensive Evaluation Study*, Program Evaluation Discussion Paper No. 9 (USAID, October 1980).

BOOTH, A., 'Irrigation in Indonesia, Part I', *Bulletin of Indonesian Economic Studies*, Vol. XIII (March 1977) pp. 33–74.

BOOTH, A., 'Irrigation in Indonesia, Part II', *Bulletin of Indonesian Economic Studies*, Vol. XIII (July 1977) pp. 45–77.

BROMLEY, D. W., TAYLOR, D. C., and PARKER, D. E., 'Water Reform and Economic Development: Institutional Aspects of Water Management in Developing Countries', *Economic Development and Cultural Change*, Vol. 28 (January 1980) pp. 365–87.

CASSEN, R., 'The Effectiveness of Aid', *Finance and Development* (March 1986) pp. 11–14.

CASSEN, R., and Associates, *Does Aid Work? Report to an Intergovernmental Task Force* (Oxford: Clarendon Press, 1986).

CASSEN, R., JOLLY, R., SEWELL, J., and WOOD, R., (eds.), *Rich Country Interests and Third World Development* (London and Canberra: Croom Helm, 1982).

CHENERY, H., AHLUWALIA, M. S., BELL, C. L. G., DULOY, J. H., and JOLLY, R., *Redistribution with Growth* (London: Oxford University Press, 1974).

CLARK, W., 'Robert McNamara at the World Bank', *Foreign Affairs*, Vol. 60, (Fall 1981), pp. 167–84.

COHN, T. H., 'Politics in the World Bank Group: The Question of Loans to the Asian Giants', *International Organization*, Vol. 28 (Summer 1974), pp. 561–71.

COLOMBO, U., JOHNSON, D. G., and SHISHIDO T., (assisted by HAYAMI Y., HEMMI K., and TAKASE K.), *Expanding Food Production in South and Southeast Asia*, Report of the Trilateral Food Task Force, discussion draft (1977).

Commission on International Development, *Partners in Development, Report of the Commission on International Development* (New York: Praeger, 1969).

COSTA, E., 'Maximising Employment in Labour-intensive Development Programmes', *International Labour Review* (1973) pp. 371–94.

COUKIS, B. P., and GRIMES, O. F., Jr., 'Labour-based Civil Construction', *Finance and Development* (March 1980) pp. 32–5.

DELL, S., *The Inter-American Development Bank, A Study in Development Financing* (New York: Praeger, 1972).

DeWITT, R. P., Jr., *The Inter-American Development Bank and Political Influence, with Special Reference to Costa Rica* (New York: Praeger, 1977).

DeWITT, R. P., Jr., The Inter-American Development Bank and Policy Making in Costa Rica', *The Journal of Developing Areas*, Vol. 15, (October 1980) pp. 67–81.

DORE, R., 'Japan and the Third World: Coincidence or Divergence of Interests', in Cassen et al. (eds.) op. cit. pp. 128–55.

FELDMAN, D., and FOURNIER, A., 'Social Relations and Agricultural Production in Nepal's Terai', *The Journal of Peasant Studies*, Vol. 4 (July 1976) pp. 447–64.

FEDER, E., 'Capitalism's Last-ditch Effort to Save Underdeveloped Agricultures: International Agribusiness, the World Bank and the Rural Poor', *Journal of Contemporary Asia*, Vol. 7 (1977) pp. 56–78.

FEDER, E., 'The New World Bank Programme for the Self-liquidation of the Third World Peasantry', *The Journal of Peasant Studies*, Vol. 3 (April 1976) pp. 343–54.

FEDER, E., 'The World Bank and the Expansion of Industrial Monopoly Capital into Under-developed Agricultures', *Journal of Contemporary Asia*, Vol. 12 (1982) pp. 34–60.

FORDWOR, K. D., *The African Development Bank, Problems of International Cooperation* (Oxford: Pergamon Press, 1981).

FORDWOR, K. D., 'Some Unresolved Problems of the African Development Bank', *World Development*, Vol. 9 (1981) pp. 1129–39.

GEYELIN, P., *Lyndon B. Johnson and the World* (New York: Praeger 1966).

GRIFFIN, K., *The Political Economy of Agrarian Change* (London: The Macmillan Press, 1974).

HAAS, M., 'Asian Development Bank', *International Organization*, Vol. 28 (Spring 1974), pp. 281–96.

HARRIS, S., 'Australia's Interests in Third World Development: The Perspective of a Resource Exporter', in Cassen et al. (eds.) op. cit. pp. 156–81.

HAYTER, T., *Aid as Imperialism* (Harmondsworth: Penguin, 1974).

HEISKANEN, I., and MARTIKAINEN, T., 'On Comparative Policy

Analysis: Methodological Problems, Theoretical Considerations, and Empirical Applications', *Scandinavian Political Studies*, Vol. 9 (1974) pp. 9–22.

HIRSCHMAN, A. O., *Development Projects Observed* (Washington D.C.: The Brookings Institution, 1967).

HOADLEY, J. S., 'Small States as Aid Donors', *International Organization*, Vol. 34 (Winter 1980), pp. 121–37.

HOLLORAN, S,. COREY, G. L., and MAHONEY, T., *Sederhana: Indonesia Small-scale Irrigation*, Project Impact Evaluation No. 29 (USAID, February 1982).

HOWE, J., and RICHARDS, P., (eds.), *Rural Roads and Poverty Alleviation* (London: Intermediate Technology Publications, 1984).

HSIEH, S. C., and RUTTAN, V. W., 'Environmental, Technological and Institutional Factors in the Growth of Rice Production: Philippines, Thailand and Taiwan', *Food Research Institute Studies*, Vol. VII (Stanford University, 1967) pp. 307–41.

HUNTINGTON, S. P., *Political Order in Changing Societies* (New Haven and London: Yale University Press, 1968).

HUANG, P.-W., Jr., *The Asian Development Bank, Diplomacy and Development in Asia* (New York: Vantage Press, 1975).

HÜRNI, B. S., 'The "New-Style" Lending Policy of the World Bank', *and Evaluation* (Boulder: Westview Press, 1980).

HURNI, B. S., 'The "New-Style" Lending Policy of the World Bank', *Journal of World Trade Law*, Vol. 13 (November–December 1979) pp. 522–34.

Independent Commission on International Development Issues, *North–South: A Programme for Survival* (London: Pan Books, 1980).

Inter-American Development Bank, *Annual Report* (1986).

International Labour Office, Bureau of Programming and Management, *Procedures for the Design and Evaluation of ILO Projects*, Volume II, Technical Co-operation (Geneva, June 1979).

ISHIKAWA S., *Agricultural Development Strategies in Asia, Case Studies of the Philippines and Thailand* (ADB, 1970).

Japan External Trade Organization, *Economic Cooperation of Japan* (Tokyo, various issues).

Japan External Trade Organization, *White Paper on International Trade* (Tokyo, 1976).

JHA, S. C., 'ADB Experience with Rural Development Projects – A Critical Review', ADB, *Rural Development in Asia and the Pacific*, Volume I, Papers and Proceedings of the ADB Regional Seminar on Rural Development (April 1985) pp. 65–76.

JHA, S. C., and POLMAN, F. J., 'Analysis of the Impact of Bank-financed Projects on Rural Employment Creation', in ADB and the International Labour Organisation, op. cit. pp. 51–78.

KING, J. A., 'Procurement under World Bank Projects', *Finance and Development*, Vol. 12 (June 1975) pp. 6–11.

KOJIMA K., 'Japan's Role in Asian Agricultural Development', *Japan Quarterly*, Vol. XIV (April–June 1967) pp. 158–64.

KRASNER, S. D., 'Power Structures and Regional Development Banks', *International Organization*, Vol. 35 (Spring 1981) pp. 303–28.

KRISHNAMURTI, R., *ADB – The Seeding Days* (Manila: ADB Printing Section, 1977).

LAAR, A. van de, *The World Bank and the Poor* (The Hague: Martinus Nijhoff Publishing, 1979).

LAAR, A. van de, 'The World Bank and the World's Poor', *World Development*, Vol. 4 (1976) pp. 837–51.

LAAR, A. van de, 'The World Bank: Which Way?', *Development and Change*, Vol. 7 (1976) pp. 67–97.

LAL, D., *Men or Machines, A Study of Labour-capital Substitution in Road Construction in the Philippines* (Geneva: International Labour Office, 1978).

LAPPÉ, F. M., COLLINS, J., and KINLEY, D., *Aid as Obstacle, Twenty Questions about Our Foreign Aid and the Hungry* (San Francisco: Institute for Food and Development Policy, 1981).

LAVRICHENKO, M., and ANUCHKIN-TIMOFEYEV, A., 'Colonialist Plans and the Asian Development Bank', *International Affairs* (Moscow), No. 2 (1972) pp. 86–9.

LEVY, I., ZUVEKAS, C., Jr., and STEVENS, C., *Philippines: Rural Roads I and II*, Project Impact Evaluation No. 18 (USAID, March 1981).

LEWIS, J. P., 'The Public Works Approach to Low-end Poverty Problems: The New Potentialities of an Old Answer', *Journal of Development Planning*, No. 5 (1973) pp. 85–113.

LLORENTE, R., 'The ADB and Road Development in the Philippines', *ADB Quarterly Review* (October 1983) pp. 13–15.

LLORENTE, R., 'Managing the Implementation of Projects: The ADB Approach', *ADB Quarterly Review* (October 1985) pp. 10–14.

LOUTFI, M. F., *The Net Cost of Japanese Foreign Aid* (New York: Praeger, 1973).

MASON, E. S., and ASHER, R.E., *The World Bank Since Bretton Woods* (Washington, D.C.: The Brookings Institution, 1973).

McCLEARY, W. A., in collaboration with ALLAL, M., and NILSSON, B., *Equipment Versus Employment, A Social Cost-benefit Analysis of Alternative Techniques of Feeder Road Construction in Thailand* (Geneva, International Labour Office, 1976).

MELLOR, J. W., *The New Economics of Growth, A Strategy for India and the Developing World* (Ithaca and London: Cornell University Press, 1976).

NILSSON, B., 'Labour-based/Equipment-supported Road Construction and Maintenance in the Philippines', A Position Paper (unpublished, March 1984).

NSEKELA, A. J., 'The World Bank and the New International Economic Order', *Development Dialogue*, No. 1 (1977) pp. 75–84.

OHKAWA K., and JOHNSTON, B. F., 'The Transferability of the Japanese Pattern of Modernizing Traditional Agriculture', in Thorbecke, E. (ed.), *The Role of Agriculture in Economic Development* (New York and London 1969) pp. 277–310.

OKITA S., 'The Proper Approach to Food Policy', *Japan Echo*, Vol. V (1978) pp. 49–57.

OPPENHEIM, V. H., 'Whose World Bank?', *Foreign Policy*, No. 19 (Summer 1975), pp. 99–108.

Organization for Economic Cooperation and Development, *Geographical Distribution of Financial Flows to Developing Countries* (Paris, 1984).

PAYER, C., 'Researching the World Bank', in Torrie, J. (ed.), op. cit. pp. 79–91.

PAYER, C., *The World Bank, A Critical Analysis* (New York and London: Monthly Review Press, 1982).

PAYER, C., 'The World Bank and the Small Farmers', *Journal of Peace Research*, Vol. XVI (1979) pp. 293–312.

PLEASE, S., *The Hobbled Giant, Essays on the World Bank* (Boulder and London: Westview Press, 1984).

REID, E., *The Future of the World Bank* (Washington, D.C.: International Bank for Reconstruction and Development, September 1965).

REID, E., 'McNamara's World Bank', *Foreign Affairs* (July 1973) pp. 794–810.

REID, E., *Strengthening the World Bank* (Chicago: The Adlai Stevenson Institute, 1973).

Republic of the Philippines, *Five-year Philippine Development Plan, 1978–1982* (Manila, September 1977).

Republic of the Philippines, National Economic and Development Authority, *Four-year Development Plan FY 1974–77. Condensed Report* (April 1973).

RIX, A., *Japan's Economic Aid, Policy-making and Politics* (London: Croom Helm, 1980).

RIX, A., 'The Mitsugoro Project: Japanese Aid Policy and Indonesia', *Pacific Affairs*, Vol. 52 (Spring 1979), pp. 42–63.

RONDINELLI, D. A., *Development Projects as Policy Experiments* (London and New York: Methuen, 1983).

RONDINELLI, D. A., 'International Assistance Policy and Development Project Administration: The Impact of Imperious Rationality', *International Organization*, Vol. 3 (Autumn 1976), pp. 573–605.

SANDERSON, F. H., *Japan's Food Prospects and Policies* (Washington, D.C.: The Brookings Institution, 1978).

SANFORD, J. E., 'Restrictions on United States Contributions to Multilateral Development Banks', *Journal of International Law and Economics*, Vol. 15 (1981) pp. 560–73.

SANFORD, J. E., *U.S. Foreign Policy and Multilateral Development Banks* (Boulder: Westview Press, 1982).

SANFORD, J. E., and GOODMAN, M., 'Congressional Oversight and the Multilateral Development Banks', *International Organization*, Vol. 29 (Autumn 1975), pp. 1055–64.

SASSOON, D. M., 'Monitoring the Procurement Process', *Finance and Development*, Vol. 12 (June 1975) pp. 11–13.

SATO E., 'Japan's Role in Asia', *Contemporary Japan*, Vol. XXVIII (May 1967) pp. 691–8.

SCHOULTZ, L., *Human Rights and United States Policy toward Latin*

*America* (Princeton University Press, 1981).

SCHOULTZ, L., 'Politics, Economics and U.S. Participation in Multilateral Development Banks', *International Organization*, Vol. 36 (Summer 1982) pp. 537–74.

SCHULTZ, T. W., *Transforming Traditional Agriculture* (New Haven and London: Yale University Press, 1964).

SCHWARTZ, H., and BERNEY, R., (eds.), *Social and Economic Dimensions of Project Evaluation* (Washington, D.C.: Inter-American Development Bank, 1977).

STEINBERG, D. I., CATON, D., HOLLORAN, S., and HOBGOOD, T., *Philippines Small Scale Irrigation*, Project Impact Evaluation No. 4 (USAID, May 1980).

STRYKER, R. E., 'The World Bank and Agricultural Development: Food Production and Rural Poverty', *World Development*, Vol. 7 (1979) pp. 325–36.

SYZ, J., *International Development Banks* (New York: Oceana Publications, 1974).

TACKE, E. F., 'Performance and Development Needs of Asian Agriculture', *Asian Development Review*, Vol. 1 (1983) pp. 63–85.

TAKASE K., 'Food Production and Irrigation Development in Asia', *ADB Quarterly Review* (July 1982) pp. 6–8.

TAKASE K., 'Irrigation Development and Cereal Production in Asia', *Asian Development Review*, Vol. 2 (1984) pp. 80–91.

TAKASE K., and KANO T., 'Development Strategy of Irrigation and Drainage', in ADB, *Asian Agricultural Survey* (University of Tokyo Press, 1968) pp. 513–51.

TENDLER, J., *Inside Foreign Aid* (Baltimore and London: The Johns Hopkins University Press, 1975).

THOMAS, J. W., and HOOK, R. M., *Creating Rural Employment: A Manual for Organizing Rural Works Programs* (Harvard University for the Agency for International Development, July 1977).

THORMANN, P. H., 'Labour-intensive Irrigation Works and Dam Construction: A Review of Some Research', *International Labour Review* (August–September 1972) pp. 151–66.

TORRIE, J. (ed.), *Banking on Poverty, The Global Impact of the IMF and World Bank* (Toronto: Between the Lines, 1983).

Trilateral Commission, 'Comments on Food Task Force Discussion Draft' (unpublished, 20 February 1978).

Trilateral Commission, 'Expanding Food Production in Developing Countries: Rice Production in South and South East Asia', Follow up Meeting, (unpublished, Paris, 25 February 1978).

TSAO J. H., 'The Asian Development Bank as a Political System' (University of Oklahoma: Ph.D. dissertation, 1974).

UL HAQ, M., 'Changing Emphasis of the Bank's Lending Policies', *Finance and Development* (June 1978) pp. 12–14.

ULLMAN, R. J., 'Trilateralism: "Partnership" for What?', *Foreign Affairs*, Vol. 55 (October 1976) pp. 1–19.

United States, Agency for International Development, *U.S. Economic Aid to Thailand: Three Decades of Cooperation* (1983).

United States, Department of the Treasury, *United States Participation in the Multilateral Development Banks in the 1980s* (Washington, D.C., February 1982).

United States, Senate, *Hearing Before the Committee on Foreign Relations, Ninety-second Congress, First Session on S.749 to Authorize United States Contributions to the Special Funds of the Asian Development Bank* (2 April 1971).

VILLEGAS, E. M., 'Japanese Capitalism and the Asian Development Bank', *The Philippines in the Third World Papers*, Series No. 38 (Quezon City: University of the Philippines, 1983).

Wade, R., 'Administration and the Distribution of Irrigation Benefits', *Economic and Political Weeky* (1 November 1975) pp. 1743–7.

WADE, R., 'The World Bank and India's Irrigation Reform', *The Journal of Development Studies*, Vol. 18 (January 1982) pp. 171–184.

WALL, R., 'Development, Instability and the World Bank', *Instant Research on Peace and Violence*, No. 2 (1977) pp. 83–98.

WATANABE T., 'The Asian Development Bank Starts Functioning', *Contemporary Japan*, Vol. XXVIII (May 1967) pp. 699–703.

WATANABE T., *Towards a New Asia, Memoirs of the First President of the Asian Development Bank* (Singapore, 1977).

WHITE, J., 'The Asian Development Bank: A Question of Style', *International Affairs* (London) No. 4 (October 1968) pp. 677–90.

WHITE, J., *Japanese Aid* (London: Overseas Development Institute, 1964).

WHITE, J., *Regional Development Banks* (London: Overseas Development Institute, 1970).

WIHTOL, R., 'The Asian Development Bank: Development Financing or Capitalist Export Promotion', *Journal of Contemporary Asia*, Vol. 9 (1979) pp. 288–309.

WORLD BANK, *Agricultural Credit*, Sector Policy Paper (May 1975).

WORLD BANK, *Annual Report* (various issues).

WORLD BANK, *Annual Review of Project Performance Results* (February 1986).

WORLD BANK, *A Guide to Institutional Changes, The World Bank Reorganization 1987* (May 1987).

WORLD BANK, *Guidelines, Procurement under IBRD Loans and IDA Credits* (May 1985).

WORLD BANK, *Guidelines, Use of Consultants by World Bank Borrowers and by the World Bank as Executing Agency* (August 1981).

WORLD BANK, *Land Reform*, Sector Policy Paper (May 1975).

WORLD BANK, *The McNamara Years at the World Bank, Major Policy Addresses of Robert S. McNamara 1968–1981* (Baltimore: The Johns Hopkins University Press, 1981).

WORLD BANK, *Rural Development*, Sector Policy Paper (February 1975).

WORLD BANK, *The World Bank Atlas* (1987).

WORLD BANK, *World Bank Operations, Sectoral Programs and Policies* (Baltimore and London: The Johns Hopkins University Press, 1972).

WORLD BANK, Transportation Staff and Consultants, *Labour-based Construction Programs, A Practical Guide for Planning and Management* (Oxford University Press, 1983).

YAMADA N. and LUSANANDANA, B., 'Rice Production in the ADB Region', in ADB, *Asian Agricultural Survey* (University of Tokyo Press, 1968) pp. 141–96.

YASUTOMO, D. T., *Japan and the Asian Development Bank* (New York: Praeger, 1983).

**Selected Periodical and Newspaper Articles**

AWANOHARA S., 'A Reprieve for Hungry Asia', *Far Eastern Economic Review* (29 April 1974) pp. 51–6.

BALFOUR, F., 'Turning a Blind Eye', *Far Eastern Economic Review* (27 November 1986) pp. 66–9.

BALFOUR, F., and CLAD, J., 'Where There is a Will, There is a Way', *Far Eastern Economic Review* (27 November 1986) pp. 63–5.

BECHTEL, H., 'Banking – Art or Science?', *Zeitschrift für das Gesamte Kreditwesen*, 19 Heft (1984) p. 6.

BOWRING, P., 'ADB: Searching for a Role', *Far Eastern Economic Review* (22 April 1977) pp. 43–63.

BOWRING, P., 'A Borrower Be', *Far Eastern Economic Review* (7 May 1982) pp. 63–4.

BOWRING, P., 'A Quiet Revolution', *Far Eastern Economic Review* (19 May 1983) pp. 54–6.

CLAD, J., 'Last-resort Lender', *Far Eastern Economic Review* (15 May 1986) pp. 64–5.

CLAD, J., 'Unhappy Returns', *Far Eastern Economic Review* (27 November 1986) pp. 60–3.

CLAD, J., 'Unpalatable Loan to Burmese Cooperatives', *Far Eastern Economic Review* (27 November 1986) pp. 64–6.

HO K. P., 'Asian Agriculture's Decade in the Wrong Direction', *Far Eastern Economic Review* (15 September 1978) pp. 47–50.

LEE, D., 'Contract Award by Asian Bank Prompts Questions', *The Washington Post* (28 April 1984) pp. A21 and A28.

LUBAR, R., 'Reaganizing the Third World', *Fortune* (16 November 1981) pp. 80–90.

OCAMPO, S., 'An Ice Age for Aid', *Far Eastern Economic Review* (23 April 1982) pp. 74–5.

ROWLEY, A., 'Clausen and a More Worldly World Bank', *Far Eastern Economic Review* (26 March 1982) pp. 131–8.

ROWLEY, A., 'Ideology Before Need', *Far Eastern Economic Review* (14 February 1985) pp. 72–3.

ROWLEY, A., 'The Tokyo Initiative', *Far Eastern Economic Review* (7 May 1987) pp. 139–40.

ROWLEY, A., 'We'll Do It Our Way', *Far Eastern Economic Review* (14 May 1987) pp. 68–70.

TAKITA K., 'ADB-ing Agriculture', *Far Eastern Economic Review* (22 December 1966) pp. 593–4.

TAN, A., 'Burma Affair Puts ADB in Bad Light', *Bangkok Post* (29 June 1984).

TASKER, R., 'Lender of First Resort', *Far Eastern Economic Review* (17 May 1984) pp. 64–5.

# Index

References to tables and figures are printed in *italic*. Under individual country entries, only tables of particular relevance to a country are included, while general tables including information on many or all ADB member countries (for example, Tables 6.3 and 6.4) are not.